Kenneth Burke's Weed Garden

Kenneth Burke's Weed Garden

Refiguring the Mythic Grounds of Modern Rhetoric

Kyle Jensen

The Pennsylvania State University Press
University Park, Pennsylvania

Library of Congress Cataloging-in-
   Publication Data

Names: Jensen, Kyle, 1981– author.
Title: Kenneth Burke's weed garden :
   refiguring the mythic grounds of
   modern rhetoric / Kyle Jensen.
Description: University Park, Pennsylvania
   : The Pennsylvania State University
   Press, [2022] | Includes bibliographical
   references and index.
Summary: "Reconstructs Kenneth Burke's
   drafting and revision process for A
   Rhetoric of Motives and The War of
   Words, placing Burke's work in historical
   context and revealing his reliance on
   the concept of myth"—Provided by
   publisher.
Identifiers: LCCN 2022006916 | ISBN
   9780271092928 (hardback) | ISBN
   9780271092935 (paper)
Subjects: LCSH: Burke, Kenneth, 1897–
   1993. Rhetoric of motives. | Burke,
   Kenneth, 1897–1993. War of words. |
   Burke, Kenneth, 1897–1993. | Semantics
   (Philosophy) | Rhetoric. | Myth.
Classification: LCC B840.B83 J46 2022 |
   DDC 121/.68—dc23/eng/20220316
LC record available at https://lccn.loc.gov
   /2022006916

Copyright © 2022 Kyle Jensen
All rights reserved
Printed in the United States of America
Published by The Pennsylvania
State University Press,
University Park, PA 16802–1003

The Pennsylvania State University Press is
a member of the Association of University
Presses.

It is the policy of The Pennsylvania State
University Press to use acid-free paper.
Publications on uncoated stock satisfy
the minimum requirements of American
National Standard for Information
Sciences—Permanence of Paper for Printed
Library Material, ANSI Z39.48–1992.

For Jack Selzer

Contents

Acknowledgments ix
List of Abbreviations xiii

Introduction 1

PART I: AN ARCHIVE OF MOTIVES

Prolegomena 11

1. Lapsing into the Unformed 17
2. A Modest Proposal 24
3. Part-to-Whole Relations 32
4. The Factors Behind Rhetoric 40
5. The Ideal Opening 53
6. Charting an Upward and Downward Path 62
7. A Pause at the Window 68
8. Writing at the Center of the Universe 77
9. Everything Is Nowhere 86

Epilegomena 92

PART II: A THEORY OF MOTIVES

Prolegomena 97

1. Mythic Palingenesis 99
2. Identification's Dimensions 127
3. Devices Old and New 145
4. Mythic Historiography 168

Epilegomena 183

Notes 189
Works Cited 210
Index 219

Acknowledgments

In the pages that follow, I argue that rhetorical critics can learn a great deal from a writer's problem-solving process. Although I encountered and solved many problems while writing this book, the absence of generosity from colleagues, friends, and family was never a problem I had to face.

This book is dedicated to Jack Selzer for reasons that will be obvious to anyone who considers him a friend. Yes, he is the foremost Kenneth Burke scholar working today. And yes, I learned a great deal from him about how to be a better writer and teacher. But the lessons I take away from our collaborations are more firmly rooted in his humanity. Imagine a scenario in which, upon retirement, students and colleagues from across the country hold a conference in your honor and spend hours telling stories about the impact you've had on their lives. I'm sure this happens to others, but it is no surprise that it happened to Jack. His generosity of spirit is the tie that binds many of us together. I hope this book makes him proud. I hope, more, that my life follows his lead.

Ron Fortune, to whom all my books could be dedicated, is the most important intellectual influence in my life. I worry that I have accrued more debts over the past sixteen years than I can possibly repay. He has read virtually every page of this book with characteristic patience and wisdom. The questions he raised during my drafting and revision process have made the argument much clearer. Simply put, he is a north star in my life, and I'm not sure a better mentor or friend exists.

If I have grown as a writer, teacher, and colleague over the years, Kris Ratcliffe is in large part responsible for it. I could fill pages listing the reasons why I am grateful for her. Instead, I'll simply say that it is a unique privilege to have her in my life.

This project gave me the opportunity to spend time with the Burke family, who welcomed me into their home several times. We told stories, played croquet, cooked food, wandered through old photos, excavated Putt-Putt (dodging a skunk, no less), went on walks, took pictures, and swam in the pond. I am grateful to Michael, Julie, and Shannon for their kindness and will look for opportunities to write about Kenneth Burke in the future simply to cross paths with them again. As for Butchie, my debt of gratitude is immense. I will always cherish our conversations, and I hope that he will continue to alert me to landmark moments in the evolution of our universe. Our field is better because of his patient work curating the Kenneth Burke Trust.

A book like this can be written only because scholars like Steve Mailloux exist. I was lucky enough to visit with him during much of my drafting process, and we even made a trip across Pennsylvania to the Burke family farm. We compared notes, he set me straight on several important archival details, and we discussed Burke's contribution to the history of ideas. He was a consistent source of encouragement, and I hope he recognizes his sizable impact on this book.

A number of colleagues and friends, probably without knowing it, have made this a much better book. Michael Bernard-Donals, Dave Tell, Jess Enoch, Roxanne Mountford, Cynthia Haynes, Ned O'Gorman, David Blakesley, Rich Doyle, David Frank, Susan Miller-Cochran, and Sandy Stelts are just a few of the most notable. Many of these incredible scholars invited me to share my research with their colleagues and students. Some, like Dave and Ned, were willing collaborators (over barbecue, no less). Their smart questions added depth and precision to my claims. I am especially grateful to Ned for helping me figure out the first part of this book; it was a breakthrough moment for me. I am also deeply grateful to Roxanne and her graduate students at the University of Oklahoma, who invited me to Norman several times to talk about Burke and modern rhetorical theory. There are sections of this book that could not have been written without their insightful questions.

I wrote early drafts at the University of North Texas, where I taught a brilliant group of students. I tested ideas in our classes together and they responded with patience and trust. To those many students, who are too numerous to list individually, *thank you*. You know who you are, and you know what you mean to me. To Sarah, Tori, Ryan, Charlotte, Cody, Kayla, Nicole, Kimberlyn, Jen, Michael, Deva, Andy, and Rebecca, you remain, as ever, in my thoughts and warmest wishes. Thank you for letting me be a part of your lives.

At UNT I also enjoyed the support of colleagues whom I miss seeing on a day-to-day basis. Jack, Nicole, Masood, and Jacqueline, thank you for being such a strong source of encouragement. Your kindness helped me move toward the finish line.

To Peter Janssen, Kristen Walker, Bill Cassell, Mike Morrill, Justin and Lizzie Ross, Randall and Rise Caldwell, Adrianna Garcia and Cesar Salas, our family couldn't ask for better friends. To Peter, Bill, Mike, and Justin, in particular, I know you will never take credit for any small success I have enjoyed, but you should. This work could not exist without you.

I finished this book at Arizona State University, where I have received enormous support in the most trying times. Our dean of humanities, Jeffrey Cohen, is the embodiment of sound leadership. I am honored to be his colleague. The same can be said of our chair, Kris Ratcliffe, and the tremendous administrative team she has built. To Demetria, Adelheid, Richelle, Pardis, and Peter: your kindness, generosity, and good humor have helped us feel at home. To my graduate students, who are routinely the highlight of my week; thank you for allowing me to teach you. Your future is bright.

Penn State University Press has proved, once again, to be an incredible partner. Many thanks to Ryan Peterson, Laura Reed-Morrisson, Jennifer S. Norton, Josie DiNovo, Brian Beer, and the design team that created such beautiful cover art. I also thank the anonymous reviewers for their insightful feedback, as well as Suzanne Wolk for her keen editorial eye.

My life has changed immeasurably since I began this book. I became a father to twin girls, Zadie and Lia, who are the most beautiful and thoughtful little girls I know. I became a father again to another little girl, Gwendolyn, whose unbridled spirit is a source of creative inspiration. And I lost a mother whose memory I carry forward in these pages and the pages yet to be written. Those who knew her will immediately recognize a separate and special dedication to her in a later chapter, which she saw in the final days of her life.

To my father, thank you for always being a man I can run toward.

To my wife, Patty, *thank you*. I know it's not enough. But knowing that you accept my love and gratitude, however imperfect, is what allows me to write with confidence. I'm not sure whether you'll read beyond this page. But if you do, I hope you'll find that your investment was well spent.

Finally, I am grateful to the Kenneth Burke Literary Trust, the Eberly Family Special Collections Library at Penn State University, Dale Davis and the New York Public Library, the Library of Congress, Robert Cowley and the Newberry Library, the University of Chicago, Princeton University Library's

Special Collections, the Shelby White and Leon Levy Archives Center at the Institute for Advanced Study, and the Beinecke Library at Yale University for allowing me to quote from unpublished archival materials written by Kenneth Burke, James Sibley Watson, and Malcolm Cowley.

Portions of Part I appeared in the "Editors' Introduction" to Burke's *The War of Words*, published by the University of California Press. I am grateful for UCP's permission to reproduce those materials.

A small portion of the "Prolegomena" in Part I appeared in "Genetic Rhetorical Criticism: An Alternative Methodology for Studying Multi-Versioned Rhetorical Works," *Quarterly Journal of Speech* 102.3 (2016): 264–85, © National Communication Association, reprinted by permission of Informa UK Limited, trading as Taylor & Francis Group, www.tandfonline.com, on behalf of the National Communication Association.

A small portion of "Devices Old and New" in Part II appeared in "Rhetorical Counteraction in Kenneth Burke's *A Rhetoric of Motives* and *The War of Words*," *Quarterly Journal of Speech* 104.4 (2018): 384–99, © National Communication Association, reprinted by permission of Informa UK Limited, trading as Taylor & Francis Group, www.tandfonline.com, on behalf of the National Communication Association.

A small portion of "Mythic Historiography" in Part II appeared in "Mythic Historiography: Refiguring Kenneth Burke's Deceitful Woman Trope," co-authored with Krista Ratcliffe, *Rhetoric Society Quarterly* 48.1 (2018): 88–107, © Rhetoric Society of America, www.RhetoricSociety.org, reprinted by permission of Informa UK Limited, trading as Taylor & Francis Group, www.tandfonline.com, on behalf of the Rhetoric Society of America, www.RhetoricSociety.org.

The background graphics for the figures in Part II were designed using resources from Freepik.com.

Abbreviations

Works by Kenneth Burke

GM   *A Grammar of Motives*

RM   *A Rhetoric of Motives*

WW   *The War of Words*

Archives

JWP   James Sibley Watson / The Dial Papers, Henry W. and Albert A. Berg Collection of English and American Literature, New York Public Library, Astor, Lenox and Tilden Foundations

KBLT   Kenneth Burke Literary Trust, Andover, New Jersey

KBP   Kenneth Burke Papers, Eberly Family Special Collections, Pennsylvania State University

MCP   Malcolm Cowley Papers, Newberry Library, Chicago

MJP   Matthew Josephson Papers, Beinecke Rare Book and Manuscript Library, Yale University

REP   Ralph Ellison Papers, Manuscript Division, Library of Congress

RMP   Richard Peter McKeon Papers, Hanna Holborn Gray Special Collections Research Center, University of Chicago Library

SHP   Stanley Edgar Hyman Papers, Manuscript Division, Library of Congress

SWLL   Shelby White and Leon Levy Archives Center, Institute for Advanced Study, Princeton, New Jersey

Introduction

In a way, perhaps, a modern Rhetoric should aim at the best of two orders—it should seek to make us realize the full extent of our national and international responsibilities, and keep us in mind to accept them as a definition of our problem as social beings—at the same time, it should keep alive, if only as a "loyal opposition" which is never expected to get its way, a critical doctrine which might at least be accepted in fragments, or heard now and then for a moment when there is a lull: the awareness that, as Candide would say, our soundest humanity is in tending our own gardens.

—KENNETH BURKE

The spring of 1948 reached full bloom as a northeast wind drove mottled clouds across the sky. Uncertain of all, save that the winter sabbatical had ended, a chime of wrens poured out a liquid song that glittered in the sunlight like new copper coins. The small waves of sound traveled across the lawn, up the porch, and into the room where Kenneth Burke sat at his writing desk. Peering up from a stack of notes, he noticed that his once tidy farm was now overgrown with weeds. This was not the first time Burke had encountered such a problem. And, up to this point, he had resisted an industrial solution. But in a surprising turn of events, he broke precedent, if not principle, and purchased a power-driven cutter bar.[1]

The cutter bar, which he named "Putt-Putt," was a revelation. "I've started reclaiming the fields," Burke wrote to his mentor and patron James Sibley Watson, "and Jeeze, what exsta-sazzy" (30 May 1948, JWP). Burke's identification with Putt-Putt was so strong that in the same letter he referred to himself by that name: "Call me Putt-Putt. I know of no act more gratifying than this extending of my dominion. Until the day when something goes wrong with the motor, I say: Bless the Industrial Revolution."

Burke's collaboration with Putt-Putt was a timely and perhaps necessary distraction from his writing. Although he had invested more than two years in drafting and revising *A Rhetoric of Motives*, he was struggling to draw

Fig. 1 Putt-Putt

its constituent parts together. In the 30 May letter to Watson, Burke wrote, "Stanley Hyman was here over the week-end and he thinks that my items on the political logomachy will just about get me tarred and feathered by the reviewers, and to the glory of no one."² The "political logomachy" was a chapter in which Burke catalogued modern rhetorical devices in the contemporary news media.³ Burke had observed, for example, that US politicians were concealing the material interests of their economic policies by spiritualizing their nation's ideals. He placed these appeals under the heading *spiritualization* and archived them along with ten other modern devices that were characteristic of the early postwar period.⁴

Defining and analyzing these devices was unusually challenging for Burke. He had a tendency to be overly critical of his contemporaries, which made his approach to rhetorical criticism feel like a "thumbs-down" activity (Burke to Cowley, KBP, Burke-1, 27 September 1946).⁵ The topical nature of Burke's analyses obscured, as well, the universal framework that his philosophy of modern rhetoric sought to establish. To solve this problem, he proposed a more allusive style: "The political incidents should be de-localized, as per the personal anecdotes. About people like the Ambassador of Preenland, his Excellency of Pronia, The Grand Apex of Onlychurch II, etc. Factions should always be the Ins and Outs, or Innables and Outables, or the Perfectists and the Loathesomites, etc. Let the anecdotes be strong in *allusive* value—but all sins of direct application *must be committed by the reader himself*" (Burke to Watson, 30 May 1948, JWP). Burke's revision—"the solushe," as he called it—had the further advantage of illustrating "the forms [of the devices] and their applications, but without having to meet the burdens of [a timely analysis] and without sacrificing what [he] consider[ed] to be the over-all attitude" (Burke to Hyman, 30 May 1948, SHP). Everything seemed to be pointed in the right direction.

Unfortunately, the proposed revision did not hold. Burke spent the better part of 1948 drafting and revising the chapter on rhetorical devices, only to suspend its completion—along with three similarly focused chapters—approximately one month before he sent the first volume of *A Rhetoric of Motives* to his editors at Prentice Hall. Burke teased the existence of these unfinished chapters in a footnote on page 294 of the published version of *A Rhetoric of Motives*, where he writes, "The closing sentences were originally intended as a transition to our section on The War of Words. But that must await publication in a separate volume" (*RM* 294). Burke would return to these chapters in subsequent years, publish small portions of them, describe them in letters to friends, and give public lectures from their contents, but he never published them during his lifetime.[6]

Despite its status as an incomplete project, *A Rhetoric of Motives* continues to inspire rhetorical critics and educators around the world. Brilliant studies of the book have deepened the field's appreciation of Burke's work.[7] And yet, for all the critical attention *A Rhetoric of Motives* has received over the years, no scholar has produced a systematic explanation of its argument. Donald Stauffer's 1950 review captures the problem that critics face: "Mr. Burke's scope is such that he includes all that he has read, heard or thought. Structure and selection are not his strong points. In his desire to bring in everything (one of his parentheses runs in length for a page), the argument is often temporarily lost, and the system itself becomes a stalwart symbol for an attempt to impose order on chaos."[8] Granted, Burke's line of reasoning is often temporarily lost—a fact punctuated each time he writes, "Where are we, now?" But Stauffer's reading is limited by the negative connotation he assigns to the term *chaos*, which, in his estimation, resists systematic thinking.[9] Like many critics of Burke, Stauffer makes the right move, but in the wrong direction. He recognizes that Burke is imposing order on a chaotic landscape but uses this observation to close down inquiry rather than open it up.

It is now time to shift the terms of the discussion and ask what lessons may be drawn from Burke's attempt to order the chaos in *A Rhetoric of Motives* and *The War of Words*. In raising this question, the incomplete status of *A Rhetoric of Motives* becomes an entry point for gauging the historical, theoretical, and personal problems that worked against Burke's drafting and revision process. The interpretive difference this question makes may be slight. But in the chapters that follow, I show how it makes all the difference.[10] Namely, we learn to read *A Rhetoric of Motives* with greater generosity, treating it not as an incoherent muddle of concepts but as a coherent and evolving philosophy of modern rhetoric that holds significant implications for the past, present, and future of rhetorical studies.

The linchpin of Burke's philosophy of modern rhetoric is the concept of *identification*—that much is clear.[11] The less obvious insight is that identification finds its transhistorical footing in the context of myth. Within this context, identification becomes a dimensional concept that appears in diverse historical periods and textual genres. Within this context, Burke's catalogue of postwar rhetorical devices participates in the long history of rhetoric and suggests the existence of a nonconscious domain of human motivation. Within this context, Burke shows that all general theories of rhetoric may be structured by mythic images and terms.

I have broken this book into two parts. Part I presents an archival account of how Burke drafted and revised *A Rhetoric of Motives* and *The War of Words* between 1945 and 1950. Over the course of nine chapters, I track the problems he encountered and attempted to solve in each volume. As we will see, Burke often turns to myth when a difficult problem requires a philosophical solution. Not surprisingly, Burke's reliance on myth creates its own set of problems, leading arguably to the greatest problem he never fully solved: completing *A Rhetoric of Motives* as a two-part work that addressed the dangers of the postwar period.[12]

Part II explains the theoretical and methodological implications of Burke's reliance on myth. The first chapter establishes what Burke means by *myth* and explains how the mythic images and terms he creates and cites support the signature concepts that distinguish *A Rhetoric of Motives*.

Once this mythic infrastructure is in clear view, I explain, in chapter 2, how *identification* functions in Burke's modern philosophy of rhetoric. Specifically, I show how myth yields a dimensional theory of identification that expands the scope of rhetorical analysis.

The third chapter focuses on how rhetorical devices—when understood in the context of Burke's mythic framework and dimensional theory of identification—organize group perception at a nonconscious level. Burke leverages his theoretical insights to create a form of rhetorical criticism that prepares audiences to consume news media more conscientiously.

The fourth chapter explains how Burke's mythic framework draws disparate historical moments into identification with one another. If, Burke argues, the problem of verbal warfare is not peculiar to the postwar period, then rhetorical critics may identify examples of verbal conflict throughout history. Burke's investigation begins with an analysis of mythic images and terms that justify, sustain, or transform verbal conflict. By making these images and terms the site of conscious reflection, Burke expands how historiographical research may be conducted in rhetorical studies. He also helps critics maintain equanimity in the face of deep political and cultural divisions.

So much for explaining why the book's subtitle is *Refiguring the Mythic Grounds of Modern Rhetoric*. Why *Kenneth Burke's Weed Garden*?

Throughout his drafting and revision process, Burke differentiated his writing from his daily chores. These distinctions began to blur, however, as he revised the remaining chapters of *A Rhetoric of Motives*. For example, just a week before purchasing Putt-Putt, Burke began characterizing the news media's rhetorical devices as weeds. "Having definitivized about 20,000 words of first chapter on the Logomachy," he wrote to Hyman, "it's an anthology: Kennel Bark's Little Golden (in psychoanalytic sense) Treasure of Rhetorical Weeds. It's fantastically easy to read, since nearly every paragraph can stand alone" (21 May 1948, SHP).

Burke's characterization of rhetorical devices as weeds indicates at least one purpose of *A Rhetoric of Motives*. Burke believed that the speed of proliferation of modern rhetorical devices made them difficult, if not impossible, to manage. By tracking these devices and teaching his contemporaries to do the same, Burke felt that he could exert a modest level of control over them. "I recognize I might be fighting two Jungles at once," he explained to his friend Matthew Josephson, "and at least the other will win, sooner or later (as usual, I feel, sooner); still, there's the Hierarchy for me, there's my Old-Man transcendence, my Putt-Putt, pot-pot, putter-putter purpose" (9 June 1948, MJP). Burke's purpose was not to dominate the landscape per se but to develop a system that explained why the landscape was so difficult to tame. As he explains in *The War of Words*, "you recognize the prevalence of the Scramble, while striving to surmount agitation by connoisseurship. And above all, you watch for the goadings of the hierarchic principle, so near to the ironic roots of human relations" (WW 185).

Ordering this chaotic landscape was difficult work. In a letter to his childhood friend the noted literary critic Malcolm Cowley, Burke wrote:

> Am still knocking off, bumpily, my first draft of the Rhetoric. The problem that emerges is this: To decide to what extent I shall make the Rhetoric simply my own contribution to the subject, and to what

Fig. 2 Kenneth Burke scything, 1947

extent I shall try to cover the field in general. The second obligation comes to the fore, as soon as one thinks of such a book from the standpoint of sheer pedagogy. But the main line is so astoundingly well traveled by Aristotle, and the new stuff (on modern propaganda, advertising, etc.) is so obvious to everyone, that only by working the marginal lands can one hope to do much that has any element of newness about it. (7 December 1945, MCP)

Burke's comments suggest that neither the classical tradition nor contemporary methods of media criticism were capable of sponsoring the attitudinal shift he imagined. Burke solved this problem by defining Aristotle's approach to classical rhetoric as a well-cultivated landscape. As a point of contrast, he then characterized the modern rhetorical situation as an unforgivingly wild space. Just as Aristotle ordered his landscape by identifying rhetorical devices in classical oratory, Burke sought order over his landscape by identifying how rhetorical devices functioned in the contemporary news media. To make this landscape new, Burke wrote a philosophy of modern rhetoric that centered on the concept of *identification*.[13] He defined identification as a persuasive effect of language that exists somewhere between conscious and unconscious awareness—what I will characterize as nonconscious identification.[14] When presenting identification for the first time in *A Rhetoric of*

Motives, Burke writes, "There is an intermediate area of expression that is not wholly deliberate, yet not wholly unconscious. It lies midway between aimless utterance and speech directly purposive" (*RM* xiii).

By tracking identification's appearances throughout history in *A Rhetoric of Motives*, Burke prepared audiences to understand the complexity of contemporary rhetorical devices in *The War of Words*. Whereas classical rhetoricians focused on conscious acts of persuasion in a primarily oratorical society, modern rhetoricians would focus on nonconscious acts of identification in a society characterized by the expedient delivery of mixed media. Identification would not eclipse persuasion but rather would coexist alongside it in order to build a more comprehensive field of study.

I admit that *weed garden* is an odd turn of phrase. One does not create a weed garden but instead removes weeds in order to cultivate a flower or vegetable garden. The advantage of this awkward phrasing is that it communicates a sense of incompletion that is crucial to understanding the textual condition of *A Rhetoric of Motives*. By choosing not to publish *The War of Words*, Burke never cleared the landscape as he had planned. Relegating the incomplete chapters to his personal archive, he allowed the weeds in postwar media to proliferate largely unchecked. And yet, by choosing not to complete the work as he had planned, Burke provides us with an opportunity to explore the historical, theoretical, and personal factors that worked against the completion of *A Rhetoric of Motives*. These factors disclose important challenges that rhetorical historians, critics, and educators face in their attempts to counteract contemporary forms of nationalistic aggression. The phrase *weed garden* thus establishes a common topos for rhetorical historians, critics, and educators.

Kenneth Burke's incomplete project is a weed garden, then, because it orders the landscape well enough for contemporary scholars to appreciate the challenges he faced and to complete, where possible, the program he established. It is now time to kneel alongside Burke and get our hands dirty.

Part I
An Archive of Motives

Prolegomena

In Part I, "An Archive of Motives," I tell the story of how Kenneth Burke drafted and revised *A Rhetoric of Motives*. To tell this story, I draw from unpublished manuscript drafts, correspondence, and lectures that Burke composed between 1945 and 1950.[1] When placed in order, these materials offer a unique glimpse into Burke's drafting and revision process for this book. Each time Burke drafted, cut, or revised his argument, he clarified what his work was and was not designed to accomplish. By following this process, critics gain a clearer picture of the theoretical coherence, historical allusions, and methodological innovations that define *A Rhetoric of Motives*.

The nine chapters in this section are guided by the principles of *genetic rhetorical criticism*, which I have defined as a methodology for "reconstructing and analyzing the chain of events" that distinguish the composition, revision, and circulation of rhetorical works (Deppman, Ferrer, and Groden 11). Critics may analyze rhetorical works with greater depth and insight when they observe how authors, editors, and collaborators respond to problems associated with the drafting process.[2] Because I use the concepts of *work*, *version*, and *revision* to differentiate the published and unpublished manuscripts in my account, it is important to pause and define each term.

A *work* is "the theoretical and material sum of extant textual versions that have been produced and collected over the course of a writing process" (Jensen, "Genetic" 269). The concept of *work* helps scholars locate an argumentative design that signals coherence between extant versions. For example, by conceptualizing *A Rhetoric of Motives* as a rhetorical work, scholars can identify organizing themes, argumentative tendencies, and distinctive concepts that obtain across published and unpublished manuscripts.[3]

Versions are the constituent parts of a rhetorical work that are created when writers revise their work in a substantive way. Versions may be outline sketches written in the margins of a notebook or letters to a trusted friend that indicate major shifts in perspective. Regardless of form, a new version must demonstrate evidence of continuity with *and* departure from the version that preceded it. Otherwise, it is simply a copy or a minor variation.[4]

Revisions are traces of textual change that signal a writer's attempt to alter his or her argument in a substantive way.[5] Unlike editing, substantive revision redefines the stated or unstated assumptions of an existing version. There is a difference between improving the syntax of a sentence and altering a sentence to create a different line of reasoning. The former refines an existing argument while the latter transforms an argument to produce a different effect. One of the main challenges of genetic rhetorical criticism is explaining why a writer revised their argument. Because Burke never furnished a reason for setting *The War of Words* aside in 1949, for example, critics must determine his reasons for doing so. A persuasive explanation requires the description and evaluation of the differences between extant versions.

I use the title *A Rhetoric of Motives* to refer to the two-volume work that includes *The War of Words* because Burke used that title when discussing his work. Still, there are times where I use *A Rhetoric of Motives* to refer to a specific manuscript *version*. For example, when Burke submitted *A Rhetoric of Motives* to his publisher in 1949, he sent a version of the work, not the work in its entirety.[6] This version is part of a long chain of writing events that includes the creation, revision, and suspension of other versions. To avoid unnecessary confusion when discussing extant versions of *A Rhetoric of Motives*, I use designations such as *version* or *published version*. Where possible, I differentiate "The War of Words," the drafted second volume of the longer work *A Rhetoric of Motives*, from *The War of Words*, the recently published scholarly edition of which I am one of the editors. By the time we reach Part II, I dispense with the "published version of" designation and simply denote published works with italics.

Given the recent publication of *The War of Words*, it is reasonable to wonder whether the status of *A Rhetoric of Motives* as a work of rhetoric has changed. Within the framework of genetic rhetorical criticism, the answer to this question is that it depends on what we mean by "change." Materially speaking, the "War of Words" manuscripts have existed largely undisturbed for about seven decades.[7] So, in a sense, the work did not change. Indeed, it would be more accurate to say that our understanding of the work has expanded as a result of the discovery of *The War of Words*, which is made up of multiple versions of the longer manuscript. In another sense, however, the work has evolved because the material publication of extant archival materials resulted in a new *version* of *The War of Words*. When transforming the manuscript versions into a scholarly edition, my coeditors and I neither circumvented Burke's wishes nor changed the content of its argument. We did, however, change the status of the work through the act of publication, even though its contents remain almost entirely consistent with the extant manuscripts.[8] *The War of Words* is no longer just a loose collection of manuscripts dispersed across different archives in the United States. It is also a bound and published scholarly edition that contains an editors' introduction, title page, copyright page, and index. These paratextual materials change the way we read the book's contents and must be factored into a historical account of the work's evolution.[9] The aspect of the work that has changed, then, is its *status* as a published text.

When I refer to drafted manuscripts (whether in the text, in an endnote, or in my list of works cited) held at Penn State University, the New York Public Library, and the Burke Literary Trust in Andover, New Jersey (for example), I differentiate them by their location.[10] Although I draw on a number of unpublished notes, outlines, and unpublished letters to tell the story of Burke's drafting process, my account is neither comprehensive nor totalizing. The volume of materials is simply too great to allow for such an account. I focus on some materials at the expense of others because my purpose is to set Burke's composition process in its historical context, establish coherence in his modern philosophy of rhetoric, and identify the rhetorical methodology that guides his approach. Not every document helps with this task. When it seems appropriate, I signal in the endnotes opportunities for future research.[11]

The chapters in Part I are conspicuously short for several reasons. First, the chapter breaks allow readers to focus on what seem to me hallmark moments in Burke's drafting and revision process. Including more details or simply extending the account by several months threatened to overstuff the narrative. So I wrote each chapter to help readers maintain focus on aspects of the story that might otherwise be subsumed by different considerations. Second, although this is an academic book, I wrote it in such a way that I hope it will be accessible to nonspecialists. I have written about Kenneth Burke for much of my career, and consistently the complaint is that his work is difficult to read. This is disheartening for many reasons, not the least of which is that Burke wrote *A Rhetoric of Motives* in order to help public audiences come to terms with the dangers of the early postwar period and beyond. Although I can't change Burke's argumentative style—which *is* difficult to follow—I do have some control over the clarity of my own writing. Third, even though I want the reading pace of the narrative to be relatively quick, I also want to encourage readers to consider the small details that distinguish each draft.

Although Burke's drafting process with *A Rhetoric of Motives* was defined by a significant decision at the eleventh hour to cut the book by half, many of its most important moments involve small shifts in argumentation that will seem minor to the untrained eye. By paring down the narrative account and presenting it in smaller bites, these archival moments become easier to see.

For simple reference, I've created a timeline that highlights signature moments in Burke's revision process for *A Rhetoric of Motives*. To underscore how early postwar events influenced his writing process, I have listed landmark events that defined this period. By implementing this tactic, I am following the lead of scholars such as Jack Selzer, who has long emphasized the value of reading Burke in context.

1945

6 August
US nuclear attacks on Hiroshima, Japan

9 August
US nuclear attacks on Nagasaki, Japan

November–December
Burke drafts and compiles notes for prospectus for *RM*

1946

2 January
Burke submits prospectus to Prentice Hall

22 February
George Kennan sends "Long Telegram"

27 February
Burke commissioned to write "The American Way"

5 March
Winston Churchill delivers "Iron Curtain" speech

12 September
Henry A. Wallace publicly urges peace with Soviet Union; President Truman asks him to resign

21 September
Burke creates a three-part outline for *RM*

1947

12 March
Truman Doctrine announced

31 March
Burke delivers "Ideology and Myth" lecture at Bennington College

27 April
Burke creates a new outline for *RM*

5 June
Marshall Plan announced

7 August
Burke finds an ideal opening for *RM* in Milton's *Samson Agonistes*

26 August
Burke creates a new, two-part outline for *RM*

October
House Un-American Activities Committee investigates Hollywood film industry

1948

15 February
Burke creates a new, two-part structure for *RM*

25 March
Watson encourages Burke to clarify the role "identification" plays in the *RM* chapter "Order"

1948 (continued)

30 May
Hyman admonishes Burke about the "Devices" chapter

3 June
Burke meets Oppenheimer at IAS

24 June
Berlin Blockade

1 September
Burke completes draft of the "Scientific Rhetoric" chapter of *RM*

2 November
President Truman reelected

22 December
Burke arrives at IAS

1949

January–March
Burke revises the first part of *RM* at IAS

19 March
Burke submits *RM*

4 April
NATO ratified

20 June
Burke suspends work on *WW* until *A Symbolic of Motives* is complete

1 October
Mao Zedong assumes power and establishes the People's Republic of China

1950

30 January
President Truman approves H-bomb development

February
Senator Joe McCarthy initiates Communist witch hunt

1 May
Publication of *RM*

17 May
Publishers report difficulty in marketing *RM*

25 June
Beginning of the Korean War

An Archive of Motives

1

Lapsing into the Unformed

After reviewing the fair copy submission of *A Rhetoric of Motives*, which for all intents and purposes became the published version of the book, Burke's editors at Prentice Hall expressed concern about its accessibility to lay audiences.[1] Although the book was ostensibly written with lay readers in mind, its argument was difficult to follow. Initially, this evaluation sent Burke into a tizzy of revisions. Like any writer, Burke wanted to build a strong audience for his book, as doing so would not only validate the argument but generate interest in his other books (Burke to Watson, 19 December 1949, JWP). But after a few days of work, Burke accepted his editors' criticism, acknowledged that difficult prose was a characteristic feature of his writing, and encouraged them to redouble their efforts (Burke to Cowley, 26 April 1949, KBP, Burke-1).

Burke was nevertheless haunted by their criticisms. We can observe him worrying over the book's readability in the opening lines of the published version of *A Rhetoric of Motives*, where he writes, "The only difficult portion of this book happens, unfortunately, to be at the start." For those needing a clear path through the woods, Burke recommends that readers go "lightly through the opening pages, with the intention of not taking hold in earnest until they come to the general topic of *Identification*" on page 19 (xiii). At that point, he promised, the difficulty would abate. Readers were expected to follow along without complaint.

However useful this lighted path may have been to past and current audiences, the need for redoubled effort in reading Burke remains. As we slog through his complicated argument, pressing questions emerge:

- Why is *A Rhetoric of Motives* so difficult to read?
- Was Albert Guerard correct when he suggested that Burke's style was a "cunning rhetorical device" that "identifies [him] with the learned, the recondite, and therefore (a very effective fallacy), the profound?"[2]

- Did undisclosed personal or historical circumstances affect Burke's writing process?
- What were Burke's purposes in writing *A Rhetoric of Motives* in light of those personal or historical circumstances?

Burke began writing *A Rhetoric of Motives* in the summer of 1945. Initially, he expected the work to follow a relatively smooth progression. However, his argument refused to play nice (Burke to Cowley, 13 October 1945, in Jay 270). "There are many pressing reasons why the writing of a Modern Rhetoric is not a joyous undertaking," he confessed to his friend Stanley Edgar Hyman in 1947, "and I am finding every one of them, the hard way" (Burke to Hyman, 21 July 1946, SHP).[3] Part of the problem was Burke's ambition. Although *A Rhetoric of Motives* had a more narrow focus than *A Grammar of Motives*, Burke was determined to "show just how deeply the militaristic ingredient in [human] vocabulary goes" ("Prospectus"). Burke planned not only to root out the sources of humanity's dangerous argumentative tendencies but also to counteract them before they coalesced into nationalistic aggression. He believed that struggling against nationalistic aggression was every citizen's patriotic duty (Burke to Watson, 3 June 1948, JWP).

In the early years of the postwar period, struggling against nationalism was no small task. The introduction of atomic weapons into world history left Burke "sputtering with wrath" (Burke to Watson, 13 August 1945, JWP). The geopolitical outlook appeared so grim that he felt "physically depressed about the heart" (Burke to Watson, 14 September 1946, JWP). And the propaganda circulating in US newspapers made the Nazis "look like honest little Jesuses" (Burke to Watson, 12 March 1947, JWP). In response to these and other problems, Burke shifted between a "benevolently caustic" and an "ironically irenic" tone in his writing (Burke to Cowley, 3 April 1946, in Jay 274–75). He explained in a letter to his friend Richard McKeon:

> Indeed, my own struggle throughout my own Rhetoric is obviously going to be the struggle to keep myself from falling into some kind of variant of the scientifico-debunko-semanticist attitude. I find that I can write of Rhetoric happily enough when I am applying Rhetorical coordinates to poetry; but as soon as I turn to consider the concealed Rhetoric in our journalistic picture of "reality," I can prevent myself from becoming homicidal only by becoming suicidal, and can prevent myself from becoming suicidal only by becoming homicidal.

At such moments, I shall remind myself of your own reasonable position, to cheer me up. (7 November 1945, RMP)[4]

As we will discover in the pages that follow, Burke's tense relation to the evolving postwar geopolitical scene is a primary theme of his drafting process, and this explains, at least in part, why he didn't publish *The War of Words* during his lifetime.

Burke took notes and drafted chapters in various locations across the United States. The bulk of his writing took place in Andover, New Jersey, where he lived with his family. He also wrote at a vacation cottage in Melbourne Beach, Florida, tested and revised his arguments while teaching at Bennington College in Vermont, and put the finishing touches on the published version of *A Rhetoric of Motives* while holding a short-term fellowship at the Institute for Advanced Study in Princeton, New Jersey.

Burke habitually corresponded with friends and colleagues throughout his writing process. James Sibley Watson, Stanley Edgar Hyman, Malcolm Cowley, Richard McKeon, Matthew Josephson, William Carlos Williams, and Ralph Ellison represent a small handful of his most famous interlocutors. Burke also delivered invited lectures at a number of prestigious universities, including Princeton, the University of Chicago, and Harvard. In fact, his lectures at Princeton formed the basis of the section "The Rhetorical Radiance of the Divine" in *A Rhetoric of Motives* and became a model for the Gauss seminars in literary criticism (Burke to Watson, 10 March 1949, JWP).

Burke catalogued modern rhetorical devices in popular newspapers such as the *New York Times* and the *Christian Science Monitor* throughout his drafting process for *A Rhetoric of Motives*. As he combed through the articles, he focused specifically on devices that incited political warfare in the name of peace. At first, this was an exercise in "self-cure" (WW 265). In search of emotional equilibrium, Burke catalogued the rhetorical devices that threatened peaceful relations in the United States and across the world. Over time, he realized that others could benefit from this method, so he began to track the devices with greater attention to clarity, comprehension, and style.

Burke's study of modern rhetorical devices both preceded and exceeded his work on *A Rhetoric of Motives*. In the opening lines of his "Foreword (to end on)"—a drafted preface to "The War of Words" written in 1976—Burke claims that he had analyzed rhetorical devices before writing *A Grammar of Motives*. Although the drafts had reached the status of a "fair copy," he set the manuscript aside in order to begin his trilogy on motives. Burke does not furnish a reason for his decision to set the devices aside. And he does not mention that rhetorical devices play an integral role in the published version of *A Rhetoric of Motives*. He does, however, indicate that setting the manuscript aside was a mistake, because the devices served as "preparation for what followed" (WW 270).

What exactly did Burke mean that the rhetorical devices were "preparation for what followed?" If his motives trilogy is organized by an attempt to purify war, then his analysis could have demonstrated why a philosophy of human motives was necessary to everything that followed. In a letter to Watson dated 2 November 1945 (JWP), Burke admitted that both *A Grammar of Motives* and *A Symbolic of Motives* could feel "pretty remote at times." So perhaps the devices are best understood as a set of resources for applying the philosophical principles he developed in the published version of *A Rhetoric of Motives*.[5]

Had Burke published his analyses prior to the release of *A Grammar of Motives*, readers might have had a reason to pursue the remote spinoffs that followed. Unfortunately, Burke chose to pursue other problems, which makes it difficult to speculate on how the motives trilogy might be read differently. At the same time, Burke's study of rhetorical devices features prominently in the two-part version of *A Rhetoric of Motives*, so we can evaluate the role they play in the broader two-volume work. This evaluation should clarify aspects of the work that remain confusing and highlight opportunities for extending his insights into the present moment.

To arrive at this point, we need to meet Burke at the moment when he set pen to page.

June–September 1945

Summer had arrived in Andover, New Jersey, as Kenneth Burke put the finishing touches on *A Grammar of Motives*. Evidently, the remaining tasks were onerous, because instead of simply completing them, Burke began daydreaming about what *A Rhetoric of Motives* might become. In a letter to James Sibley Watson dated 22 June 1945 (JWP), he offers a glimpse into the earliest moments of his drafting process: "For the next phase, I am going to have to keep supplying the advertising dept. with promotion material, to work over proofs, index, and the like—and, in general, to be going over the Grammar, Grammar, Grammar. And all the while all that I want to do is lapse into that stage of sheer formlessness necessary prerequisite to the lining up of the Rhetoric." *A Rhetoric of Motives* lacked material form; that much is clear. But Burke was circling around an important target: the relationship between war and words. In the same letter, he asserted that war is dreadful because "it is so <u>rational</u>" and noted that it would be possible to locate "the very essence of form, method, and purpose" once he had identified a site of criticism. Had Burke identified options at this point? Not exactly. In a self-conscious aside, he admitted that his ideas were not yet unfolding in a clear progression. As fate would have it, however, Burke's site of criticism would reveal itself in short, albeit devastating, order.

On 6 August 1945 the US military dropped an atomic bomb on Hiroshima, Japan. Three days later, it dropped a second bomb on Nagasaki, with equally destructive force. Burke responded to the news with grave concern over the fate of the human race. The only hopeful response to this tragedy, he felt, was to invest in the "ironic 'worse the better' principle," which assumed that "people simply <u>must</u> reform their thinking this time, so as to make their terminology of human action adequate to the powers of inhuman motion" (Burke to Watson, 13 August 1945, JWP).

Burke was not confident that public audiences could reform on their own. He resolved, therefore, to build a terminology of human action on their behalf. Specifically, he set out to explain how modern rhetorical devices incited war in the name of peace and thus garnered consent for nationalist aggression. This project would be extraordinarily difficult given the foment of postwar antipathy. But he seemed game for the challenge.

Burke's comments about the atomic bomb were designed to elicit Watson's assent, but Watson did not take the bait. Curious about his stance, Burke asked Watson his opinion a couple of weeks later:

> Where do you place this one in Rhetoric: When the Japs first surrendered, our papers began vigorously attributing their surrender to the atomic bomb. This explanation was obviously considered a good move politically, since it played down the effect of Russia's entry as an ally. But a few days later I read indignant reports that the dirty Japs were attributing their defeat to the atomic bomb, as a way of gaining sympathy. Presumably, if we are to spread our influence internationally, we can't plan just one hold at a time, as Rhetoricians in control of a press dearly love to do. It must be adjusted to several antagonists variously placed. (Burke to Watson, 10 September 1945, JWP)

Wary of offending his mentor and patron, Burke must have felt that news media representation was a safe subject of discussion (Burke to Watson, 13

August 1945, JWP). Rhetoric would in turn provide a framework for their subsequent discussion, serving as a heading that categorized the example of Japan's surrender (e.g., "Where do you place this one in Rhetoric"?) and functioning as a heuristic *for* identifying actors within this tradition (e.g., news reporters "as Rhetoricians"). All the while, rhetoric would be neither immune to the dangers of misapplication nor specific to formal argumentative training.[6]

Because Burke's investment in rhetoric was well documented, his proposal should have made sense to Watson. And yet Burke never explains why rhetoric provided the *best* framework for interpreting the early postwar scene. To answer this question, it is helpful to consider how Burke frames his unique approach to rhetorical criticism. The first task was to define the rhetorical situation ("Where do you place this one in Rhetoric"?); since the early postwar period was volatile, rhetoric would help audiences establish order by exposing argumentative tendencies that typified and sustained the existing situation ("It must be adjusted to several antagonists variously placed"). Once he had established this rhetorical situation, Burke could demonstrate how people acted against their best interests. Eventually, the concepts of *myth* and *form* would play important roles in his argument, but at this stage in the drafting process, Burke's ideas were not fully developed.

October–November 1945

Long practiced in cataloguing rhetorical devices, Burke expected that *A Rhetoric of Motives* would be easy to write. At this point, his notes were composed primarily of case studies drawn from contemporary news reports, suggesting that, unlike *A Grammar of Motives* and *A Symbolic of Motives*, it would be more topical in focus. "The Rhetoric is, I believe, going to be by far the 'lightest' of the three books," he explained to Watson in a letter of 2 November 1945 (JWP), adding, "sometimes I feel almost like a kind of academic Will Rogers, commenting on metropolitan ways while twirling my lasso, and in a mood benevolently caustic." The lightness in Burke's mood indicates that he had not moved much beyond tracking devices in the press. He was simply having too much fun chasing down and lassoing the arguments of his contemporaries, a process that in all probability offered a much-needed vent for his concerns.

Although Burke may have felt that *A Rhetoric of Motives* was not the intellectual equivalent of *A Grammar of Motives*, his characterization of it as a light work was overdrawn. Burke would learn quickly that his study of rhetorical devices, if it was to carry any weight, needed a complicated philosophy of motives that synthesized, among other things, rhetorical, literary, and psychoanalytic theory. Initially, he developed his philosophy around the tripartite terminology "simplicity, duplicity, and complicity." In a letter to Watson written on 4 October 1945 (JWP), he outlined the advantages of this approach: "The Rhetoric, it seems, may have to do some weaving in and out of the distinctions between simplicity, duplicity, and complicity. There is Edenic unity in human utterance; then there is an unrecognized division; then there is conscious division consciously exploited, but for an end shared in common; then there is the state of division consciously made to look like unity, for the ends of division. Usually, however, a good ruse flutters back and forth among all these stages. Oof!"

With simplicity, duplicity, and complicity lighting the path forward, Burke could explore such issues as an original unity (simplicity), known and unacknowledged divisions (complicity), and conscious efforts to increase division under the guise of unity (duplicity).[7] The fact that these terms appear in the published version of *A Rhetoric of Motives* suggests that they remained helpful to him throughout the drafting process. However, the tentativeness in his descriptions in the aforementioned passage suggests that he was not yet fully sold on the approach: "The Rhetoric, it *seems*, *may* have to do some weaving in and out of the distinctions between simplicity, duplicity, and complicity," and "*I want it to be* rather a philosophizing on rhetoric" (Burke to Watson, 4 October 1945, JWP, emphasis added). In order to gain confidence, if not clarity, he needed to develop a more formal proposal, which is precisely what he began to compose as the sun disappeared over the autumn horizon.

2

A Modest Proposal

When Burke began drafting *A Rhetoric of Motives,* he felt that it was important to place contemporary verbal conflict within the broader history of rhetoric. Doing so, he reasoned, would demonstrate that verbal warfare was not peculiar to the early postwar period but was symptomatic of language use in general ("Prospectus"). As he began to collect examples, he encountered the unexpected problem of determining "to what extent [he would] make the Rhetoric simply [his] own contribution to the subject, and to what extent [he would] try to cover the field in general," as he put it to Cowley in a letter of 7 December 1945 (MCP). The latter approach, he surmised, had obvious pedagogical value, so the issue of rhetoric's relevance was not a concern. Instead, the problem was one of novelty: "the main line [of rhetoric] is so astoundingly well traveled by Aristotle, and the new stuff (on modern propaganda, advertising, etc.) is so obvious to everyone, that only by working the marginal lands can one hope to do much that has any element of newness about it." Burke's reflection is important because in it we find his first reference to the *marginal lands* of rhetoric.

Investigating the marginal lands of rhetoric required that Burke "indicate at what point rhetoric and poetic diverge" (ibid.). This step was necessary because, according to Burke, rhetoric could not achieve a universal scope on its own. A specific function of the dialectic principle, rhetoric was designed to address local situations and motivate attitudes and actions in specific audiences. To prevent his book from disintegrating into a series of loosely connected case studies (e.g., "Another instance of this is . . . and still another instance is . . . 'etc.'"), Burke needed to enlist an accomplice such as poetry. Unlike rhetoric, poetry was consciously de-localized and thus accessed the universal more easily (Burke to Cowley, 13 October 1945, in Jay 270).

The tension between rhetoric and poetics compelled Burke because it allowed him to explain how a poetic approach to rhetoric could temporally expand the study of rhetoric without subsuming it. Those who have read the published version of *A Rhetoric of Motives* have noticed that Burke reads poetic texts rhetorically. But the inverse is also true: Burke also reads rhetoric texts poetically. As we will discover in the pages that follow, Burke used this core insight to connect the immediate events of the early postwar period to a broader rhetorical situation he called the war of words.

2 January 1946

After four months of note-taking, Burke submitted a prospectus to his editors at Prentice Hall in which he divided *A Rhetoric of Motives* into five major sections:

1. On the War of Words, the "Logomachy"
2. The Rhetorical Situation
3. The Boundaries of Rhetoric
4. Landmarks of Rhetoric
5. Catalogue of Rhetorical Devices

Under each heading, Burke provided a brief explanation of the section's contents. Of the first section, for example, Burke wrote:

> Part One (on the War of Words, the "Logomachy") is designed to show just how deeply the militaristic ingredient in our vocabulary goes. This section is intended to place the whole subject, and to show why Rhetoric is not just a matter for specialists, but goes to the roots of psychology and ethics, including man's relation to his political and economic background. It deals with two major trinitarian clusters (Love-War-Work and Mine-Thine-Ours), showing how each member of a given cluster implicates the other two, and how basically such interweaving affects the formation and use of the communicative medium. Above all, we seek to disclose the ingredients of war lurking undetected in language that may seem on its surface to be the language of peace. ("Prospectus")

The first and most striking feature of Burke's 1946 prospectus is that none of the proposed sections or chapters appear in the published version of *A*

Rhetoric of Motives. The chapter that bears the closest resemblance is "Landmarks of Rhetoric," which, like its published counterpart, "Traditional Principles of Rhetoric," offered "a kind of long review of the various works of the past and present [that he] consider[ed] particularly useful as contributions to the study of Rhetoric" ("Prospectus"). This remnant of the original prospectus is all the more remarkable because, at the time of composition, Burke viewed it as a somewhat marginal consideration. Burke's notes explain that the chapter would probably fall to the cutting room floor once he "made sufficient reference to those works in passing" earlier in the book.

Burke identified "On the War of Words" as the most important section because it would "disclose the ingredients of war lurking undetected in language that may seem on its surface to be the language of peace." The war of words was not specific to the postwar scene but was "rooted in human psychology and ethics." Where considerations of politics and economics arise in human societies, the war of words would be present and available for analysis. Eventually, Burke would use the concept of *identification* to select and analyze episodes in the history of the war of words. However, at this point in the drafting process, he simply used the "trinitarian clusters Love-War-Work and Mine-Thine-Ours" to organize his analysis. Again, these clusters were valuable because they helped him "find ways whereby working and loving may be done without warring" ("Prospectus").

A close reading of Burke's plan for "The Rhetorical Situation" reveals that it was the most underdeveloped component of the prospectus.[1] Burke defined the rhetorical situation as "the scene for which particular rhetorical utterances are the appropriate act, or strategy." The section would address "extra-literary factors that contribute to the persuasiveness of rhetorical expressions."[2] From his correspondence, we know that Burke planned to consider rhetorical expressions both in the universal human situation and in the local economic and political situation. But there is little else to indicate that he had moved beyond this point.

"The Boundaries of Rhetoric" was a more developed section, if not on paper then at least in Burke's mind. It focused on the relationship between rhetoric and poetics as it related to the "literary battles of recent years." In a letter to Watson dated 2 November 1945 (JWP), Burke provided some detail about the literary battles he planned to address:

> Am now thinking of including a section that goes over some of the literary squabbles I went through. I was recalling the other day, for instance, how things went about the time of the first Writers

Congress. I had been haggling for months with Cowley and Josephson[3] about their relation between art and the politico-economic situation. And they had just about flattened me out with the unswerving assurance that I was a "petty bourgeois," and that's all there was to it. So finally, by the time things got around to the plans for the first Writers Congress in behalf of the Proletariat, I had become convinced that I was, hopelessly and forever a petty bourgeois. And when they asked me to write a paper for delivery at the Congress, in a mood of abject sorrow I gave a paper, on how the problem of propaganda looked as seen from the standpoint of a petty bourgeois. When I had finished, up jumps Joe Freeman, throbbing like an engine, shouting, "We have a snob among us."

Though he could "write a whole book" on these 1930s episodes, he would focus on "representative moments" that differentiated rhetoric, poetics, and esthetic criticism ("Prospectus"). "What I'd like to do," Burke explained in the same 2 November 1945 letter, "would be to give enough of the literary situation in order to make my point about the element of use that underlies so many of the apparently 'pure' criticisms." This approach would not only expose elements of the rhetorical motive but would also make the analysis more "engaging." Although Burke periodically returned to this topic in his notes and revised outlines, he never fully drafted the chapter. Instead, he used the relationship between rhetoric and poetics as a heuristic to sharpen his definition of rhetoric in the published version of *A Rhetoric of Motives*.

Finally, "Catalogue of Rhetorical Devices" would "list, classify, and analyze the many examples of rhetoric" that Burke had been "assembling over the years." The purpose of this section was to present a group of rhetorical devices organized around a "greatly reduced set of principles." These principles would emerge from "developments purely internal to the book" ("Prospectus"). In other words, they would exemplify the core principles that organized Burke's philosophy of modern rhetoric.

10 January 1946

Burke launched his post-prospectus drafting process by creating a taxonomy of criticism that differentiated *rhetorical criticism, esthetic criticism, poetic criticism, reviewings*, and *textual analysis*. According to this unpublished taxonomy, which Burke titled "Kinds of Criticism," there were two varieties of rhetorical criticism: genetic and implicational. Genetic criticism focused on the environmental or psychological conditions that sponsored specific rhetorical actions. For example, it explained how a cramped theater space could agitate an audience and thereby affect its interpretation of a film. By contrast, implicational analysis referred to the relationship between an act and its audience.[4] For example, it explained whether a rhetor's turn of phrase engendered a trusting relationship with the audience.

Whether genetic or implicational, Burke argues that rhetorical criticism is always directed outward. Genetic criticism focuses on extra-literary factors, or the immediate and measurable nontextual factors that make an argument persuasive. Implicational criticism was similarly focused on the persuasiveness of an argument, but it homed in on the measurable changes in an audience's attitude. Either way, rhetoric and rhetorical criticism was constitutively bound to a specific time and location.

Poetic criticism, by contrast, was exclusively textual in its orientation. Whereas "genetic criticism is par excellence the temporalist approach," Burke wrote, poetic criticism was "thoroughly timeless" in its focus on the internal textual relationships created by a work of art ("Kinds of Criticism"). Poetic criticism considered the work "in itself, without reference to its emergence from a context." Burke's definition of poetic criticism does not imply that literary works possess stable meaning. Instead, it argues that works of art can be interpreted independently of any specific reference point. According to this view, art can be counted upon to convey meaning regardless of where it is situated. This constitutional feature of literary art allows poetic criticism to advance "speculative or theoretical" insights that span time and space.

The most provocative implication of Burke's argument is that critics can interpret the evolution of rhetoric poetically. A poetic approach to rhetoric would focus on the conditions of its self-referentiality *irrespective of time or place*. Per the tenets of poetic criticism, acts of self-reference would obtain across time and point toward a universal truth regardless of who was writing and in what context. As we will discover, Burke's "universal" truth was the dialectic principle that the war of words helps render.

February–April 1946

The detailed chapter outlines in Burke's prospectus, combined with the successful completion of *A Grammar of Motives*, encouraged Prentice Hall to pick up the option on *A Rhetoric of Motives* (Burke to Cowley, 20 December 1945, KBP, Burke-1). On 23 February 1946 (JWP), Burke announced the good news to Watson: "The publisher has taken up the option on the Rhetoric, and has sent me a contract." When Burke received this news, he was studying contemporary warfare through the lens of fourth-century Christianity and anticipating his work on the devices: "The central motive in primitive Christianity," he told Watson, "is not in sex austerities but in a radical attempt to avoid war.... Today we are 'contemporary' with early Christianity in the sense that we must again face just as radically the problem of war, and must (albeit by a different route) be as enterprising in trying to discover just how deep the motives of the 'irascible appetite' go."

Burke learned about the fourth-century anchorites from Helen Waddell's translation of *The Desert Fathers*. As he explained in the letter to Watson and more elaborately in his essay draft, primitive Christianity "sought to propound a structure of motives that would bring about a condition of peace, not as with a mere bowing of the conquered to the conqueror, but by a more substantial kind of understanding, got by spiritualizing and universalizing the tribal concept" ("Desert Fathers," 1). Burke believed that his *love-war-work* cluster explained the "substantial kind of understanding" sought by this religious group and thus extended the study of rhetorical devices to a much earlier period history. Like the fourth-century anchorites, Burke sought ways to transcend factional *identifications* by "spiritualizing and universalizing" the tribal concept, which was not a relic of the past but was symptomatic of the human impulse toward factional conflict. According to this view, he wrote Watson, "we are 'contemporary' with early Christianity" because "we must again face just as radically the problem of war."

Whether one is an early church father or a witness to nuclear explosions, facing war requires that one "discover just how deep the motives of the 'irascible appetite' go." As the opening line of Burke's letter attests, rhetorical devices provide an entry point to the discussion because they often incite war in the name of peace. By defining the function of rhetorical devices within the broader postwar scene, Burke could question every "single aspect of warfare" and thereby remain "vigilantly skeptical even of [his own] vigilance" ("Desert Fathers," 7).

Burke drew from the desert fathers two important insights about the relationships among love, war, and work. First, rhetorical critics must identify *moral equivalents of war*, which refer to repressed aggressions that manifest themselves in the form of rhetorical devices.[5] By characterizing these devices as acts of war, Burke could determine how and to what extent US rhetorical tendencies were sponsoring violence in the name of peace. He could then devise a set of tactics that counterbalanced the nation's warlike tendencies.

Second, Burke believed that rhetorical critics must "make [themselves] absolutely, systematically, programmatically, without malice" by examining how episodes in rhetorical history (such as those revealed in Waddell's book) exposed the interminability of the war of words ("Desert Fathers," 5). These two levels of order—historical and universal—would not only address the temporal scope of humanity's warlike tendencies but would also approximate better solutions in the present by learning from episodes in the past. Burke's solutions were organized by Candide's claim that our "soundest humanity is in tending to our own gardens" ("Conclusion"). *Tending to our own gardens* meant coming to terms with one's mortality and thus allowing "each day [to have] a fit measure of retreat, meditation, and frank regret." In effect, one must remove "the frantic pressures" that characterize "our office" in life ("Conclusion"). By placing these pressures within the broader scope of human history, critics may assess whether the uncritical consumption of warlike devices is acceptable. If the answer to the question is no, then critics may seek an alternative path that disassociates oneself from nationalistic aggression.

Initially, Burke planned to publish his essay on the desert fathers separately from *A Rhetoric of Motives*, but he didn't pursue the essay beyond an initial draft and a minor revision. Although Burke never explained why he abandoned the topic, he indicated in a letter to Malcolm Cowley that *A Rhetoric of Motives* had hit rough waters: "First draft of the Rhetoric goes bumping along. Instead of writing it from start to finish, I seem to be writing it from the middle out. Each day I drive in more wedges that push the two ends farther apart. And there's just the possibility that I may, this time, be lambasted for being too easy to read. . . . I gave as the formula, 'benevolently caustic,' but out of some correspondence with Knickerbocker I have found a more tonal way of expressing the same design 'ironically irenic'" (Burke to Cowley, 3 April 1946, in Jay 274–75).[6]

This was not the first time Burke expressed difficulty managing *A Rhetoric of Motives* as a coherent work. In an earlier letter to Cowley, he likened his work on the devices to "bunching the cards preparatory to a shuffle." Although Burke anticipated that the cards would form into a "square pack," they were, instead, jutting out every which way (Burke to Cowley, 16 January 1946, MCP). "The book is as anecdotal as T.B.L.," Burke told Cowley a few months later, "except that this time the anecdotes are strung along an idea instead of a story. The clothesline method. Except that there is a shortage of clothespins, so that you have to hang several items at each spot along the line" (Burke to Cowley, 3 April 1946, in Jay 274–75).[7] Burke discovered, in other words, that there were not enough categories to contain the rhetorical devices he had identified in the popular press. As new devices emerged, he found himself attempting to hit a moving target, which, for obvious reasons, left him feeling "irascible" (Burke to Cowley, 16 January 1945, MCP).

Burke also struggled with the tone of his analysis. Initially, he viewed the "benevolently caustic" tone of his argument as an asset, likening himself to a lassoing Will Rogers (Burke to Cowley, 3 April 1946, in Jay 274–75).[8] But his caustic criticism gave way to an "ironically irenic" tone that addressed the popular press somewhat less aggressively. If Burke wanted to expose how "the *superficial* uses of persuasion . . . have in them the *ultimates* of persuasion" (*RM* 179), he needed a stylistic approach that invited audiences to think critically about their rhetorical habits. He hoped that an invitation to irony would do the trick.

To draw the ironies of war into clear relief, Burke imagined diplomatic negotiations as equivalent to what his sons "Butchie and Michael say at the sand pile" (Burke to Cowley, 3 April 1946, in Jay 274–75). By creating such an equivalence, Burke showed how the impetus to war lurks in every act of persuasion, regardless of one's social standing. If audiences learned to observe these tendencies, they could scrutinize them wherever they stood. According to Burke, warlike tendencies do not manifest themselves exclusively in the international political scene; they exist in everyday argumentative habits. This shift in focus allowed Burke to expose the mundane quality of war, in which "a myriad of constructive acts" can coalesce into a major "destructive one" (*RM* 22). If citizens did not learn to recognize their warlike tendencies, they risked identifying with nuclear destruction. Afraid of this eventuality, Burke began playing in the sandbox differently.

3

Part-to-Whole Relations

As the summer of 1946 approached, reviews of *A Grammar of Motives* began arriving in the mail. Predictably, Burke worried over the negative assessments. In particular, he was upset with Isaac Rosenfeld, a positivist philosopher whose unfavorable review had just appeared in the *Kenyon Review*. "The review in Kenyon makes me wrathful," he wrote to Stanley Edgar Hyman, "because it was given to one of the stinks of the Phartisan (which was inevitably the foreordaining of a stinkeroo treatment)" (20 April 1946, SHP). Burke's thinly veiled reference is to *Partisan Review*, a scholarly journal affiliated with his intellectual nemesis, Sidney Hook.[1] Although Rosenfeld's bad review was not surprising given the journal's political leanings, Burke demanded that Hyman "be honest and helpful" by determining whether any of Rosenfeld's concerns "seem[ed] convincing." Hyman responded by calling Rosenfeld a "phat and phony philosopher" and dismissing the review as nothing more than "high-level red-baiting." If Rosenfeld could not follow his own advice and write with "greater formal clarity, or greater material commitment," then he deserved no further consideration (Hyman to Burke, 24 April 1946, SHP).

Burke, for the most part, heeded Hyman's advice. In a letter to James Sibley Watson dated 8 May 1946 (JWP), he wrote, "[I am] trying to get Munson[2] to publish an anthology that pits Positivists vs. Dramatists: It should be the Next Phase (first the Humanist controversy, then the Proletarian one—and now, shall we say, 'Critical Substantialism,' since so many object to 'Dramatism'). At least, I think that that is the way I shall line things up in my Rhetoric, on the section to do with literary controversy." Burke's reference to the "Positivists" makes it seem as if he is preparing to settle scores with Rosenfeld in the chapter titled "Boundaries of Rhetoric." But that wasn't his goal. Distance from the literary debates of the 1930s had taught Burke to view his combatants as "tough" examiners who "forced [him] to learn [his] subject"

(Burke to Cowley, 14 April 1946, MCP). Because they helped him find a place for his ideas, there was no longer a need to be aggressive. With an even hand, he could present the evolution of the debate as "a kind of belated inventory" of literary values, he told Cowley. Given that "Boundaries of Rhetoric" was part of *A Rhetoric of Motives* and consciously extended his ideas from *A Grammar of Motives*, Burke's belated inventory would demonstrate the superiority of his "dramatistic" method.

But what exactly did Burke mean by the phrase *belated inventory*? The term *belated* refers, obviously, to something that arrived after an appointed time, and an *inventory* is a catalogue or survey that places different objects or ideas in order. If we consider the timing of Burke's comments, along with his reference to Cowley's *Exile's Return* in the letter of 14 April ("It is the equivalent, in my way of doing, to *Exile's Return* in your way"), Burke probably meant that he would write an overview of the debate from the perspective of dramatistic criticism. Had dramatistic criticism existed in the 1930s, the debates might have unfolded differently. Critics might have recognized how a humanist controversy led to a proletarian controversy, which in turn would have created a need for dramatism. By using dramatism as a frame for this historical arc, Burke could show audiences how to disentangle themselves from the ideological weeds. The work would be difficult, of course. In the 8 May letter to Watson, Burke modified "Dramatism" to "Critical Substantialism" in response to the negative reviews that *A Grammar of Motives* had already received. But the trouble of crafting this belated inventory would be worthwhile because it would show audiences how to deliberate peacefully.[3]

June–August 1946

As the belated inventory in "Boundaries of Rhetoric" took shape, Burke began working on smaller writing assignments. Earlier that spring, Hyman had invited him to give a lecture at Bennington College, where Burke had been teaching as an adjunct lecturer. As payment for the lecture, Hyman promised to "have the velvet carpet laid" for him and Libby (his wife) and ensured that "half the student body" would attend (Hyman to Burke, 24 April 1946, SHP). The lecture, titled "Words, War, and Peace," would introduce the study of rhetoric by demonstrating how it related to the postwar situation. Because the audience would be full of nonspecialists, Burke would offer practical applications relevant to their everyday lives.

From a letter to Watson on 11 June 1946 (JWP), we learn that the lecture went well. Burke emphasized the distinction between rhetoric and poetics, characterizing the former as "applied poetic[s]" because it considered "the extra-literary situation involved in the expression." He also discussed the relationship between rhetoric and "the Logomachy" (the war of words), a constitutive feature of the rhetorical situation that "involve[d] part-whole relations." Although each part has an "independent nature," the individual episodes in history "all belong to a greater whole, and depend for the existence on such universal participation."

Burke's argument about the "greater whole" of rhetoric was important to the evolution of his argument because it required that he consider the role that identification could play in a modern philosophy of motives. War occurs because "the fact of partiality" creates a sense of individual property, Burke told Watson, a "mine-own-ness" that leads to division and may spark conflict. Thus there is "recourse to <u>identification</u> (whereby the individual part, while maintaining its individuality and seeking advances for it, also must, with varying degrees of sincerity, <u>identify</u> itself with larger wholes)" (Burke to Watson, 11 June 1946, JWP). Identification, facilitating both the act of individuation (part) and group formation (whole), helps create the immediate rhetorical situation (local), which is constituted by an unrelenting invitation to war over property (universal).

Burke connected his insights on the universality of war to modern political ideologies, focusing specifically on how the impersonality of group identifications allowed routine and potentially catastrophic violence. In the same letter to Watson, to explain how such violence could occur, he recounted his experience with an exhibitor at the World's Fair who sterilized a drop of water with an electric ray: "It was filled with live bacteria of some sort, which cd. be seen scurrying about happily . . . then, of a sudden, the death flash, whereupon everything on the screen was reduced to total stillness . . . and the audience, at the contrast, broke into a cry of sympathy for the poor dead bugs, whose destiny had been brought to the imagination, given at least as much appeal as a forest full of birds." This demonstration revealed a powerful feature of identification in the war of words. Because the audience was caught off guard, their cries of sympathy signified no predisposition toward apathy. The audience's identification with the bacteria allowed it to identify with the fate of humans who were subjected to the threat of nuclear and biological weapons. The problem was not associated with apathy, then, but with the naturalization of "certain aspects of our vocabulary" that encouraged apathetic responses. To address this problem, Burke needed a vocabulary to shake people free from their naturalized habits, one that would collapse the distance between "personal feelings and public results" and thereby redirect their sympathies toward more humane outcomes.

Reading through Burke's notes and early drafts, one gets the impression that identification, war, and the rhetorical situation are fundamental to his argument. He uses these terms to analyze the "sorry rhetoric of the U.N, of our diplomatic meetings, etc., and the war of nerves in the press" in a clear and compelling manner (Burke to Watson, 11 June 1946, JWP). And yet Burke does not define identification, war, and the rhetorical situation coterminously until this moment. Reading his notes, one expects (or maybe hopes) that his reference to identification is the functional equivalent of an intake of breath. But Burke moves on without further comment. His major theoretical leap forward would have to wait for another day.

In the meantime, Burke continued to evaluate US involvement in early postwar geopolitics. While preparing his Bennington lecture, he began an essay titled "The American Way." The Office of War Information, a newly created branch of the US State Department, commissioned the essay on 27 February 1946. Evidently, the editor of the French magazine *Esprit* had contacted the office and requested that Burke identify the characteristic qualities of American philosophies, ideologies, and language differences.[4] Although the job didn't pay well, the office believed that writing the essay would be worth Burke's time and hoped he would contribute (Helen Louise Johnstone to Burke, 27 February 1946, KBLT, C12).

What the magazine lacked in payment, it made up for in the prestige of its contributors. *Esprit* had secured commitments from Margaret Mead, Katherine Anne Porter, Reinhold Niebuhr, and Claude Lévi-Strauss (to name only the most famous contributors). Burke probably didn't care much about the company his essay kept. He seems to have taken the bait because it provided an opportunity to counteract the ill will that characterized the United States' rhetorical tendencies. He writes in the essay:

> It is questionable whether, for the atomic age, *any* kind of militant assertion, however justified on moral grounds, is a fit condition for human society. Resistance is heroic; and the warm and brilliant poetry of Aragon written during the Nazi occupation of France shows how felicitously it unites the elements of love, war, and work, as the poet employed his medium to recruit allies against the enemy, inspiriting his side with the love of all good things traditionally associated with country; indeed these three motives form so consubstantial a trinity, that man's attempts to modify his thinking profoundly in any

one of these ways will demand equally profound modifications of the other two. But we shall not be really radical (in the sense which the threat of atomic and biological war imposes upon us) unless even such songful felicity as that of Aragon's poetry of the Resistance becomes suspect. ("American Way" 8–9)[5]

Burke's reference to military aggression is provocative, but the phrase "form so consubstantial a trinity" steals the show. Because love, war, and work are in identification, the modification of one term requires a corresponding revision to the other terms. To demonstrate his point, Burke refers to the French poet Louis Aragon, who, in his resistance to the Nazi occupation of France, modified his countrymen's understanding of war and work by appealing to their love of country.

Three features of Burke's argument concerning Aragon merit close consideration. The first is Burke's alternative approach to political resistance, which centers on "criticism and analysis" ("American Way" 9). Burke defines political resistance as renegotiating the relationship between love, war, and work. In this essay, Burke does not cite or analyze any passage from Aragon's poetry. He simply describes it as felicitous in its songful delivery and claims that it recruits "allies against the enemy, inspiriting his side with the love of all good things traditionally associated with country." By enlisting Aragon's poetry for rhetorical purposes, Burke initiates a corresponding shift in his definitions of love and war.

The second feature is the universal reach of Burke's criticism. Although Aragon's poetic resistance (individual) was context-bound (Nazi occupation of France), Burke's characterization of it as "heroic" places it firmly within a universal frame.

How so? The answer could be as simple as: "Aragon wrote poetry; thus it occupies a universal orbit." But Burke does not make this argument. Instead, he argues that Aragon's resistance is heroic because all forms of political resistance are heroic ("American Way" 8). The heroic, as we will discover, is a core feature of myth, in which the actions of heroes are repeated as meaningful irrespective of time and context. So while Aragon's resistance was by definition tied to temporal conditions, Burke's identification moves it into the universal. The upshot is that rhetoric can become poetic via a mythic framework.[6]

The third feature is how individual examples of rhetoric can be collected under the aegis of a universal order. Burke viewed Aragon and fourth-century anchorites as contemporaries because they resisted war by reconfiguring the terms *love*, *war*, and *work*. When placed in identification, they form a curve of history[7] that exposes an elemental feature of human motivation. Burke's curve of history would not collapse the material differences that distinguish individual wars. The fact that Burke differentiates "atomic and biological warfare" from other forms of warfare makes this point clearly. But in their capacity to point toward a larger whole, these episodes in the war of words expose a motivational principle that transcends individual contexts. This motivational principle does not appear in the content of individual poems or sayings but in the form of scrutiny that consciously reconfigures the relationship between love, war, and work. By tracking this form of scrutiny over time, Burke believed that he could build a pathbreaking philosophy of modern rhetoric.

21 September 1946

To document the evolution of his thinking, Burke wrote a new outline for *A Rhetoric of Motives*, which is distinguished by its "September 1946" heading. Unlike the previous outline, Burke now organized the work into three major sections: "The Range of Rhetoric," "Rhetoric and Poetic," and "The Logomachy."

Like the "Landmarks" section from his earlier prospectus, "The Range of Rhetoric" surveyed the field of rhetoric and used Aristotle's definition as a starting point. Burke would then define "The Rhetorical Situation"—now a subsection of the larger section—within his long history of rhetoric. In a parenthetical aside, Burke explains that the major challenge of this section would be to control rather than fix his definition of rhetoric. Rather than treat rhetoric as a logical concept that existed independent of history, Burke proposed to treat it as a "<u>title</u>, used in <u>history</u>, by many different kinds of men having many different views and activities" ("Outline [Sept. 1946]"). This tactic allowed him to extend the range of works that contributed to the rhetorical tradition and, through such extension, determine the "basic definition [of rhetoric], and methods of transformation that could account for the many departures from it." Although Burke does not make the point explicitly in his outline, this description correlates with the part-to-whole relationship he associates with *identification* in "Words, War, and Peace."

Unlike his initial prospectus, the September 1946 outline contains a section dedicated to "Rhetoric and Poetic" in which Burke planned to "isolate the good side of rhetoric" by distinguishing works considered in themselves (poetic) from works intended for an audience (rhetoric). Burke surmised that this approach would counterbalance the negative assessments that appeared in the "Logomachy" section because the formal qualities of literary art are oriented more toward contemplation than toward verbal combat. "I think that a <u>systematized</u> treatment of the rhetorical between internal structure and external address, as exemplified in the study of <u>good</u> plays," he explained to Watson, "can restore the balance in the book, without requiring me to peddle my previous stuff over again." In addition to focusing on good plays, Burke planned to include "recipes for tragedy, comedy, satire," and sermons (Burke to Watson, 21 September 1946, JWP).

The final section, "The Logomachy," remained largely consistent with the description in the original prospectus, but with two noteworthy revisions. First, the outline for this section introduced new terms such as "Malice and the Lie" and "Scientific Rhetoric." Second, Burke incorporated the section on literary controversy titled "Boundaries of Rhetoric" and gave it the new title "While They Last."

The terms *malice and the lie* and *scientific rhetoric* would play an important role in both the published version of *A Rhetoric of Motives* and the (previously) unpublished version of *The War of Words*. But at this point in the drafting process, Burke does not offer specific details about how these terms figure in his argument. What we do know is that his assessment of the contemporary political scene would continue to adopt a negative tone. In the same letter to Watson of 21 September 1946, Burke explained that "The Logomachy" "wd. deal with all the variants of malice and the lie, the thumbs-down side of rhetoric, and wd. contain our specialty, analysis of rhetorical devices (operated about the ambiguities of competition and cooperation)." In "While They Last," Burke would present an "analysis of news, literary polemic, etc. (I see a chance to smack at some of my old enemies, under favorable, even enjoyable, conditions.)" In other words, he told Watson, it would interpret the literary debates of the 1930s in terms of the contemporary political climate.

Placing "The Logomachy" at the end of the book resolved some of Burke's stylistic problems. By opening with more traditional and poetic contributions to rhetoric, Burke would enable audiences to define rhetoric as more than polarized political argumentation. Rhetoric could provide ways of orienting oneself toward the problem of division and suggest new strategies for bridging divisions without resorting to direct violence. Having developed this perspective, readers would be better prepared to examine the dangers of their immediate historical context. They could place it within a long history of conflict and find comfort in the fact that resolution was possible no matter how dire the circumstances seemed to be. Burke felt that this ending would also prepare readers for *A Symbolic of Motives*: "If one ends [*A Rhetoric of Motives*] on the theme of the Universal Wrangle, as goaded by unnecessary itches and appetites," he explained to Watson, "then one has the best lead into Book Three, which is the study of these Itches and Appetites in themselves (as grounded in motives <u>not competitive or invidious at all</u>)" (21 September 1946, JWP). The unnecessary itches and appetites characteristic of the early postwar period were, in fact, part of a larger thematic of conflict caused by the "Universal Wrangle." By observing the historical arc of human conflict, audiences could accept its inevitability and scrutinize it more carefully. *A Rhetoric of Motives* would prepare them to do so through the study of external address; *A Symbolic of Motives* would prepare them to do so through the study of self-referentiality in literary texts.

The evolving postwar scene weighed heavily on Burke as he composed this revised outline. In a letter to Watson dated 14 September 1946 (JWP), Burke complained of physiological and psychological illness. He felt frustrated that his book was "all over the place," but the larger problem was the "so very damned gloomy" state of the world, which left him feeling "physically depressed about the heart." Burke was concerned that the only ideas gaining traction in the early postwar period were ones that led to "Great Devastation." Maybe rhetorical education could help. But its success hinged on the ability to bring "[the hubris of Science] compellingly to both men's understanding and their imagination."

Two days earlier, on 12 September, Henry A. Wallace had delivered a speech suggesting that a political sea change was possible. With a tinge of hope, Burke wrote to Watson, "The Wallace speech is the first thing I've seen pointing in the other direction, for a long time." Among other things, Wallace urged that Americans be dedicated to peace, which could be attained by abandoning anti-Russian policies and modifying the country's military spending. Unfortunately, Wallace's proposal did not gain much traction. In a postscript written the next day, Burke observed that Truman's response to Wallace signaled a long-term commitment to "Atom Diplomacy." Still, Burke remained convinced that *A Rhetoric of Motives*, if it became more balanced in its assessment of the contemporary rhetorical situation, could improve his "morbid gloom over the homicidal and suicidal corruption of the contemporary press" (Burke to Watson, 21 September 1946, JWP). In time, such improvement would find its place at the core of his argument.

4

The Factors Behind Rhetoric

Early on, Burke reveled in the "sheer formlessness" of his drafting process (Burke to Watson, 22 June 1945, JWP). But these positive feelings dissipated as his argument evolved. After several unsuccessful attempts to impose order on his drafted chapters, Burke worried that his argument was overly topical and unnecessarily negative (Burke to Cowley, 27 September 1946, KBP, Burke-1). To solve this problem, he turned to the distinction between rhetoric and poetics. This distinction propelled Burke forward because it placed him on familiar terrain. Identifying the rhetorical upshot of poetic texts could, as it had in previous books, establish a new curve of history. By extending the range of rhetoric along these lines, Burke could demonstrate that rhetorical works, whether they consciously contributed to the rhetorical tradition or not, all responded to a generating principle—what he called a *minimum grounding in unity*.[1] From this vantage point, his modern philosophy of rhetoric could become more systematic in quality.

September–December 1946

Burke's students at Bennington College deserve credit for propelling his revision process forward. In a letter to Cowley dated 27 September 1946 (KBP, Burke-1), Burke explained that one student's question "required of me an answer which incidentally organized a whole third of my book for me. Whereas previously this part of the book was a clutter of loose ends," Burke told Cowley, "I was suddenly able to find requirement no. 1, ye olde 'generating principle,' so that the many parts could be derived from one source."

Testing his argument on students had always been a part of the drafting plan. Once Burke had completed a rough first draft, he would focus on case studies and "start pinning them into [his] outline, supply new matter, transitions, etc." and then "mull over the material until September," at which point he would "try teaching it from September to mid-December" (Burke to Cowley, 25 November 1945, in Jay 272–73). In the past, Burke had benefited immensely from this approach. "The particular cunning I am aiming at," he told Cowley, "is a scheme whereby my teaching can be wholly an aid to me, in greatly extending the possibilities of experimental testing. My Grammar was wholly rewritten after such a test."

Burke's comments clearly refer to his draft of "The Range of Rhetoric" (Burke to Cowley, 27 September 1946, KBP, Burke-1). In the chapter overview of his "September 1946" outline (KBP, Burke-3), Burke writes in a parenthetical aside, "when on 'controlling' the definition [of rhetoric], rather than trying to keep it fixed: cite on student who asked which one we opted for." Although Burke does not offer any more details, we can imagine that the student's question went something like: "Well, which definition of rhetoric do *you* prefer?"[2]

Picking sides was not an option, of course. If Burke was to demonstrate how rhetoric formed attitudes and actions across history, then his philosophy of modern rhetoric needed to present *variations* of rhetoric in varied *and* coherent relief. These variations should gesture toward universal principles without losing track of the material exigencies that called them into being. To accomplish this task, Burke defined rhetoric as a heading used throughout history that indicated the existence of a generating principle of language. This principle would, in due course, emphasize the capacity of definitional transformations.

Burke did not name a generating principle for another three months. In a 7 October 1946 letter to Cowley (KBP, Burke-1), he reported, "Meanwhile, know me for one who is naught but Rhetoric. I don't know what the class is getting out of my courses, but I am profiting hugely. At each lecture I find some shift in presentation that makes a lot of difference; also, I see new areas to mine. I now doubt whether I could finish the revision during the winter vacation, and I don't give a d--n." In the drafting history of *A Rhetoric of Motives*, Burke's final line is a watershed moment. More often than not, Burke expressed impatience with the fact that *A Rhetoric of Motives* was not yet finished. But in this letter to Cowley, he seems delighted that the finish line has receded from view. The discovery of persuasive "shift[s] in presentation" and "new areas [of research] to mine" transformed his attitude about the work. Although arriving at this point had been difficult, the discovery of "an A-to-B-to-C, etc." made it worth the trouble (Burke to Cowley, 27 September 1946, KBP, Burke-1).

By the end of the semester, Burke had collected exemplary literary works that constituted "broken fragments of a single object," as he wrote to Watson in late December. Although his collected literary works had received treatment in the past, scholars acted as though they "had found . . . each [work] in a different place, and named it not from the whole to which it originally belonged, but from the place in which he found it." According to Burke, this interpretive tendency structured "much modern analysis of language" (Burke to Watson, 22 December 1946, JWP).

In a December 1946 review of Ernst Cassirer's *The Myth of the State*, Burke extended this observation by claiming that modern language critics tended to split language into magical (incantatory) and semantic (descriptive) categories. This limited framework encouraged them to pit "science against some antithetical term" and thus overlook "the motive that goes into rhetoric." Without a systematic treatment of rhetoric, public audiences would characterize nondescriptive uses of language as a magical "reversion to savagery in the modern world." For Burke, this tendency made it difficult, if not impossible, to "approach the modern political 'myth' . . . more directly" ("*Homo Faber*" 668). So he would need to develop a systematic method for approaching modern political myths.

Burke approached modern political myths via the ultimate terms that permeate all language use. In a letter to Richard McKeon dated 2 December 1946 (RMP), he explained:

> For the Rhetoric, I am sure you will be glad to hear, I have finally perfected my early weak hankerings after a doctrine proclaiming the "Symmetrical Necessity for the Existence of God." Carrying out my post-Kantian reduction from "God" to "God-term," I have founded the New Semantics designed to show that, <u>if</u> you use language at all, you vow yourself to its ultimate logic, which winds up in a "God-term." And then, by some very expensive maneuvers which I have worked out but are too cumbersome for tossing off here, I contrive to get from "God-term" back to "God." . . . Let us hope I can get it published before your bomb-happy colleagues blast us all to nothing, leaving plenty of room for super-personality but a vast absence of just plain personality.

This passage is remarkable not simply because Burke announces an approach to semantic analysis in which mythic terminologies function as the sine qua non of all language use. It is also remarkable because this approach focuses on the lived experiences of everyday language users. Notice, for example, how Burke turns McKeon's attention to his "bomb-happy colleagues," whose research threatens the human race. This comment suggests that the superpersonal quality of language is indifferent to the everyday dealings of personality. Like a nuclear chain reaction, it may find a perfect state in sheer desolation. And yet, if the tension is controlled, language may produce unprecedented amounts of energy that cultivate personal life rather than destroy it.

January–March 1947

Burke gave his generating principle a formal name on 27 January 1947, when he updated Watson on the progress of *A Rhetoric of Motives*: "Have got it all down to three words: for the Grammar, Substance. For the Rhetoric, Identification. For the Symbolic, Identity," he explained. "The rest is but to draw out all the implications, transform them into explications. One does not 'synthesize the complexities of the contemporary scene.' One <u>begins</u> with synthesis, and shows how the many things are from it, out of it, spun and spawned" (JWP). Burke's confidence in this letter is arresting. Remember, his conception of *A Rhetoric of Motives* had not yet been formalized; an unmistakable tentativeness characterized his prospectus, and the frequency with which he revised his outlines suggests that his argument remained fluid. Choosing identification as the book's organizing term seems to have stuck, however, because it systematized not only *A Rhetoric of Motives* but the entire motives trilogy. Just as *substance* had organized the *Grammar*, *identification* and *identity* would organize *Rhetoric* and *Symbolic*, respectively. The step from *Grammar* to *Rhetoric* would involve a shift from substance thinking to common-substance thinking. To arrive at identity, Burke needed to place local conflicts within a universal war of words and focus on the nature of external address. Then he could examine the war of words as it was manifested in internal (or poetic) address.

Burke's new focus disclosed an exciting evolution in *A Rhetoric of Motives*. If "one <u>begins</u> with synthesis," then everything that follows "shows how the many things are from it, out of it, spun and spawned." This assertion is more about delivery than methodology. Just as he had begun *A Grammar of Motives* with a consideration of substance, so he would also begin *A Rhetoric of Motives* with a discussion of identification. Once established, he could then "mark off the areas of rhetoric, by showing how a rhetorical motive is often present where it is not usually recognized, or thought to belong" (*RM* xiii).

Having established identification as the organizing principle of *A Rhetoric of Motives*, Burke began a concentrated study of myth. By his own admission, this turn was unexpected (Burke to Watson, 21 February 1947, JWP). However, there were a number of scholars working on myth at the time; as Cowley explained in a letter to Burke dated 3 March 1947 (KBP, Burke-1), myth had become, to his disappointment, "the fashionable word" in academic circles. In short order, Burke had been invited to review Ernst Cassirer's *The Myth of the State* for the *Nation* and to participate in a lecture series devoted to myth at Bennington College. Along with Peter Drucker, Max Salvadori, Joseph Campbell, and Erich Fromm, he would address myth's relevance to the postwar geopolitical scene.[3]

Burke did not study myth because it was fashionable. As we have noted, he needed the resources of poetry to help rhetoric gain a universal reach. Since myth was a type of poetry, arguably the oldest type, it was ideally suited to his study of the relationship between love, war, and work. As he told Watson, Virgil's "mythology should be considered equivalent for a modern terminology of the 'unconscious.' . . . He had many enterprising variants of the love-war equation" (Burke to Watson, 21 February 1947, JWP).

As we might expect, Burke's study of myth ranged well beyond the boundaries of literary studies. Bronislaw Malinowski's *Freedom and Civilization* and *Myth in Primitive Psychology*, Karl Mannheim's *Ideology and Utopia*, J. A. Stewart's *The Myths of Plato*, Thorstein Veblen's *Theory of the Leisure Class*, J. W. Mackail's *Virgil and His Meaning to the World Today*, and Wilhelm Reich's *The Function of the Orgasm* are just a handful of the works he consulted during this stage in the drafting process. Of the lot, Reich's was probably the most unusual. Burke had learned about Reich's research from a plucky Bennington student who saw in Reich's books "a sanction for picking up tail." Curious about the lead, Burke wrote to his friend William Carlos Williams to learn more (Burke to William Carlos Williams, 8 January 1947, in East, *Humane* 103).

Williams's response was encouraging but measured. Although he endorsed Reich's findings from a medical perspective and drew some interesting distinctions between Freud's and Reich's research, Williams suspected that the book might not be worth Burke's time because it was "a medical treatise more than anything else" (Williams to Burke, in East, *Humane* 105). Nevertheless, Burke read the book, took extensive notes on it, and sent his notes to Watson. As Burke told Watson in a letter dated 17 March 1947 (JWP), he was "batting the book into [his] bean" in part because "the stupidity and corruption of the rhetoric which has been let loose around the Truman message finally got [him] so disturbed that [he] simply had to dig into something else for a few days." The malaise of the early postwar scene was evidently getting under Burke's skin.

Burke's notes on Reich and myth are provocative because they indicate how his work on identification was evolving. For example, following a definition of myth as "stating dialectical principles in concrete terms," Burke considers how the "'transmigration of souls' is based on real experience. growth (transformation) by successive abandoning of selves. Succession of selves . . . Development as a succession of selves, grounded in continuity of the one nervous system with its related 'consciousness'" ("myth—"). The phrase *transmigration of souls* refers to *metempsychosis,* or the notion that a soul can pass from one body to another. Burke did not seem to be interested in the possibility of reincarnation but rather in the role that symbol systems could play in transforming and extending the self—or representing the "truth" of one's transformations and extensions.[4] If one shared, or could be persuaded that one shared, a common substance with another person, one could vicariously participate in another person's actions and thereby transform that person's identity. In other words, identity is by definition a complex braid of identifications that are not entirely one's own. Myth, as a concrete figuration of the dialectic principle, draws the formal operations (e.g., identification, transformation, transcendence) of such braiding into clear relief.[5]

As influential as Cassirer's, Malinowski's, Mannheim's, and Reich's works were in the development of Burke's argument, J. W. Mackail's *Virgil and His Meaning to the World Today* played the most important role. In his preparatory notes for the Bennington lecture—eventually titled "Ideology and Myth"—Burke says that he became "interested in Virgil because of his relation to the pax Romana," which carries "many important correspondences [with] the situation today" ("Ideology" 202). Virgil encouraged a desire for peace by creating a vision of Rome "that transcended the political, yet . . . had political attitudes interwoven into it" (201). He did so by establishing a transhistorical curve of history that positioned Rome's political power in terms of a *mythic destiny*.

For Virgil, the emperor of Rome was not just a political figure or conqueror but also the manifestation of a divine idea called *peace*. "The real emperor" thus became "mythically resonant" as "the bridge that brought a myth and an ideology together." The myth was "tolerant," Burke explains, because it did not require theological conversion from non-Roman citizens; it only demanded "that [citizens] accept inclusion into the Roman political economy." Virgil's *Aeneid* thereby stood in sharp contrast to Hitler's Third Reich, which governed according to a "theory of racial domination" that "marked for a systematic destruction or great weakening" any form of difference or dissidence ("Ideology" 202). It is little wonder Burke felt that the "whole hopeless turmoil of human motives" could be found in the pages of *The Aeneid* ("on myth").

Virgil's strategy was provocative because it responded to the dangers posed by "modern weapons." The "inexorable demand" of atomic weapons, Burke explains, "is that they offer peace without pacification, that is, a peace without war, a peace *before* war." In these lines, Burke anticipates how the postwar geopolitical scene would become deadlocked in an ideological struggle and thus create "a peace *before* war," which was no peace at all ("Ideology" 202). Without a transcending perspective, warring factions would become deadlocked in an argumentative endgame—until, that is, tensions reached a fever pitch and "a third world war" became inevitable (203).

Burke felt that *The Aeneid* was preferable to contemporary works that aimed to transcend ideological conflict. For example, although Karl Manheim's *Ideology and Utopia* built "up a science" to transcend the factionalism of competing ideologies, it could not find a deeper "source of motives" ("Ideology" 198). Independent of this source, critics would become caught in a spin cycle of ideological critique. To transcend ideological struggle, which Burke characterizes as *profoundly* rhetorical in nature, one must identify or create a new order of motives around myth.

At the end of his lecture, Burke outlines a twelve-step method for creating a new political myth and thus a new political order. He appropriated this method from Mackail and modified it to account for the impossibility of attaining a "peace of pacification" in postwar geopolitics ("Ideology" 202). Each step emphasizes the need to establish a universal vision of politics that attends to the material conditions that distinguish local historical scenes; Burke's vision celebrated the heroic but emphasized that "much courage, power, [and] ambition have been misdirected." In doing so, Burke defined "human motives in the most incisive and comprehensive terms, as regards both conscious and unconscious orders of experience" (205). Finally, it seems, Burke had developed a coherent vision for the work.

From "Ideology and Myth"
Kenneth Burke's Twelve Steps for a Hypothetical Myth of Today

1. The work must transcend nationalism. But it must survey the pageant of nationalism's emergence, the quality of its exaltation, even

while considering it inadequate as an over-all political motive. The "mission" and "supremacy" of national strength could be fulfilled only in the attempt to go beyond it, not by mere decay (the usual way in which it is "transcended") but by a positive new step.
2. It must establish and vindicate the cult of the *region* (the piety of loyalty to a particular location), presenting it in ways that do not at all require the domination over other regions, but recognizing each as having its own peculiar motives differentiating it from the totality of world-motives but not setting it against such world-motives.
3. It must establish the vital interconnection between the modern world and as much of the past (not only Greek, but universal) as can be imaginatively encompassed.
4. It must consider the modern world, not as "superior" to other ages, but in terms of first and last things, motives which confront all ages, though in ways varying with the conditions of time and place.
5. It must be intensely concerned with the momentous conflicts that center in technology and property, and that now threaten to pit the United States against the Soviet Union somewhat as Rome and Carthage were once opposed.
6. It must celebrate the feats of heroes, great deeds in battle and council and government, such as had lent immortal greatness to the *Iliad* and *Odyssey*. But above the sincere praise of great deeds, should hover the thought of human folly, the concern ever with the ironic possibility that much courage, power, ambition have been misdirected: not the "explaining" of this so much as the constant meditating upon it.
7. It must give expression of love and adventure, though as modified by the perspective of modern psychology.
8. "It must possess direct vital human interests," but its aim to "create men and women drawn to the heroic scale and on the heroic plane" should be confined within the limits of ironic sophistication. (The "heroic" would be conceived along the lines of mythic identity treated by Thomas Mann in the Joseph story, conceiving of role in terms of its ritual completion, with its formal perfection being seen as its essence. Here would be the archetypal figure, situated in the mythic past, as "temporal" way of stating the "essential" aspect of the role, the aspect which is concealed behind the accidents and particulars of the role as enacted in one specific set of circumstances. Cf. also the kind of thinking preserved in the

Aristotelian concept of the entelechy, a being's "perfection" residing in its fulfilling the highest potentialities of its kind.)
9. "It must connect its figures with larger and more august issues," with the laws of nature—pondering always on the direction of human destiny as regards life in general and the individual in particular.
10. It must look, as towards a Messiah, towards a new regime which it could exalt, giving "shape and colour to its ideals of peace and justice development and reconstruction, ordered liberty, beneficent rule." But never forgetting that this cannot be the peace of pacification, the Roman peace.
11. It should draw the lineaments of an ideal citizen (at once ruler and ruled). He would be gravely conscious of his mission (even to being conscious of the possible self-congratulatory deceptions in such a posture). He would be in favor of "rising towards its high demands, subordinating to it all thoughts of ease or luxury, all allurements of pleasure and temptation of the senses," except insofar as moderate relaxations and concessions to one's own weaknesses help to prevent militant austerities and to make one less uncharitable.
12. It must think of human motives in the most incisive and comprehensive terms, as regards both conscious and unconscious orders of experience.

April–June 1947

The evolution of Burke's thinking led to another structural revision, which appears in an unpublished outline dated 27 April 1947. In this new outline, Burke breaks *A Rhetoric of Motives* into nine major sections:

1. Ideology and Myth
2. The Rhetorical Situation
3. Rhetoric and Poetic
4. Rhetoric of the Drama
5. "While They Last"
6. "Scientific Rhetoric"
7. Bureaucracy
8. Devices
9. Conclusion

As Burke began drafting the book from his September 1946 outline, he discovered that his opening chapter missed the mark. Although it began with a definition of rhetoric that seemed "pedagogically correct," in application it left him "drooping" (Burke to Watson, 27 April 1947, JWP). He tried to solve this problem by reviewing "briefly all the things [he] had previously said on rhetoric," he wrote to Watson, but that made him "droop even more." To maintain forward momentum, he began taking notes for the section titled "The Rhetorical Situation."

From earlier outlines, we know that this section was to examine "the grounds, or resources, available to the Rhetorician in giving urgency and poignancy to his utterance" ("Prospectus"). It would do this by demonstrating how resources available in local situations were connected to resources available in all situations. Initially, "The Rhetorical Situation" seemed to offer the "panoramic quality" Burke sought, as he told Watson. But after further consideration, he concluded that "beginning a book on rhetoric by a long chapter on something else" distracted readers from the work's "main subject." So he turned to his recent lecture "Ideology and Myth" instead (Burke to Watson, 27 April 1947, JWP).

In the September 1946 outline, Burke had folded "The Rhetorical Situation" into "The Range of Rhetoric." In this new iteration, he allowed it to become a freestanding section, or chapter, once again. Although Burke had taken notes for the chapter, he does not offer much description beyond what we have already discussed. One important detail stands out, however. In the chapter description for "Ideology and Myth" Burke proposes to study "the factors behind rhetoric" ("Outline [April 27, 1947]"). This phrasing seems to replicate the description of "The Rhetorical Situation" from his prospectus, which promises to survey "the formal and the extra-literary factors that contribute to the persuasiveness of rhetorical expressions." Burke goes out of his way in the 1947 outline to differentiate "Ideology and Myth" from "The Rhetorical Situation." The argumentative distinction thus needs further clarification.

We have already seen that Burke was concerned about the "obvious drawbacks" of beginning a book on rhetoric with a chapter titled "The Rhetorical Situation" ("the Rhetorical Situation being the factors behind rhetoric"), as he had written to Watson on 27 April 1947 (JWP). Although "The Rhetorical Situation" and "Ideology and Myth" both focus on factors behind rhetoric, the former deals in *extra-literary* factors, whereas the latter would focus on *literary* factors such as the poetic form of myth. As Burke told Watson, "this Myth racket seems to be just the thing. For it is panoramic, it gives a fairly good sampling of characteristic rhetorical moments and it shows the kind of factors that are behind rhetoric."

In a letter to Watson on 11 February 1947 (JWP), Burke drew the distinction into even clearer relief: "Resolved: that property is (a) the very core of moral integrity; (b) the very core of war. Hence, if we are not to carry out the logic of the new weapons, the need for a 'New Myth' aimed at new dissociations (in the de Gourmont sense) at precisely this point." *Property* and *nuclear weapons* constitute here the *extra-literary factors* (e.g., the rhetorical situation) that affect an argument's persuasiveness. If the goal was to help audiences become aware of these factors, then rhetoric needed a new myth (e.g., poetic form) that placed such factors within a broader historical framework. Again, this form of criticism was consistent with the successful strategies Burke had identified in the work of Aragon and Virgil.

In the subsequent chapters, Burke expanded his discussion of rhetoric and poetics. He imported the chapter "Rhetoric and Poetic" from the September 1946 outline, created a new chapter titled "Rhetoric of the Drama," and reintroduced "While They Last" as a separate chapter. We have noted how "Rhetoric of the Drama" was to balance his negative assessments of the popular press. In his 27 April letter to Watson, Burke explained that the chapter was "getting some additions" because his students at Bennington "forced [him] into finding what [he] needed" for it: "an over-all vocabulary" for student papers that could explain how the different plays related to one another. We catch a glimpse of this vocabulary in a set of drafting notes in which Burke outlines such terms as "(PC) Pointing Up the Conflict," "IR(ony)," "IN(cidental)," and "ST(eps)."[6] As Burke told Watson, each of these terms focused on "just what 'dialectic' means."

The chapter "While They Last" also returned to Burke's plan for *A Rhetoric of Motives*. As before, it would focus on "the litry racket; a kind of Inferno, where we might consign enemies and theories to hell; attack, intermingled with litry theory" (Burke to Watson, 27 April 1947, JWP). However, instead of figuring in the "Logomachy" section, "While They Last" would serve as Burke's transition point to local rhetorical debates, which he would address in the sections "Scientific Rhetoric," "Bureaucracy," and "Devices." Evidently, he felt confident enough to address these debates, with the positive side of rhetoric being pointed up in "Rhetoric and Poetic" and "Rhetoric of the Drama."

What we know about "Scientific Rhetoric," "Bureaucracy," and "Devices" is limited to the notes that accompany each section heading in the outline and letter to Watson. In the unpublished outline, Burke offers no further elaboration on how the section "Scientific Rhetoric" would unfold. In the letter to Watson, he explains that it would provide a "perspective by incongruity by the Aristotelian point of view," because Aristotle "treats the scientific as the opposite of the rhetorical." By scientific rhetoric, Burke informed Watson, he meant the "'honest' ways in which news can be fallacious." In particular, he would focus on "concealed persuasion natural to the 'best' news-purveying" (Burke to Watson, 27 April 1947, JWP).

In "Bureaucracy," Burke would study the "social organizations behind rhetoric, legal finagling as rhetoric, tax reports as a form of rhetoric, accountancy as rhetoric, parliamentary tactics, etc." According to Burke's definition, social organizations constituted *extra-literary* factors related to persuasion. As this section was "an aspect of The Rhetorical Situation," it might "eventually merge" with the earlier chapter (Burke to Watson, 27 April 1947, JWP). In his unpublished outline, Burke wrote in the margins that this chapter would include considerations of the "U.N. & peace conference" ("Outline [April 27, 1947]"). Though this detail does not appear in the letter to Watson, it suggests that Burke would also consider how the rhetorical motive structured institutional processes in topical postwar events.

Finally, the "Devices" section would be composed of Burke's "catalogue of strategies, in the cooperative-competitive Scramble," as he put it in the 27 April letter to Watson. As in the prospectus, he would "list, classify, and analyze the many examples of rhetoric" ("Prospectus"). But in a departure from the 1946 outline, "Devices" would become its own chapter. There are two important features of Burke's description of this chapter. First, he refers to the devices as his "Neo-Machiavellian" lore, by which he means, presumably, the administrative tactics one uses "to move [an audience] to your purposes" (Burke to Watson, 27 April 1947, JWP; see also *RM* 158). As Burke explains in the published version of *A Rhetoric of Motives*, administrative tactics "cannot be confined to the strictly verbal; [they are] a mixture of symbolism and definite empirical operations" (*RM* 161). So "Devices" would extend the discussion Burke advanced in "Bureaucracy." Second, Burke asserts that the "Devices" chapter was "the origin of the whole project" and, in so doing, demonstrates that *A Rhetoric of Motives* was still engaged with the warlike tendencies of the contemporary news media (Burke to Watson, 27 April 1947, JWP).

Burke's April 1947 outline was clearly evolving into a two-part project in which the philosophical heavy lifting would occur at the beginning of the book and the topical analyses would follow, once the philosophical terms had been set. In addition, the outline seems less itinerant in its argumentative progression. For example, by establishing the *literary* factors that motivate rhetorical action in "Ideology and Myth," Burke would set the stage for addressing the *extra-literary* factors that motivate rhetorical action in "The Rhetorical Situation." Because both chapters would demonstrate how representative examples were symptomatic of a broader terminological order, they would together provide a formal symmetry that made the work's underlying structure more apparent to readers. Notice, too, how general chapters such as "Rhetoric and Poetic" would prepare readers for the more specific "Rhetoric of the Drama" and "While They Last." Presumably, this progression would reveal an increasingly narrow focus that would help audiences understand, by the end of the book, how they were meant to use its insights.

5

The Ideal Opening

Although "Ideology and Myth" seemed to provide the ideal opening for *A Rhetoric of Motives*, it did not stay in place for long. By midsummer, Burke had moved "The Range of Rhetoric" to the front of the line, where it stayed until the book's publication. He wrote to Watson on 26 July 1947 (JWP) that he had decided he needed to begin "a bit differently, after all": "Opening section is evidently to be: 'The Range of Rhetoric.' Start with 'identification.' Note how, implicit in it, lurks division. Then, swing around, somewhat generously, covering all sorts of cases." Burke's discussion of identification and division would draw extensively from John Milton's mythic poem *Samson Agonistes* because, as an "informative anecdote," it contained "*in nuce* the terminological structure that is evolved in conformity with it" (Burke to Watson, 7 August 1947, JWP; see also *GM* 60). For Burke, *Samson Agonistes* represented "implicitly what the system that is developed from it contains explicitly" (*GM* 60). Through a close reading of Burke's engagement with this poem, the core themes of *A Rhetoric of Motives* come into clear relief.

July–August 1947

Burke's decision to open *A Rhetoric of Motives* with Milton's *Samson Agonistes* was a shift more in *delivery* than in *focus*. Although "Ideology and Myth" offered a compressed version of Burke's argument on the relationship between rhetoric and poetics, it was inelegant and difficult to follow. As Burke explained in a letter to Watson dated 7 August 1947 (JWP), "instead of beginning with the abstract reduction, we begin with the 'informative anecdote,' and draw the reduction from it." Elaborating further on the poem's strengths, Burke added, "We have here the war theme (so much of Rhetoric being under the sign of malice and the lie, an anecdote proper to this book should be on the side of invective). And by looking into the allusions behind the poem, we have ample material for our key term: 'identification.'" The most significant advantage of this new beginning is that it highlights the complexity of identification, a complexity on full display in a letter Burke wrote to Hyman on 31 July 1947 (SHP). "Began, for my anecdote, with Milton: Samson Agonistes, and the cantankerous old fighter's identification with same," Burke told Hyman. "As Yeats slept on a board to hard[en] his style, so I, to prepare for this opening blast, went nearly two months without a haircut. And then told my secret to a woman. Now, myself my own dungeon, I hugely lament, in servitude, though frankly, I'd like, if possible, to see whether I could arrange to have the temple fall down just after I scaped with the vulgar."

The heartbeat of Burke's argument is Milton's identification with Samson. But Burke's identification with Milton and others is crucial to the definition of identification that he advances here. In the letter to Hyman, Burke simultaneously identified with Yeats (who slept on a board to harden his style), Samson (going nearly two months without a haircut and telling his secret to a woman), and Milton (who identified with Samson because his blindness—both physical and political—transformed his body into a dungeon). With each new identification, Burke demonstrates how different historical moments, organized by disparate material and ideological exigencies, can be brought together under one mythic heading (identification and division). Here, myth refers not just to the content of a poem (Samson and Delilah) but to the formal act of producing a poem (Yeats slept on a board to harden his style, so Burke, "to prepare for this opening blast..."). In terms of both form and content, Burke's identifications blur the distinction between poetry and rhetoric, showing that poetry can constitute an argument's content and at the same time provide a structure for revealing the capacities of the dialectic principle.

However blurry the distinction between rhetoric and poetics may be, Burke emphasizes their differences as a framework for criticism. He draws this distinction early in the opening passage of the published version of *A Rhetoric of Motives*, writing, "One can read [the poem] simply *in itself*, without even considering the fact that it was written by Milton," but one can also read it as the translation of "political controversy into high theological terms" that "sanction the ill-tempered obstinacy of [Milton's] resistance" (*RM* 5). Rhetorical analysis emphasizes that Milton wrote the poem to "sanction the ill-tempered obstinacy of his resistance," whereas poetic analysis would analyze the poem without reference to Milton. Burke does not invoke poetic analysis in order to dismiss it as misguided or limited. Instead, he introduces it as a *formal consideration* to show how organizing concepts such as *identification* can be analyzed without regard to the writers who invoke it in their work. For Burke, we need both rhetoric and poetics to advance a philosophy of rhetoric. We need rhetoric to analyze local, timebound examples, and we need poetics to understand the universal scope of dialectical insights.

Milton identified with Samson in order to transform his immediate rhetorical situation. By suggesting that "a blind Biblical hero *did* conquer," Milton himself sought to conquer by slaying "the enemy in effigy" (*RM* 5). Milton's symbolic aggression required both identification and dissociation. Samson's "Philistines and Dagon implicitly [stand] for [Milton's] Royalists . . . who have regained power in England, while the Israelites stand for the Puritan faction of Cromwell" (5). By couching his symbolic act in theological terms, Milton "by such magnification . . . sanction[s] the ill-tempered obstinacy of his resistance" (5).

Burke's use of the phrase *by such magnification* is key to the argument. His theory of the rhetorical situation analyzed the relationship between local and universal scenes of rhetorical action to disclose how local ideologies are entangled with governing myths that exceed ideological partisanship. Much like Virgil's *Aeneid*, *Samson Agonistes* employs a theological (or ultimate) terminology to establish a prepolitical (or universal) ground that explains the local political situation. It does so by appropriating the Samson myth, the catalyst of which is the Judeo-Christian god Yahweh. Samson is punished for disobeying God's commands. Samson's contrition encourages God to return his heroic powers, which Samson then uses to crush the enemies of his god. All the while, *Samson Agonistes* discloses the universality of the rhetorical situation because the constancy of the invitation to war is not specific to a local struggle over property. The hero Samson thereby functions as an example of local conflict that discloses a universal strife rooted in the struggle over property. Burke felt that audiences in his immediate rhetorical situation needed to reconsider how local situations were connected to universal ones. As we will discover in the next chapter, he was not alone in this conviction.

In sum, we find in Burke's informative anecdote the following themes: the organizing function of myth in revealing how identification functions in rhetoric, the distinction between rhetoric and poetic criticism, and identification's role in disclosing the connection between the local and the universal rhetorical situation. Although offering a definition of identification could have allowed Burke to delineate each of his core themes, it would not have demonstrated the process by which such themes can emerge out of rhetorical criticism. By dramatizing this process, Burke taught his audience how to carry out a similar process within their own local rhetorical situation. Obviously, this pedagogical lesson anticipates later chapters in the book that discuss dangerous rhetorical devices. It also recalls earlier drafts that seek a moral equivalent of war capable of transforming nationalistic aggression. What remains consistent is Burke's tendency to address homicidal tendencies by imagining a suicidal counterpoint.

Shortly after completing it, Burke sent a draft of his new opening to Watson for feedback. In a cover note, Burke underscored the intimate connections between myth, identification, and war:

> Anyhow, do assure me that this should be the way to start. We have here the war theme (so much of Rhetoric being under the sign of malice and the lie, an anecdote proper to this book should be on the side of invective). And by looking into the allusions behind the poem, we have ample material for our key term: "identification." So, today, after 20 pages scrutinizing Milton's Samson and two by Arnold (Empedocles on Etna and the one we studied at high school: Sohrab and Rustum), we are ready for the abstract reduction. Lo! out pops "Identification." (7 August 1947, JWP)

Although Watson believed that Burke would need to carefully define *Samson Agonistes* in terms of identification (rather than identity), he was eager to see how the rest of the argument would unfold. Burke responded to Watson by writing a new outline for *A Rhetoric of Motives*, which he described in a letter dated 26 August 1947.

Burke's revised plan is a key moment in the composition of *A Rhetoric of Motives* because it marks the first time he breaks the work into two major sections. In order to bring clarity into Burke's description of the work, I have created an outline from his prose:

Section I: The Range of Rhetoric

1. The systematic <u>extension</u> of the term "rhetoric" to include areas not traditionally so named
2. The examination of all the typical traditional meanings, with our devices for deriving them all from the same source or generating principle
3. A reworked version of "Ideology and Myth"
4. Conclusion

Section II: The Rhetorical Situation

1. Situation in the scenic sense
2. Reworked version of "The American Way"
3. Situation in the instrumental sense
4. Rhetoric and poetic
5. Rhetoric of education
6. Rhetoric of drama
7. Rhetoric of New Yorker cartoons
8. Scientific rhetoric
9. Catalogue of devices
10. Conclusion pointing toward the symbolic

Burke organizes the book into two main sections that focus on rhetoric's universal and local qualities. For example, when he refers to "Situation in the scenic sense" in the opening of section II, he means "nature and problems of identification as regards technology, politics, etc." (Burke to Watson, 26 August 1947, JWP). Burke's discussion in this section focuses on the local, extra-literary factors that inform persuasive appeals. We know enough about "The American Way" to conclude that it would address specifically the capacity of economic ideologies to coordinate human action—regardless of how Burke "reworked" the argument. Once the scenic properties of the rhetorical situation had been established, Burke would then outline its instrumental function. He doesn't provide much detail about what he had in mind for the chapter, but we can infer from his use of the term *instrument* in *A Rhetoric of Motives* and *A Grammar of Motives* that it would serve as the *agency* or *means* for identifying rhetorical communications. This section would show how poetics, education, drama, *New Yorker* cartoons, information, and argumentative devices all drew from extra-literary factors available in the rhetorical situation to shape attitudes and induce actions in local rhetorical situations. Again, Burke defined the universal rhetorical situation as a constant invitation to war over property (e.g., the logomachy). So we can deduce that each instrumental chapter would demonstrate how the general war over property exposed rhetoric's capacity for motivating change in local situations.

"The Range of Rhetoric" will strike a familiar chord with contemporary readers of Burke, since it serves as the first chapter title in the published version of *A Rhetoric of Motives*. In this August 1947 outline, "The Range of Rhetoric" is a general section heading for chapters focused on the extension of rhetoric, the traditional meanings of rhetoric, and ideology and myth. The chapters collected under this heading would extend the range of rhetoric along different axes. In the first chapter, Burke intended to focus on "areas [of rhetoric] not traditionally so named." The second chapter would focus on "all the typical traditional meanings" of rhetoric, "with our devices for deriving them all from the same source or generating principle." And the third chapter would offer a "reworked version of the 'Ideology and Myth' business," which we discussed at length in the previous chapter (Burke to Watson, 26 August 1947, JWP).

Following the detailed outline of this new section, Burke delved into the details of the first chapter. From subsequent letters between Burke and Watson, we can infer that the chapter included a fully elaborated definition of identification that closely approximates the one in the published version of A Rhetoric of Motives. In fact, the archival record demonstrates that Burke sought Watson's feedback on this definition and revised his argument according to Watson's comments. "Many thanks for the hecklings anent Identification," Burke wrote to Watson; "kept them in mind as I deposed" (26 August 1947, JWP).

With the first chapter in place, Burke turned his attention to the second, which focused on the traditional definitions of rhetoric. This chapter (tentatively titled "Landmarks of Rhetoric") was not a comprehensive survey of the rhetorical tradition but a focused account of the history of rhetoric guided by Burke's "devices for deriving the[m] all from the same source or generating principle" (Burke to Watson, 26 August 1947, JWP). Adopting this approach allowed Burke to establish coherence between the two chapters and thereby provide a substantial demonstration of how the rhetorical motive could be tracked throughout history. As he explained to Watson in a letter dated 28 September 1947 (JWP), "At moment, am wrestling with the job of telling about Aristotle's art of Rhetoric, Cicero's De Oratore, Quintillian's [sic] Institutio Oratoria, and fourth book of Augustine's De Doctrina Christiana (with side-glances at Longinus on the Sublime) as ground-work for our section on the standard definitions of Rhetoric. Problem: don't want merely to peddle these gents over again, don't want merely to give superficial smattering of them, and above all don't want to get into the old rut in talking about them." To solve this problem, Burke treated each book as "stages in one 'curve.'" In this way, he could put the ancients to use rather than allow their definitions of rhetoric to use him. Once Burke had established this curve of rhetorical history, he told Watson, "the rest of the section should be speedy and easy going."

Whereas the first section is tightly organized around the systematic extension of rhetoric through a focus on identification, Burke gropes for coherence in the second section. Of course, the core features that he introduces in the first section set the stage for their application in the second. For example, by opening with an analysis of *Samson Agonistes*, Burke prepares for a sustained engagement with contemporary approaches to factional identification. But when we consider what he had accomplished in his new opening for *A Rhetoric of Motives*—particularly in his effort to include areas of rhetoric "not traditionally so named"—chapters on rhetoric and poetics, the rhetoric of drama, and the rhetoric of *New Yorker* cartoons seem misplaced (Burke to Watson, 26 August 1947, JWP). By systematically extending the range of rhetoric to include works not traditionally associated with rhetoric, Burke appeared to have found the necessary counterbalance to his negative assessments of contemporary politics and news media. What's more, his engagement with *Samson Agonistes* demonstrates that nontraditional extensions of rhetoric could expose the distinctions between rhetoric and poetics in a manner that pointed up rhetoric's good side. Still, those concerns seemed a long way off as he worked on the remaining chapters of the first section.

September–December 1947

Burke's turn to the universal grounds of identification could have distracted him from the postwar scene, but his notes and letters indicate that contemporary geopolitics remained clearly in view. For example, in a letter to Watson of 23 October 1947 (JWP), he explains how even though the "Landmarks" chapter was outlined and ready to be composed, he had become distracted by contemporary political debates. "Some of it must be psychology," he told Watson, "for the whole damned current wrangle is in me. I suffer it daily. I head-shake at the signs of folly that mark every moment of the international situation. I am horrified at the thought that, despite the suicidal nature of war today, patriotism and the call for another war are so often identical. The need to dissociate these two ideas seems to me cultural requirement No. 1 for all humanity, yet it is the association that is being built up with greater earnestness and organizing ability than ever before." We hear in this call resonances of an earlier engagement with Virgil, in which Burke sought a new myth that could reorder the argumentative priorities of the prevailing rhetorical situation. His observation about "the suicidal nature of war today" also represents a dangerous counterpoint to Milton's *Samson Agonistes*. Whereas Burke's contemporaries sought to eradicate the enemy via the threat of direct violence,

Milton sought to avoid direct violence by imagining a transformational form of poetic suicide (Burke to Watson, 23 October 1947, JWP).

After a series of intense physical reactions to the popular news media, Burke realized that his concern was predicated on the assumption that those who read newspapers did so with the same level of attention that he did. This assumption was wrongheaded, in his view, because newspapers were designed for inattention. "I had an intellectual revolution in which I vowed never again to read a newspaper carefully," he wrote Watson in mid-November. "Those filthy things are obviously designed for the maximum of inattention. And if you read them as I have been doing, with maximum attentiveness, you simply punish yourself cruelly. Hereafter, I'll confine my close analysis to good poetry and philosophy. And I'll read the newspaper, like everybody else, in a slovenly haphazard way of mind." Burke's revelation was so profound that he describes himself as "enjoying the sight of much ineffectuality where before I had seen only the most disastrous of effectivity. Oof! and what a load is thus removed. That alone helps one to breathe easier" (Burke to Watson, 14 November 1947, JWP). At first glance, this letter marks the end of Burke's study of the war of words and even provides strong reasons for his ostensible abandonment of major sections devoted to contemporary rhetorical devices. But the archival materials tell a different story.

While it is apparent that Burke's concern with newspaper media had waned in intensity, he did not abandon his work. On the contrary, the archival records suggest that we interpret Burke's claims above as an ironic affirmation of the challenge he and his contemporaries faced. Recognizing that the news media were designed for inattention did not make them any less persuasive. Public audiences would remain attentive to the claims of news media no matter how much inattention they engendered. Moreover, Burke would not suddenly begin reading the newspaper "in a slovenly haphazard way of mind" unless this interpretive strategy helped him conceptualize how the contemporary news media cultivated *attentive inattention*. Burke's self-imposed confinement thus marks a formal distinction between different types of media. Philosophy and poetry required great attention because they were designed to be read closely; newspapers needed to be read with less scrutiny because they were designed for inattention. Recognizing this subtle point provides critics with greater insight into the formal distinctions that Burke introduces throughout the published and unpublished version of *A Rhetoric of Motives*. We also gain a better sense of the factors that motivated Burke's eventual revisions to the structure of the book.

As Burke contemplated the dangers of the news media, he prepared for his winter leave in Melbourne Beach, Florida. On 18 November 1947, he announced to McKeon, "I go with a trunk full of notes, which are expected to be transformed into a book by spring. On Rhetoric, on Rhetoric extended, on Rhetoric as per the basic texts, on Rhetoric and Dialectic, Rhetoric and Poetic, Rhetoric and Myth, Rhetoric and the News (the quasi-scientific), Me and Rhetoric, Rhetoric and the Non-Verbal, Rhetoric and the End of the World" (RMP). In a letter to Watson written several days earlier, Burke explained that he had "stopped straight-ahead writing on my chapter, to do bits here and there that require reference to books in my library" so that he could travel Florida without much "to lug . . . besides my notes, so far as the book is concerned." Evidently, "the chapter on 'Landmarks,'" in which Burke had now found himself knee-deep, had ceased to be a chore and "finally took on some vitality" (Burke to Watson, 14 November 1947, JWP).

The incongruity between Burke's reference to the "Landmarks" chapter and his list of headings in the McKeon letter indicate that the latter is more descriptive of the proposed content. While Burke would go on to write about "rhetoric and dialectic" and "rhetoric and the news," he never made a serious attempt to draft chapters along these broadly defined lines.

By the end of December, Burke had nearly completed the "Landmarks of Rhetoric" chapter, which he was now calling "Traditional Principles of Rhetoric" (Burke to Watson, 24 December 1947, JWP). The progress he had made in the fall and early winter of 1947 had energized him. "Am coming out for the book quite zestfully," Burke wrote Hyman, "particularly since I think I can love myself all the more by loving it" (14 December 1947, SHP). On that high note, he packed up his family and headed south.

6

Charting an Upward and Downward Path

As we noted earlier, a chapter titled "Landmarks of Rhetoric" was part of Burke's original prospectus for *A Rhetoric of Motives*. In the chapter description, Burke characterized it as a small, pedagogical section that would probably be cut when he filled out the chapters that preceded it. As he began drafting "Landmarks," however, he discovered that it offered much more than a pedagogical lesson in the history of rhetoric. Specifically, it allowed him to aggregate key episodes in the history of rhetoric that pointed toward the functions of the dialectic principle. By January 1948, the chapter had grown so large that Burke relegated the majority of his writing on "rhetoric and poetic" to *A Symbolic of Motives* (Burke to Watson, 17 January 1947, JWP). He also decided to rename the "Landmarks" chapter "Traditional Principles of Rhetoric."

Over the course of successive drafts, "Traditional Principles of Rhetoric" became a crucial counterpoint to the critical assessments that would appear in later, more topical chapters. Burke would collate these chapters under the general title "The World of Publicity" and address topics associated with modern rhetorical devices, the role of facts in modern argument, and the phenomenon of bureaucratic identification. Since composing these chapters involved "sorting, revising, and arranging" notes that Burke had already composed, he grew hopeful that *A Rhetoric of Motives* would soon be complete (Burke to Cowley, 26 January 1947, KBP, Burke-1). Unfortunately, like so many of Burke's plans for *A Rhetoric of Motives*, this one, too, turned out to be overly sanguine.

January–February 1948

Burke celebrated the arrival of the new year in Melbourne Beach, Florida. Accompanied by his wife, Libby, and sons Anthony and Michael, he walked along the shoreline, retreated to the sulfur pool on inclement days, and made steady progress on the remaining chapters of *A Rhetoric of Motives* (Burke to Watson, 13 January 1947, JWP). The trip to Florida must have felt long overdue for the Burke family. They had planned to visit in 1945 when Burke began writing *A Rhetoric of Motives*, but they couldn't quite work out the living arrangements. "After my grand talk of going to Florida," Burke told Watson at the time, "here I am, back heaving snow.... So it looks as though I'm to stay right here, batting away at the Rhetoric (the first draft of which is progressing as per schedule, though somewhat bumpily)" (30 November 1945, JWP). With the living arrangements now settled, Burke could enjoy a respite from the northeastern winter.

Burke had made significant headway with "Traditional Principles of Rhetoric" before heading to Florida. With much of the chapter now drafted, his plan was to complete the remaining sections upon arrival and then revise the next chapter, "Dialectic, Ideology, and Myth." This plan proved to be a good one. In a 13 January 1948 letter to Hyman (SHP), he announced, "So far, Florida has been a success, I've been able to cut exactly the path I wanted to cut." He wrote to Watson the same day, telling him that "Traditional Principles" opened with "the old gents" (meaning Aristotle, Plato, Cicero, and Quintilian) and moved into discussions of "Augustine, Marx, [and] Bentham" (JWP). In a letter to Ralph Ellison written the next day (REP), Burke described how the chapter analyzed Marx, Carlyle, and Empson, which he thought would be of interest to Ellison. Although the argument had been challenging to write, Burke's effort had produced a "wholly new thing anent mystery," which allowed him to export much of his work on rhetoric and poetics to *A Symbolic of Motives*.

Burke now began characterizing the first three chapters of Part I as the "Upward" section—a term he begins to use in reference to *A Rhetoric of Motives* in January 1948 and would continue to use even after publishing its first half. The "Upward" section would be followed by a corresponding "'Downward' section," which included the chapters "Catalogue of Devices," "The Rhetorical Situation," "Scientific Rhetoric," and "The Rhetoric of Bureaucracy." Again, Burke called Part II "The World of Publicity" (Burke to Cowley, 26 January 1947, MCP). From the published version of *A Rhetoric of Motives*, we learn that the upward and downward way is a process in which a critic "aims at a systematic withdrawal from the world of appearances, a crossing into a realm that transcends everyday judgments—after which there may be a return: the Upward Way is matched by a Downward Way; or the period of exile, withdrawal, and negation terminates in a new vision, whereupon the visionary can once again resume his commerce with the world, which he now sees in a new light, in terms of the vision he earned during his stage of exile" (*RM* 95).

In Part I, Burke would produce a distinctly modern philosophy centered on the concept of identification. With a new vision in place, he would then return to his contemporary moment with "a totally different vocabulary to chart its motivations" (*RM* 245).[1] Had Burke developed a fully formed vision of the rhetorical motive at this point in the drafting process? Not entirely. The challenges posed by this difficult problem explain, in part, why the chapter "Dialectic, Ideology, and Myth" still yearned for improvement. And yet Burke had developed a strong enough foundation to begin analyzing how the rhetorical motive was manifested in human communications. Consider, as a case in point, his invocation of myth early in "Traditional Principles of Rhetoric."

Following an overview of the canonical contributions to rhetoric (Aristotle, Cicero, Quintilian, Augustine), Burke writes, "Though these meanings are often not consistent with one another, or are even flatly at odds, we do believe that they can all be derived from 'persuasion' as the 'Edenic' term from which they have all 'Babylonically' split, while 'persuasion' in turn involves communication by the signs of consubstantiality, the appeal of *identification*" (*RM* 62). In characterizing persuasion as *Edenic*, Burke couches his argument in terms of a Western mythic image that assumes that all acts of persuasion are fragments of a unified whole that can no longer be recovered. To amplify the mythic tenor of his argument, Burke employs the image of the Tower of Babylon, which represents not only the desire for a perfect union with God but also the impossibility of attaining such perfection. Unlike the mythic image of the Garden of Eden, the source of failure in the Tower of Babylon myth is humanity's reliance on language. According to the myth, humans are able to communicate purely with one another and thus build a tower to the heavens. To stop their progress, God confuses their language so that they are no longer able to communicate with one another. Humans are subsequently left to their divisions and thus prevented from building such towers in the future.

Although both mythic images seem to look back on the prehistoric grounds of rhetoric, Burke suggests that each is in fact forward-looking (*RM* 200). Specifically, both mythic images—Eden and Babylon—explain how linguistic division is derived from a single source and thus explains what language users can reasonably expect in the present and future.

15 February 1948

On 15 February 1948 Burke wrote Watson to thank him for his helpful feedback on the first two chapters of the upward section ("The Range of Rhetoric" and "Traditional Principles of Rhetoric") (JWP). On the back of the letter, Burke included a general outline of the chapter that would complete the upward section and a skeleton outline of the chapters that would make up the downward section. Burke explained that he had written "about 20,000 words" of the final chapter of the upward section and expected to finish it in another ten thousand. Burke mentioned in a parenthetical aside that he planned to end the chapter with "the Ideology and Myth stuff, Virgil etc., with which we originally planned to begin." This disclosure reflects his evolving vision for the final chapter, which had now adopted a more ambitious philosophical argument focused on the relationship between motive, hierarchy, courtship, and myth.

in general, contents of the last section of Upward Way:

three order [sic] of vocabulary (positive, dialectical, and ultimate)

view of Marxist vocabulary from this point of view

view of Mannheim's Ideology and Utopia, in light of the three orders—and as tour de force, we show how Mannheim's book would have been written, if he had used the same material, but given it the treatment of a Platonic dialogue (not from the standpoint of division into competing voices, but from the standpoint of dialectical operations for transcending the positive order and establishing an ultimate order)

analysis of Book of the Courtier, as paradigm for the rhetoric of courtship

analysis of Kafka's The Castle, in light of the pattern disclosed by analysis of The Courtier. (side references here to Kierkegaard)

transition leading into

revision of material in Ideology and Myth article.

Downward Way:
    Catalogue of Devices (social sparring, etc)
    Bureaucracy (rhetoric of institutions)
    "Scientific Rhetoric" (news, accountancy, etc)
    The Rhetorical Situation (attempt to reduce contemporary conflict to its fundamentals, seeking for the propositions that will be enough and no more).

Conclusion:
    Fairly brief, and including am [sic] "In our next" note on the Symbolic

In this thumbnail sketch of how to pursue the upward path toward greater levels of abstraction, Burke's discussion of positive, dialectical, and ultimate terms discloses the rhetorical motive in the works of Marx, Mannheim, Castiglione, Kafka, and Kierkegaard. What draws these varied works together is their response to a universal rhetorical situation characterized by the effort to transcend social estrangement via dialectical resources such as identification. Again, Burke studied the rhetorical motive in order to help audiences understand how the news media fomented nationalistic aggression in the early postwar period. The material he had written on ideology and myth would serve as a key turning point, leading to the chapters in the downward section that addressed contemporary rhetorical devices directly.

In the end, Burke did not need the "Ideology and Myth" essay to conclude his chapter. On 24 February 1948 he wrote to Watson explaining that he had completed a first draft of the upward section and had found, to his surprise, a natural conclusion to the chapter that did not include the lecture. "Incidentally, while trying to write the pages that were meant to serve as transition into the original Ideology and Myth lecture, lo! I came instead upon an _ending_—whereupon, bing, down went the curtain, and the lecture was relegated to the Appendix. I'll probably add an addendum to it there; but there was great rejoicing when I discovered definitely that I would not have to attempt fitting it into the book proper" (JWP). Burke does not explain why he was happy to have completed the chapter without integrating the lecture. But we can infer from the general outline that parsing the distinction between ideology and myth was no longer necessary. By the time he reached the end of the chapter, it had developed a theoretical scope that greatly exceeded what he had proposed in "Ideology and Myth." The scope of Burke's argument would come into full view over the next couple of months and during the revision of the upward section in 1949. It is possible, then, that Burke was happy to relegate "Ideology and Myth" to the appendix because its sudden lack of fit meant that the argument of *A Rhetoric of Motives* had reached a new level of coherence and sophistication. The new level of sophistication, in particular, hinged on Burke's introduction of "pure persuasion" into the argument.

7

A Pause at the Window

As Burke's time in Florida drew to a close, so too did his work on the upward section of *A Rhetoric of Motives* (Burke to Watson, 25 March 1948, JWP). By his own admission, the chapter now titled "Order" should have been complete. But the Cowleys had come to town to engage in an "old-fashioned alcoholic stage of a midnight swim in the boisterous breakers" (Burke to Watson, 23 March 1948, JWP). Besides the welcome distraction of socializing with old friends, Burke had encountered some unforeseen problems during his revision process. Specifically, he realized that he needed to expand the sections on Kierkegaard and D. H. Lawrence. Since these revisions would have to wait until his return to Andover, he spent the remaining time in Florida drawing together notes for the first chapter of the downward section, "Catalogue of Devices."

April 1948

Burke sent a version of the newly titled chapter "Order" to Watson on 25 March 1948 and pronounced the upward section complete pending Watson's feedback. Burke was nervous about his friend's response, but his trepidation vanished when he received a positive assessment on 4 April (KBP, Burke-3). Watson declared the section on pure persuasion "most fascinating" because it clarified how Burke was "working toward two explicit aims, one general and one immediate—for this year, for this moment even." To improve the chapter, Watson recommended that Burke engage psychoanalysis a little less perversely. If Burke wanted to provide a viable counterpoint to psychoanalysis, Watson reasoned, he needed to identify a logical priority that existed in "a vacuum 'deep in the heart of' dialectic." And what, Watson wondered, had happened to identification?

Watson's feedback was always helpful to Burke, but these comments took on an altogether different level of value. As Burke responded in a letter of 9 April (JWP), "Many thanks indeed for your last note plus the two valuable admonitions ('what happened to identification' and 'isn't the treatment of psychoanalysis perverse?') The concerns with 'hierarchy,' 'order,' 'courtship,' etc. are all variants of the identification business. But I had better point that up." Watson's questions helped Burke recognize that identification could be both "realistic" (as when a social class is courted in a social order) and "idealistic" (as when a citizen wishes to be identified with a nation). Burke resolved to parse these differences more carefully in his revisions. As to the question regarding psychoanalysis, Burke agreed that some revision was necessary. Writing *A Rhetoric of Motives* had become so engrossing that Burke had forgotten he would soon "write a Symbolic." Whereas the former dealt with the properties associated with a "class or group identification," the latter was more focused on the "particulars composing individual *identity*." Rather than treat individual and group identifications as antithetical to each other, Burke proposed to treat them as extensions of each other. This approach would allow a cleaner transition from *A Rhetoric of Motives* to *A Symbolic of Motives*. It would also require him to follow Watson's encouragement to look more deeply into the dialectical vacuum.

Besides ironing out the delivery of his arguments, Watson's comments helped Burke clarify the role of hierarchy in his modern philosophy of rhetoric. Burke believed that psychoanalysts erred when they assigned universal status to individual symptoms. This assignment, Burke surmised, relied on the identification of an "extra hierarchic" factor (e.g., a childhood trauma) that explained why individuals who were subject to the same "hierarchic psychosis" acted differently in response (e.g., some thrived while others struggled). However, this explanation obscured how social hierarchies structure human motivation from early childhood. Although Burke's admiration for Freud was "tremendous," he sought a theory of identification that did not interpret original myths "literally" (Burke to Watson, 9 April 1948, JWP). Myth, in his philosophy of modern rhetoric, would be more indicative than representative.

May–June 1948

Early in his drafting process, Burke was comforted by the thought that most people did not read newspaper articles very closely. As he completed revisions to the upward section, however, his assessment changed. Within the framework of his discussion of concepts such as collaborative expectancy, courtship, and pure persuasion, Burke now felt that the news media were persuasive *because* they encouraged inattention. This form of delivery could persuade readers to think, act, or feel a certain way, even if, upon careful consideration, they disagreed with the content of the argument. The capacity to sponsor inattention thus became Burke's greatest cause for concern as he turned his attention to the "downward" chapters. With a renewed sense of purpose, Burke would help audiences pay attention to the formal characteristics of everyday arguments that persuaded them on a nonconscious level.

Burke's multifaceted theory of identification was the key to this task. By establishing identification and its variants as a feature of the dialectic principle—as opposed to, say, an extra-hierarchic factor—Burke moved rhetorical criticism beyond guilt or shame. As symbol-using and symbol-misusing beings, humans are caught up in a language game defined by vulnerability. In the upward section, Burke had built a vocabulary for explaining why shared responsibility is a necessary response to linguistic vulnerability. He was now ready to present new methods of rhetorical criticism that put this new vocabulary to work.

Throughout the month of April 1948, Burke collected the notes he had written on rhetorical devices. His progress was slowed, in part, by the workaday labor of "digging out" his Andover home. The editors of the *Hudson Review* had also invited Burke to assess Thomas Mann's works in light of his recently written criticism on rhetoric and courtship (Burke to Watson, 23 April 1948, JWP). Despite these distractions, Burke maintained his momentum from Florida. On 5 May he sent an update on the "Devices" chapter to his friend Stanley Edgar Hyman, writing, "Only today have I finally got into manageable shape my notes for the Catalogue of Devices. (Or rather, for the opening 15,000 words or so.) Have made several beginnings, some of them quite extensive. But now at last I think I have hit upon the right approach" (SHP). Two days later, on 7 May, he wrote Watson to announce that he had completed his "Bland" device section and would now proceed to "Shrewd Simplicity," "Undoing by Overdoing," "Deflection," and then the "Spokesman" device. He enclosed the opening pages of the "Devices" chapter, titled "Of the Devices in General," which proceeded "mainly by example," so if "any particular item seemed dull, or forced, or unconvincing," to Watson, Burke would drop it immediately (JWP). With regard to his writing process, he wrote:

> Lo! I am back at the part of my project where, some several years back, when I began to write up these same notes (though many have

been added since), I found all the other stuff interposing itself (plus the h.b.p). So now, after the Grammar, and the Mlbrn Bch section of the Rhetoric, I am caught up. The puffed-upness has now abated. The particular kind of tension and impatience that went with these unwanted but necessary preliminaries is gone. The writing becomes more of a driving, less of a being-driven. (Which means that, if something is gained, something also will be lost.)

Burke's systematic engagement with myth and identification had relieved the frustration he felt in earlier drafts. With his philosophy of modern rhetoric now driving the argument, he could locate the dangers of war in all language use. Burke's analysis thus focused on understanding contemporary politics in terms of a broader curve of history rather than taking a stand in a volatile political environment. If his analysis was correct, the problems of the contemporary moment were not unique, as he had initially supposed; they were and would continue to be characteristic of all rhetorical action. The upshot of this insight was that audiences were involved in a long war of words rather than an immediate battle over postwar geopolitics. Of course, Burke's stylistic difficulties were not over yet. But, for the moment, he proceeded with confidence through the first chapter of the downward section.

By the third week of May, Burke had completed the first half of the "Devices" chapter, which now included considerably more devices than he had listed in his 9 May letter to Watson. The five devices he had originally envisioned had now grown to fifteen. In addition to the aforementioned devices (blandness, shrewd simplicity, undoing by overdoing, deflection, and spokesman), Burke added, "Yielding Aggressively; . . . Reversal; Say the Opposite; the Nostrum (Spiritualization); Say the Word; Say Anything; Putting Two and Two Together; the Pointedly Unsaid; Failing to Make the Connections" (Burke to Watson, 17 May 1948, JWP).

Burke told Watson that he worried that his anthologizing might make the chapter "*too damned easy* to read." But he justified this approach on the grounds that it revealed "how much is going on" in contemporary reporting of national and international politics (Burke to Watson, 17 May 1948, JWP). Two days later, Burke sent Watson the first half of the "Devices" chapter. In the accompanying letter, he described himself as "dreadfully anxious" to hear Watson's assessment. Unlike the chapters in the upward section, the "Devices" chapter functioned like an anthology in which each device served as a separate entry unto itself. Burke characterized this new section as an "anthology of rhetorical wild-flowers (weeds?)" (Burke to Watson, 19 May 1948, JWP).

In earlier chapters, we noted how Burke, in an attempt to chart a new path for modern rhetoric, pursued rhetoric beyond Aristotle's well-manicured gardens. By his own account, Burke had traveled into the uncultivated badlands of rhetoric, where weeds abound. That he characterized his devices as "rhetorical wild-flowers (weeds?)" at this stage in the writing process is significant because it underscores the continuity of his thinking from earlier drafts. It is one thing to imagine a chapter that involves collecting, arranging, and adapting previously written notes. It is an entirely different thing to have composed significant portions of the chapter and remain committed to the language that described the initial draft. Burke was back in the badlands of modern rhetoric. But this time he was armed with a new vocabulary that would help him navigate it with a greater sense of scope and purpose.

On 30 May 1948, Watson responded to Burke's chapter with superlative praise. Watson described Burke's opening preamble, "Of the Devices in General," as "excellent" and claimed that the "bland" device was his favorite. Watson's observation that the chapter would "go over . . . well with people who have trouble with other parts of the book" provided an additional boost to Burke's confidence (KBP, Burke-1). Watson's comments indicated that the upward and downward sections needed to be read alongside each other so that each could clarify and support its respective purpose.

Burke responded to Watson's feedback the same day with two important announcements. The first was that he had shown the half-completed "Devices" chapter to Hyman, who had visited Andover over the weekend. Unlike Watson, Hyman did not approve of the chapter. Hyman was concerned that "the political logomachy will just about get [Burke] tarred and feathered by the reviewers, and to the glory of no one" (Burke to Watson, 30 May 1948, JWP). In response to Hyman's concerns, Burke proposed a new stylistic strategy by which the examples of each device "should be de-localized, exactly as I de-localized the personal anecdotes. They should be about subjects such as the Ambassador of Preenland, His Excellency of Pronia, The Grand Apex of Onlychurch II, etc. Factions shd. be not Democrats and Republicans, or Stalinists and Trotskyites, etc. but Ins and Outs, or Innables and Outables, or Perfectists and Loathesomites, etc." (Burke to Hyman, 30 May 1948, SHP).

The advantage of this approach, Burke told Hyman, was that "the sins of direct application [would] be committed by the reader himself" and thus would absolve Burke of the responsibility of making the connection on the reader's behalf. In addition, Burke believed that this approach would more clearly point up "the form (that is, the 'permanent element') in each anecdote." Recognizing the permanent element in Burke's analyses of rhetorical devices was crucial because the upward chapters focused so strongly on developing a philosophy of modern rhetoric.

The second announcement was that Burke had been contacted by the Institute for Advanced Study in Princeton, New Jersey, about holding a short-term fellowship (Burke to Watson, 30 May 1948, JWP). The informal offer had come about a week before, in letters from both Richard Blackmur and Francis Fergusson, who were attempting to secure a position for Burke so that, together, they could "straighten out the problems of literature in the modern world" (Fergusson to Burke, "Tuesday," 1948, KBP, Burke-1). Burke had known Blackmur for nearly two decades and considered him a friend. Blackmur had originally contacted Burke in 1929 about publishing a piece in *Hound and Horn*, a magazine he edited (Blackmur to Burke, 26 February 1929, RBP). Over time they grew closer, and the Blackmur family made several visits to Burke's farm in Andover.

In May 1948, Blackmur served on the faculty of Princeton University's English Department. Fergusson, a noted scholar of literary drama, was a colleague of Burke's at Bennington College. At the time, Fergusson held a short-term fellowship at the Institute for Advanced Study, where his childhood friend Robert Oppenheimer had recently been appointed director.[1]

June–July 1948

Burke traveled to Princeton and met with Oppenheimer to learn more about the short-term position at the IAS. He reported to Watson in a letter of 3 June 1948 (JWP) that the meeting had gone well and that Oppenheimer expected to provide office space for one year. If he could arrange housing, Oppenheimer also hoped that the Burke family would live on campus for three months, from January to March of 1949. This living arrangement worked seamlessly with Burke's schedule, as he was on leave from Bennington during that period.

In the interim before his appointment at the IAS commenced, Burke worked steadily on the remaining chapters of the downward section. In the 3 June letter to Watson, Burke reported that he would send another installment of the "Devices" chapter soon, but that he had once again run into stylistic difficulties that were slowing his progress. Specifically, Burke discussed the challenges associated with maintaining an "anthology" of devices. The "spiritualization" device had become too essayistic in form and was threatening the coherence of the chapter. In addition, he told Watson, Hyman's concerns had caused him to revise each political reference, making all of them much more allusive in nature. But the most important stumbling block to his progress was the evolving nature of the Cold War.

> I believe the primary duty of every patriot is to work against war. But the resistances to be overcome are terrific. Hence, my great concern lest the paragraphs go too far. Hence, my vacillations as to the exact way in which the political anecdotes shd. be handled, the percentage, etc. Fundamentally, I take the situation to be this: Our imperialists are trying to uphold capitalism in parts of the world that simply lack the material conditions necessary for the thriving of capitalism; if they keep on with such idiotic efforts, they will destroy the material conditions for capitalism even here. We are beset by a batch of journalistic goons systematically coaching international ill will at a time when things would be nasty even if everybody were trying his best to be of goodwill. (Burke to Watson, 3 June 1948, JWP)

As Burke continued to analyze the news media's representation of the Cold War, he worried that his "paragraphs go too far" in their political criticism, he told Watson, and thereby supported the war's forward momentum. He needed to revise the style of his approach in order to overcome the terrific resistance that characterized prevailing political debates.

Over the next several months, Burke continued to encounter political resistance. In a 19 June letter to Watson (JWP), Burke admitted that his proposed solution to Hyman's critique was not complete and worried that if Hyman kicked, "others will kick much more." From a tonal perspective, Swiftian allusions could become "much more drastic than [one] would have been had [one] treated the incidents factually." To maintain forward momentum, Burke suggested that his argument could be "toned down later."

On 15 July 1948, Burke wrote to Hyman to update him on the progress of *A Rhetoric of Motives* (SHP). Having completed the "Devices" chapter the day before, Burke would turn his attention to the remaining chapters of the downward section. He had begun to draft "Scientific Rhetoric," pointing "out what the resources for misrepresentation are, and leaving it for the reader to decide whether these resources are exploited." The resources for misrepresentation came in the form of reports from the *New York Times* and the *Christian Science Monitor*. Burke would present these reports as hypothetical cases so that readers could "decide for [themselves] to what extent ... the yellow press is a guardian of our freedom," he told Hyman.

A week later, Burke wrote to Watson with a dejected update. "Our project has hit a spell of droop. As were it a paper flag in a downpour. The thought of doing the sections on News and Bureaucracy seems of a sudden so forbidding, that I gasp and belch and heart-flop at the mere idea" (22 July 1948, JWP). In response to the challenge of completing these chapters, Burke proposed a "revision-by-omission" strategy, which would involve cutting down a "bulging folder" of already collected materials. In addition, Burke asked Watson to identify unnecessary passages in the "Devices" chapter because Burke now lacked the "vitality [to] repair things." Burke's dejection is understandable. His imminent return to Bennington meant that he would have considerably less time to write. To add insult to injury, he had also "picked up some briar scratches and poison ivy blisters" while "racing about with putt-putt."

September–December 1948

Burke began the "Scientific Rhetoric" chapter during the final week of July 1948 and completed a draft on 1 September. In a letter to Watson dated 29 July, he reported once again on stylistic concerns, writing, "Stylistically, it is perhaps the most difficult problem in the book. For one must look closely at things that don't deserve a glance. So it is a search for subterfuges." On 1 September, he announced to Watson that he had completed the chapter, which he broke into seven subsections:

1. "Facts" are Interpretations
2. Headline Thinking
3. Selectivity
4. Reduction (Gist)
5. Tithing by Tonality
6. News as Drama
7. Polls, Forums, and Accountancy

Burke characterized this chapter as "the most dogged accomplishment of [his] areercay." Against all odds, he had managed to write in a less polemical style. And though there were "still a few flare-ups here and there," he believed that they could be tossed out during the final revision (Burke to Watson, 1 September 1948, JWP).

Burke sent a typed manuscript titled "Scientific Rhetoric" to Watson on 25 September (JWP). In the accompanying letter, he admitted once again to being concerned about its style, explaining that it was dangerously on "the edge of platitude." He also confessed to "peddling the *Rhetoric*" in his courses at Bennington, which had been well received by his students.

Burke's updates on *A Rhetoric of Motives* slowed considerably during the fall and winter months of 1948—presumably because he was busy teaching his Bennington courses. However, once he arrived at the Institute for Advanced Study in late December, they picked up again. In a 22 December letter to Watson (JWP), Burke reported:

> As for my War of Words pages: My problem there is too complex to be settled by a mere post-election shift. I want the analysis of polemic to be seen now and to count, but I don't want it to look like the whole thing (as the newspaper crooks can very easily make it do, in case they do not decide to give it the Quietus). My job is to make it count for just enough, a job involving conditions that (cf. Hierarchic Anguish) are in large measure beyond my control (unless I were willing to drop all items like the Say Anything pages, but in that case the W of W pages wouldn't count for enough).

Here, Burke is responding to a suggestion from Watson that he either revise his critique of the Truman administration or publish *A Symbolic of Motives* before *The War of Words* (Burke to Watson, 5 December 1948, JWP). Burke's response is significant because it demonstrates that he was continuing to work through the challenges of *The War of Words* while serving as a member of the Institute for Advanced Study. At the end of the letter, Burke explained that he would devote the next three months to "the final revision" of the first half of *A Rhetoric of Motives*, hoping that its completion would give him "the needed footing" for executing the book as he had planned it. In a letter to Malcolm Cowley dated 3 January 1949 (MCP), Burke reiterated his plan, announcing that *A Rhetoric of Motives* had grown "into two sizable tomes . . . the second not quite finished."

8

Writing at the Center of the Universe

Kenneth Burke arrived at the Institute for Advanced Study in Princeton, New Jersey, on a blustery winter evening in late December 1948 with his wife and two sons (Burke to Watson, 22 December 1948, JWP). He would spend the next three months completing the published version of *A Rhetoric of Motives* as we have come to know it. Again, Burke's appointment was made by Robert Oppenheimer, who had taken over as IAS director in 1947. Convinced that the IAS faculty needed diversification, Oppenheimer negotiated a "Director's Fund" to make long- and short-term appointments that capitalized on his intellectual interests and professional connections.[1] Francis Fergusson, an old friend and a college roommate of Oppenheimer's, was his first short-term appointment (Monk 546). At Fergusson's recommendation, Kenneth Burke became the second.[2]

Although Burke's time at the IAS was relatively short in duration, it proved to be a landmark moment in the history of rhetoric. Burke's lectures at neighboring Princeton University established a model for the Gauss Seminars in Literary Criticism. In addition, Burke's membership coincided with the IAS's Electronic Computer Project, which, under the guidance of Hungarian polymath John von Neumann, produced the first digital computer on US soil and successfully calculated the equation for the hydrogen bomb.[3] Finally, and most relevant to our story, Burke suspended work on the downward section of *A Rhetoric of Motives*, which he now referred to as "The War of Words" (Burke to Watson, 2 March 1949, JWP).

There's no reason to bury the lede: Burke never furnished an explanation for suspending work on "The War of Words." We know that he had planned to finish the two-volume work long before his visit to the IAS, so fatigue was a likely factor. We also know that he was struggling to maintain argumentative equanimity as he analyzed the evolving geopolitical scene (Burke to Watson,

5 December 1948, JWP). The postwar rhetorical situation may have simply become too overwhelming to manage. And we know that Burke was eager to move on to the next phase of his writing, *A Symbolic of Motives*. Perhaps that next phase was too appealing to keep him tilling the postwar landscape.

In any case, we must consider how "The War of Words," as a section in *A Rhetoric of Motives*, is connected to its historical moment. Because each of Burke's chapters examines rhetorical devices that enacted war in the name of peace, his decision to suspend work suggests a provocative convergence point between the formation of modern rhetorical studies as defined in the published *A Rhetoric of Motives*, the dawn of digital computing technology, and postwar atomic geopolitics.

January-February 1949

Burke arrived at the IAS with a plan. While there, he would smooth out the first three chapters of the upward section and, once those revisions were complete, finish drafting and revising the remaining chapters in the "War of Words" section. According to Burke's letters, the space and time afforded by the IAS helped with both of these tasks—at least in a manner of speaking. In letters to Cowley, Watson, and Hyman, Burke described a relatively productive revision process, going so far as to call himself a "revision machine" (Burke to Cowley, 17 January 1949, KBP, Burke-1). In a letter to Hyman dated 20 January 1949 (SHP), Burke explained that his revision process was still yielding new material: "(. . . instead of revising by omission, I've tended to revise by addition). Some parts don't have the fuoco they had while I was writing them. They seem so tame, it's hard to think that during some of the said elucubrations the author was puffed up like a pouter pigeon."

Though productive, Burke felt out of joint in his new surroundings. Part of the problem was the absence of his natural environment in Andover. In a letter to Watson dated 20 January 1949 (JWP), he explained, "The almost total elimination of chorelessness leaves me somewhat rootless. Everything seems suspended in a vacuum. (I write in a handsome, brand-new office. Everything splongdeed. But so far as permanent production goes, it would be like trying to meditate in a store window. I guess old Kaspar Hauser must cry for his dungeon.) The fields I see from my window are almost exactly the way I would have them, with my putt-putt, they seem as remote as something on a mortuary slab." Evidently, Burke had grown so accustomed to working in the weeds that, upon his arrival in a highly ordered "vacuum," he struggled to find purpose. As Burke would put it eloquently in "The War of Words," the value of rhetorical criticism lay in the struggle to maintain order while living within a fraught landscape. Returning to the world after a self-imposed period of exile was therefore not just a turn of phrase. It was an ethic of living and a tactic for invention that the IAS did not support.

Burke also had difficulty interacting with his IAS colleagues. In the same 20 January letter to Watson, Burke described how these colleagues exhibited "the morbidities of Hierarchy." It "is one of those ironic situations," he wrote, "wherein everything is done to support production, and yet I believe nobody could continue productive work here for any length of time." Despite the prestige associated with an IAS appointment,[4] "The Institute as a whole has an inferiority complex envers [Princeton] University," which engendered "positions of pantomime" that were manifested in highly formalized exchanges between colleagues. "I shall never be able to live down my first mighty error," he continued. "(Appearing at a festivity sans Uniform, while all were bedecked except me and a few forlorn youngsters—I know what a vast rhetorical blunder that was, having already cited La Rochefoucauld rule no. 1 for the rhetoric of social relations: Pour s'établir dans le monde, on fait tout ce que l'on peut pour y paraître établi" (To establish yourself in the world, you do everything you can to seem established there).

Burke's observations regarding social pantomime were not, in and of themselves, a critique. According to this letter, and to passages that appear in the published version of *A Rhetoric of Motives*, pantomime is an attending feature of our symbolic inheritance. Instead, Burke's critique lies in his characterization of the social interactions as *grotesque forms* of pantomime. Faculty members' efforts to maintain an air of superiority compromised genuine intellectual collaboration, which, in Burke's view, functioned as a form of self-interference akin to the dynamics of pure persuasion. It did not matter how much acclaim Burke's research had garnered, or how important his current work would eventually become. The game at the IAS was not primarily intellectual in nature but social—a fact that undermines Oppenheimer's once famous claim that the IAS faculty met every day for tea to "explain to each other . . . what we don't understand" (Bird 387).

As Burke revised the upward section of *A Rhetoric of Motives*, he was careful to chart his progress in letters to friends. In the 20 January 1949 letter to Watson, he enclosed a new section called "Traditional Principles of Rhetoric" that analyzed Dante's *De vulgari eloquentia*. By the following week, he had finished "Traditional Principles" and moved on to "Order." In a letter to Malcolm Cowley dated 24 January 1949 (MCP), Burke described the "Order" section as being focused on "the law-n'sort" and claimed that his revisions had produced a thesis and "maybe even an obsession." By the end of the month, Burke was revising his analysis of *Venus and Adonis*, which "in [the] original text was not very sturdy" (Burke to Watson, 31 January 1949, JWP). This revision was a boon because it helped Burke develop a better framework for "socioanagogic" interpretation.

In the preceding chapter, we noted how Watson relayed two concerns after reading Burke's initial draft of "Order." First, he felt that Burke's explanation of mental disturbances was not yet a viable counterpoint to psychoanalysis. To solve this problem, Watson recommended that Burke identify a logical priority in the heart of the dialectic that was capable of explaining why humans tended toward transcendent explanations. Second, he was concerned that Burke had lost track of identification as he discussed the concepts of *courtship*, *order*, and *hierarchy*. Socioanagogic interpretation was Burke's formal response to Watson's concerns. Burke never identifies the sources of the term *anagogic*. But we can pick up the trail by noting important influences on his work. For example, in *A Rhetoric of Motives*, Burke writes in a footnote, "In this chapter, we are adapting for our purposes the account of Platonist transcendence given in *The Myths of Plato* by J. A. Stewart" (200). The term *anagogic* appears in Stewart's introduction to the book, in his discussion of the relationship between writing and spirit: "The fourth sense is called *anagogic*, that is, above sense and this is when a writing is expounded spiritually which, even in its literal sense, by the matters signified, sets forth the high things of glory everlasting: as may be seen in that Song of the Prophet which says that in the coming out of the people of Israel from Egypt, Judah was made holy and free" (Stewart 20).

When a text appeals to the spiritual or supernatural, it holds open the promise of a supersensory experience. For example, the union between people and their God unfetters them from familiar social hierarchies ("coming out of the people of Israel from Egypt") and, by implication, the social estrangements that result from such hierarchies ("Judah was made holy and free"). The creation of a new spiritual order subsequently organizes group actions around accessibility to its supersensory source. Greater accessibility signifies greater value, which in turn produces estrangement between different classes of people. Anagogic interpretation is designed to explain how spiritual orders establish and maintain relationships between different groups via estrangement. Burke believed that examining spiritual orders from an anagogic standpoint could explain how "members of a group promote social cohesion by acting rhetorically upon themselves and others" (*RM* xiv). In other words, he could explain how rhetorical devices mediate the social estrangements created by a spiritual order and thus promote war in the name of peace.

There is more to Burke's adaptation of anagogic interpretation. In the history of psychoanalytic theory, anagogic interpretation was a flashpoint for debate. Herbert Silberer introduced anagogical interpretation in order to explain the relationship between myths and dreams. Like Freud, Silberer believed that certain abstract ideas are best expressed through concrete symbols—particularly if one wishes to conceal the abstract idea from others or if the idea cannot be explained by existing symbols. And, like Freud, Silberer believed that symbolic creation occurred in the unconscious and was thus metaphorical rather than allegorical. But, unlike Freud, Silberer sought a nonpathological approach to spiritual meaning. He placed anagogic interpretation in competition with psychoanalysis.

Although Freud praised Silberer's "theories of hypnagogic hallucinations, myths, and alchemy," he rejected Silberer's implicit claim that psychoanalysis dealt with less noble problems (Merkur 91). In "Dreams and Telepathy," for example, Freud argued that Silberer's anagogic approach required a "deeper investigation" that would undoubtedly reveal "a chain of phenomena belonging to the region of the repressed life of the instincts [that] displays its *psycho-analytic* content" ("*Dreams*" 216). More specifically, Freud believed that anagogic interpretation did not resolve the problem of neurosis or the fact that "virtue does not reward a man with as much joy and strength in life as one would expect, as though it brought with it too much of its origin" (216–17). In other words, Freud believed that Silberer's anagogic approach was overly sanguine about the spiritual content of dreams, and, as many critics have noted, he was upset with Silberer's modifications to the underlying tenets of psychoanalysis.

If Silberer's modifications were upsetting to Freud, Burke's would have been even more so. But what did that matter to Burke in 1949? He was trying to put the finishing touches on the first volume of *A Rhetoric of Motives*, which required a viable counterpoint to the psychoanalytic explanation of mental disturbances. To maintain coherence with preceding chapters, Burke needed to navigate the immediate and the universal simultaneously, without capitulating to a theory of human motives that relied on the psychosexual unconscious. So Burke appropriated anagogic interpretation by claiming that mystical appeals were neither symptomatic of man's universal spiritual quest (Silberer) nor reducible to an unconscious psychosexual pathology (Freud), but rather were outgrowths of the hierarchic function of the dialectic principle.

The *socio-* in Burke's *socioanagogic* interpretation bears the weight of the argument because it signifies that the spiritual is a function of the dialectic principle, not something that stands outside or in excess of it. Insofar as human language possesses a dialectical function, appeals to hierarchy—spiritual or otherwise—will emerge in human discourse. The task of socioanagogic interpretation is to recognize the motivational capacity of spiritual appeals within societies. Burke's revision allowed anagogic analysis to approach the mystical as something other than an introverted spiritual quest. By looking deep into the heart of the dialectic, Burke developed a method for identifying, describing, and explaining why spiritual appeals (1) produced alienation between classes and thus (2) motivated the maintenance of social order vis-à-vis courtship.

It is no coincidence that Burke opens his discussion of socioanagogic interpretation by analyzing Shakespeare's *Venus and Adonis*. The example, which Burke might call a representative anecdote, is a poem, organized around a myth, that conceptualizes social alienation in "sexual terms" (*RM* 212). At every point of contact (social, symbolic, mythic, sexual), it addresses the psychoanalytic explanation of mental disturbances without accepting its governing assumptions. In addition, Burke addresses the universal and immediate problems of his contemporary moment by extending the value of poetry in his philosophy of modern rhetoric. In the example of *Venus and Adonis*, Burke "reduces" the "main elements" (212) of the poem to excavate a "motivational cluster" (213) built around an explanation of "hierarchy"; this explanation clears away "mother-son implications . . . lest their unformulated presence keep the reader from following another line of explanation" (215). In this section, Burke shows how Shakespeare's hierarchy is a "bridge" that connects the divine with the secular, the universal with the immediate. This hierarchy is not specific to Shakespeare's poem but appears as well in any argument where "one class is struggling to possess the soul of another class" (117).

Burke finished the section on *Venus and Adonis* and sent it to Watson on 10 February 1949 (JWP). While he awaited Watson's verdict, he rounded out the remaining subsections of "Order" and tested them at parties and lectures. To capitalize on Burke's expertise and close proximity, Richard Blackmur scheduled five guest lectures at Princeton University, where Burke would discuss his theories of symbolic action, as Burke told Watson in the same letter. Burke had recently given a lecture on mysticism and poetry titled "Mysticism as a Solution to the Contemporary Spiritual Problem" at the Institute for Religious and Social Studies in New York, so, he informed Watson, he planned to "peddle" it along with his material on Castiglione and Henry James.

Burke delivered the first of these lectures on 16 February to Richard Blackmur's class at Princeton, which left four remaining seminars dedicated to Burke's theories of symbolic action. Evidently, the first class was well attended. After completing the first lecture, Burke reported to Hyman, "Quite some interest has been manifested" (16 February 1949, SHP). Burke interpreted this situation as an indication that the group would get "cozier each time, until there are just a few gentle stalwarts who are too tender-hearted to pull out."

Burke's gloomy mood would soon be chased away by a visit from his closest friends. Together with his wife, Libby, he had been planning a get-together in the area (Burke to Watson, 20 January 1949, JWP). Burke secured commitments from "the Cowleys, Oppenheimers, Blackmurs, Fergussons, and Walter Stewart," along with "Max Radin and his daughter," his neighbors at the IAS residence (Burke to Watson, 31 January 1949, JWP).[5] According to Burke's account, the party was a success even though Watson could not attend.

March–April 1949

By 2 March 1949 Burke had delivered two lectures at Princeton, both drawn from his completed work on the upward section of *A Rhetoric of Motives*. In the remaining three lectures, he told Watson, he planned to test his revisions to the sections on socioanagogic interpretation. In the meantime, he had been developing a new section of "Order" titled "A 'Dialectical Lyric' (Kierkegaard's *Fear and Trembling*)." Burke's initial plan at this point in the book was to write a "Where are we then?" recapitulation of his argument and then move on to a section he referred to as "The Kill and the Absurd." However, Burke tarried over Kierkegaard's work, hoping that a "second, and closer, look" would turn "up something" (Burke to Watson, 2 March 1949, JWP). What was that "something"?

Evidently, Burke felt that a clarification of the relationship between the upward and downward ways was more important to the argument than a recapitulation. "A 'Dialectical Lyric'" opens with an anecdote about how employees working in department stores would use little carriages to send communications to one another. Just as the cashier in a department store sends a message up to headquarters (infinite) and receives a different message in response to his immediate situation (finite), so too does Kierkegaard's dialectician send "up one thing," have something "abstracted from it," and have it return "as another thing" (*RM* 244). For Burke, this exchange is important because it demonstrates how the dialectic can *transform* identifications via abstraction. Recognizing the trajectory of this process, critics may identify the emergence of a "totally different vocabulary" that organizes how a rhetorician perceives, and thus interacts with, the world (245). It does so by defining the origin points of basic motives via myth.

As an interval between the two sections "The Caricature of Courtship: Kafka (*The Castle*)" and "The Kill and the Absurd," "A 'Dialectical Lyric'" extends Burke's discussion of the relationship between *hierarchy*, *mystery*, and *courtship*; elaborates the role of the "incommensurable" infinite in Burke's Neoplatonist "Upward" and "Downward Way"; and, in so doing, adumbrates his discussion of pure persuasion, which represents "an absolute, logically prior to any one persuasive act" (*RM* 252). Perhaps most important, though, it helps the first volume of *A Rhetoric of Motives* become more self-contained in its delivery.

In his 2 March letter to Watson, Burke explained that although he was "batting away [at the first volume] at a good clip," he had grown "weary" from the work. At the end of the month, he would be returning to his regular teaching schedule at Bennington and thus become less able to carry on with the project. As a result, he decided to postpone completion of "The War of Words." "Hope to be turning in the MS in about a week," he told Watson. "(That is, the first volume, Rhetoric and Dialectic. Have definitely decided to offer this by itself, and to postpone decision about the War of Words stuffo until I can make up my mind. If the publisher doesn't like this idea, he can go do to himself what publishers do to themselves under such circumstances—which is, namely, publish five more pieces of nefandum by some dirty sons of Winchell)." A week later, Burke completed his lectures at Princeton. He eventually delivered his lecture on socioanagogic analysis in *Venus and Adonis*, which also included "the Kierkegaard, the Castiglione-Kafka matching, and Pure Persuasion, winding up with the mildly perverse interpretation of the Apocalypse" (Burke to Watson, 10 March 1949, JWP). He told Watson that there had been no protests but worried that the argument was not as convincing as he had hoped.

By 19 March 1949, Burke had completed the first half of *A Rhetoric of Motives* and sent a revision of the "Preface" (renamed "Introduction" in the published work) to Watson: "With the sunset sun on our typewriter, we finished up the book this aft. Enclosed are the pages of the preface, as finally reduced. (We originally had got ourselves into about 30 pages, and were still going, when all of a sudden I saw that if I didn't stop I'd just write the book all over again, in the preface)" (JWP). The timing was appropriate, as Burke was scheduled to return to Bennington the following Monday. He admitted to Watson some concern about the final chapter, "The Rhetorical Radiance of the Divine," which had "engrafted itself onto the organism" at the last minute. But he planned to proceed with confidence, given that he had delivered several portions of it at Princeton to a warm reception.

As for "The War of Words," Burke had not yet decided what to do. For the time being, he was preparing for his Bennington classes, writing an essay on the poetry of Theodore Roethke for the *Sewanee Review*, and entertaining a recent offer to lecture alongside Gregory Bateson, George Boas, Frank Lloyd Wright, Marcel Duchamp, and Andrew C. Ritchie at the Western Round Table on Modern Art in San Francisco (Burke to Watson, 19 March 1949, JWP; see also *WW* 6).[6] For the moment, it was enough to pack up the family and travel north.

9

Everything Is Nowhere

Burke sent Watson revised sections of "Order" for feedback almost as soon as they were complete. But as the spring of 1949 approached, his communications met with radio silence. Naturally, he began to worry about both the quality of his argument and the well-being of his friend and patron. In a 10 March 1949 letter (JWP), he told Watson flatly, "I'm beginning to fear that you are doing a pocket veto of the items I sent you." When no response arrived, he followed up on 19 March 1949 (JWP), writing, "If your silence concerns Toilet Flower, and my proposal to dedicate the first volume to him, then hell let's forget it. But I hope you'll at least let me quote the line from him, as at bottom of p. 2 herewith attached."

It turned out that Watson had been ill. In a note dated 21 March 1949 (KBP, Burke-1), Watson informed Burke that he had only recently been capable of reading the socioanagogic interpretation of *Venus and Adonis*, which he enthusiastically endorsed. In response to Watson's fragile condition, Burke offered to swing by on his way back from Bennington so that he could help. "About the physicalities of the matter, I know nothing," he wrote, "but insofar as these things also involve mental attitudes, God damn it I am sure I could contribute something that would be under the sign of utterance. I am sure" (Burke to Watson, 26 March 1949, JWP). In the meantime, he sent along the final chapter, "The Rhetorical Radiance of the Divine," and declared the first volume of *A Rhetoric of Motives* "delivered" to his publisher.

Watson responded quickly with a note of encouragement. "I don't think the closing chapter is slow going at all—extremely engrossing. Nice way to handle William James and H. J. too. The preface read now at least is most helpful" (30 March 1949, KBP, Burke-1). Unfortunately, Burke's publisher was less encouraging. Following his trip to San Francisco, Burke learned that his editor was having difficulty making heads or tails of the argument. "I sent in the Rhetoric to the publisher some weeks ago," Burke explained to Malcolm Cowley, "and he seems to be undergoing sorrows of some sort. Last week, one of the editors said, plaintively, 'But you have to study the book!' Whereupon rearranging my lines hastily, I came back indignant and thunderous, 'Of course, you have to study all my books.' Presumably he's still studying" (26 April 1949, KBP, Burke-1).

The publisher's tepid response to *A Rhetoric of Motives* made Burke hesitant to reveal the existence of "The War of Words." He wrote to Watson on 29 March 1949, "Meanwhile, publisher has not as yet sent word of plans anent Rhetoric book. And I have not, accordingly, discussed at all the problem as to whether the War of Words business should preceed [*sic*] or follow the Symbolic. So, at the moment, let our slogan be: Everything is Nowhere" (JWP). Everything may have been nowhere, but that didn't shield Burke from the "sheer instrumentalities of living," he told Watson. Following the completion of the first volume of *A Rhetoric of Motives*, Burke had hoped to "huddle with himself" and "decide what would be the Next Phase." Unfortunately, his teaching schedule at Bennington, existing writing commitments, and lecture opportunities prevented any respite.

Earlier that winter, Frederick "Champ" Ward had approached Burke about a teaching opportunity at the University of Chicago (Beasley 38).[1] Ward was tasked with bolstering both the quality and the reputation of the university's undergraduate writing curriculum, and he, along with R. S. Crane and Richard M. Weaver, felt that Burke was the person for the job. Ward invited Burke to submit a one-page précis of his recent work. Burke obliged shortly thereafter with a document that, for all intents and purposes, was a snapshot of the recently completed first volume of *A Rhetoric of Motives* (Beasley 39). "The Rhetoric is both traditional and original," he told Ward. "Beginning with five classical texts . . . we note the main principles that we consider vital to modern rhetoric. Next, we consider what sort of developments have been, or can be, made atop these early principles. Here we offer our own theories, though using at every step some related modern work" (Burke to Ward, 1 February 1949, KBP, Burke-1).

Ward found the document compelling, and Burke received a formal invitation to teach for two semesters (Beasley 40). Although he wanted to "turn down the Chicago offer entirely" in order to focus on his writing, the offer intrigued him. "The boys out there are very much on their toes," he explained to Watson, "so a season with them would be all to the good. And Hutchins' stand in the face of the warmongering, etc. has been something to stand up and cheer about" (29 April 1949, JWP). Meanwhile, Burke continued to worry over the news, the status of his book, and his garden, which had once again grown wild (Burke to Watson, 13 May 1949, JWP).

As July approached, Burke received positive news about the first volume of *A Rhetoric of Motives*. "The publishers as I interpret the letter, seem minded to go ahead on the project with zest," he informed Watson. However, the positive news did not inspire Burke to reveal the existence of "The War of Words." "Am thinking more than ever of holding the War of Words section until after the Symbolic has appeared. Also, by then, things should have swung around a sufficient number of times for me to be surer of my over-all perspective. Meanwhile, I think I'll try to carve out bits of the material for possible magazine publication, lest someone else get a scoop on me" (Burke to Watson, 20 June 1949, JWP). For the time being, it was enough that the first volume of *A Rhetoric of Motives* was scheduled to be published in January 1950.

A couple of weeks later, Burke's Andover farm was wired for electricity. To celebrate, Burke lamented the state of education at Bennington and worried about his impending trip to Chicago. If there was any solace in his upcoming appointment, it resided in the thought that socioanagogic interpretation would guide one of his courses on "literary poetics/taste/aesthetics" (Burke to Watson, 5 July 1949, JWP). Although, initially, socioanagogic interpretation was a solution to a local problem he encountered while drafting *A Rhetoric of Motives*, it now served as the bridge from that book to *A Symbolic of Motives*.

Watson supported Burke's decision to withhold "The War of Words." Although he said he would be "sorry not to [see it] in print next year," he thought "the hierarchy is quite enough subject for a book" and felt the popular material "should indeed make some good articles" (Watson to Burke, 26 June 1949, KBP, Burke-1). Watson's endorsement of Burke's plan for "The War of Words" meant that Burke had finally cleared a runway for the next phase. One would expect, given the chapter drafts Burke had already completed for *A Symbolic of Motives*, that he would be able to get to work right away. And he did. Within the year, he had drafted new chapters and produced a formal outline.

As Burke closed *A Rhetoric of Motives*, the state of US and international politics continued to weigh on him. In a letter to Watson dated 9 August 1949 (JWP), Burke enclosed a poem titled "A Prelude and a Prayer" that conveyed his overall attitude:

Were everybody to spit in the ocean at once
It would make little difference. Hence our hero

Though siclied o'er with the pale thought of caste
and ailing physically, found no good ground
For public bellyaching.

Assailed by radio
Blasting vug-music for brigs and gunds to blank by,
He said: It stinniks. Noting the free press's
Indoctrination towards greater global frenzy,
He but felt a dull pain in the pain-receiver. Confronting
Professional pronouncements, he glumly edsay itshay.

He knew the country was so God-damned rich,
The rest of the world would sit up all night trying
To keep its politicos from making monkeys of themselves.
He knew there was less religion in a carload of cigarettes
Than in Cardinal Francis Pukeman's spiritual mug,
And wondered if they had a pissant for President.

Burke figured that this poem would concern Watson. In subsequent letters, he admitted that he wasn't sleeping well and wondered if Watson could prescribe a medication to help (1 September 1949, JWP). Evidently, Burke was growing increasingly anxious about his upcoming Chicago appointment. To channel his nervous energy, he took copious notes on *Hamlet*. However, Burke's "Prelude" poem suggests a real sense of despair. Because it is a "Prelude," it introduces a principal event. A worse fate, Burke seemed to suggest in the poem, awaited him just over the horizon.

September 1949–May 1950

Burke's pills arrived in mid-September, just in time for his departure to the University of Chicago. He had finished his essay on Roethke and sent it off for Watson's review. By the end of November, Burke's courses on rhetoric and literary criticism were in full swing. He described the class on rhetoric as a "prima-donna . . . seminar for five teachers of college English. Mainly I have been peddling the Rhetoric (except that I gave them the MS to read, and let the seminar develop from there on, rather than building the course out of the gradual release of this material itself). As a result, I have had to work harder, but I think I profited more than I would have, had I used the husbandry method" (Burke to Watson, 26 November 1949, JWP). The course on literary criticism was more enjoyable because he was engaging in friendly debate with students about definitions of key literary terms. As at Princeton, Burke attended parties with colleagues where he no doubt sharpened "up the points in the book." Of course, that work would have been much easier once the galleys of *A Rhetoric of Motives* arrived.

The galleys finally appeared in mid-December, much later than Burke had expected. Having just completed his first term at Chicago, he was busy teaching his recent and forthcoming work. "I have a vast amt. of notes to be sifted and shifted (some for the Symbolic, some for the War of Words section of the Rhetoric, and lo! some for Epilegomena to the Grammar)," he wrote Watson (19 December 1949, JWP). What's more, he continued,

> The head of the college English dept., a younger man who was in my Seminar, has taken quite a shine to the Rhetoric material, and has started a backfire on the publishers (by himself acting to get the Prentice-Hall "field men" acquainted with the book, which is being published by the "trade book" division, and was thus a kind of secret, as regards the textbook trade). I dare hope that the book will do fairly well. (My prognostications bring up vast mathematical problems. For I have said that the Rhetoric will sell at least three copies to each one of the Grammar. But I have also said that the sale of the Rhetoric will also re-stimulate the sale of the Grammar. . . .)

Burke would "rest" over the holidays in the glow of this potential outcome, correcting his galleys, reviewing Francis Fergusson's new book for the *Kenyon Review*, and preparing for the next term (Burke to Watson, 19 December 1949, JWP).

The lightness in Burke's attitude did not last long. By year's end, he was describing the galleys of *A Rhetoric of Motives* as "hideously unclean." Distance from his manuscript showed him that there were "hundreds and hundreds of cases in that book where I thought I was hitting the bull's eye and now fear I too often wasn't even hitting the target," he told Watson. Although he felt that "'the idea' is there," the particulars were not "worked out" as neatly as he had believed after his most recent revision. The problem of his style had resurfaced once again. "Trouble seems to be something like this: The sentences hurry along so that they make you read faster than you should for that sort of material; hence, the demonstrations don't take. Well, the next time . . . " (Burke to Watson, 31 December 1949, JWP).

Unfortunately, it was too late to change course now. Burke finished marking the galleys and carried on with his lecture circuit, fielding and declining offers to teach elsewhere and testing out material from "The War of Words." He even delivered a public talk on the radio (ibid.).

By the first week of April, the published book had arrived. Burke promptly sent a copy to Watson, who read the book again and sent along his praise: "Stopping here and there I think I see that the Range of Rhetoric section begins as before and that you have tied identification in at various points later. The opening pages of the section Order seem new to me (perhaps I merely understand them better). I remember pretty well from the bottom of p. 189 on" (Watson to Burke, 16 April 1950, JWP). The official publication date was set for 1 May 1950, which left Burke daydreaming about "a Windy-Joe McCarthy of the reviewer's guild making capital of that," as he put it to Watson. He eventually decided to transform sections of the "Devices" chapter into individual articles. The "reason for haste," he told Watson, is that "at Chicago, I gave some talks before the sociologists on the theory of the devices, plus some illustrations; and since it's obviously a line of thought they should have been following all along, and since they immediately began to discover that one or another of them had already been following it, I decided I had better publish mine, before I found myself obliged to do some fantastic apologetic squirming, etc" (Burke to Watson, 7 April 1950, JWP). As with *A Rhetoric of Motives*, all that remained was the arrival of the reviews.

Epilegomena

As my coeditors and I explain in the introduction to the scholarly edition of *The War of Words*, and as noted above, Burke chose not to publish "The War of Words" during his lifetime. He returned to the manuscript at various points in subsequent years, publishing a small portion of the manuscript in his famous essay "Rhetoric—Old and New," and delivering various lectures about rhetorical devices throughout the country. Life's complications seemed to work against the project. For example, in an unsent letter written, presumably, in 1951, Burke wrote Watson to gauge his interest in completing the volume as a collaborative effort. Burke's mother was dying of cancer and he needed financial support, so even though he had never written with "monetary ambitions," the haunting look in his mother's eyes was enough to motivate him to make an exception (Burke to Watson, undated, KBP, Burke-1).

"I have many notes," Burke explained to Watson, "for a fourth volume on my Motivation business. (Primarily, the stuff beyond the third comprises those Devices which you approved of)." So, he wondered, "can I prevail upon you to join me in this fourth volume?" The project, Burke believed, would benefit from Watson's "sensitive qualifications" and thus could "add up to something as human as is humanly possible, in this most humane of activities, methodic inquiry into the ways of symbols." Burke made this request to Watson "without the slightest embarrassment," but he promised that "if this notion in any way seems exorbitant or unreal," he would never mention it again (ibid.).

As far as I can determine, there is no archival evidence to suggest that Burke actually sent the letter. It is written in draft form, and if he did send it, there is no extant evidence that Watson responded. I mention it so as to underscore the humanity of Burke's (and, really, any author's) writing process. As editors of *The War of Words*, we make a similar gesture when we note that Burke planned to publish "The War of Words" with the University of California Press in 1968 before his wife, Libby, suffered a stroke; she eventually died after a long battle with ALS (*WW* 30). As Debra Hawhee has demonstrated so eloquently in *Moving Bodies*, rhetoric, especially Burke's conception of rhetoric, is an embodied phenomenon (2).

As for *A Rhetoric of Motives*, the post-publication response was tepid. Although the publishers had delayed publication for nearly five months beyond the originally proposed date (January 1950 versus May 1950), they didn't wait a month before suggesting—in none too subtle terms—that Burke find another press for *A Symbolic of Motives* (*WW* 32). Evidently, sales of *A Rhetoric of Motives* were "proceeding slowly" and there were not many reviews, which was a problem given that "this is one kind of book for which review attention is important in developing sales." If there were some way to "increase the intelligence level of all readers" or "at least, to multiply the number of intelligent, thoughtful readers," then perhaps they would see greater sales figures (L. E. Christie to Burke, 31 May 1950, KBP, Burke-3).

The reviews were mixed as well. I opened the introduction of this book by noting how reviewers such as Donald Stauffer had found *A Rhetoric of Motives* provocative but unwieldy. In a letter dated 16 June 1950, Burke wrote a response to Stauffer, conceding some of his points while noting that the review, "on the whole," made him feel "quite miserable" (KBP, Burke-3). At least Stauffer's review was not entirely ham-fisted. In a pithy review published in the *Boston Herald* under the headline "Kenneth Burke Not Easy to Read," Arthur E. Jensen denounced *A Rhetoric of Motives* as "a tangled growth between [what] the reader [is hearing] and what the author is saying," though he conceded that Burke's mind was "remarkably erudite and complex" (KBP, Burke-3). Albert Guerard made a similar observation in the *New York Herald Tribune's* review, in which he expressed the wish that Burke "had spent a couple more years making it lucid." Still, if nine readers were turned off by Burke's erudition, at least one would be attracted, which was, all totaled, "an excellent bargain" (Guerard, "Kenneth Burke").

It was not all bad news, of course. Both Stanley Edgar Hyman and Malcolm Cowley, along with other reputable scholars in various fields, soon published short essays and reviews, all of them full of unqualified praise.

There is more to the story, of course. But we must end here in order to pick up the theoretical and methodological trail that Burke blazed in *A Rhetoric of Motives* and *The War of Words*.

Part II
A Theory of Motives

Prolegomena

In Part II, I use the lessons we've learned from Burke's drafting and revision process to reassess his philosophy of modern rhetoric. Specifically, I demonstrate how the philosophical infrastructure of *A Rhetoric of Motives* relies on mythic images and terms to extend the range of modern rhetoric.

In the first chapter, "Mythic Palingenesis," I define the war of words as a mythic image, track its relationship to the other mythic images and terms in *A Rhetoric of Motives* and *The War of Words*, and explain how a focus on mythic images and terms helps manage the vicissitudes of contemporary politics.

In the second chapter, "Identification's Dimensions," I redefine Burke's concept of identification in the context of the war of words myth. Specifically, I characterize Burke's theory of identification as a dimensional phenomenon that includes but ultimately exceeds rhetorical considerations. By locating verbal conflict in the dialectic principle, Burke's theory of identification expands rhetorical history and helps rhetorical criticism avoid ideological gridlock.

In the third chapter, "Devices Old and New," I identify and analyze the modern rhetorical devices Burke presents in *A Rhetoric of Motives* and *The War of Words*. Specifically, I show how a myth-oriented form of rhetorical criticism may counteract dangerous political tendencies such as concealing violence in the name of peace. I also show how Burke's analysis of rhetorical devices helps audiences achieve tolerance and contemplation in the face of nationalistic aggression.

In the fourth chapter, "Mythic Historiography," I outline Burke's guiding methodology in *A Rhetoric of Motives* and *The War of Words*. Specifically, I demonstrate how Burke's definition of rhetoric attains depth and scope because it identifies, analyzes, evaluates, and denaturalizes mythic images and terms in modern social philosophies. To advance this argument, I identify the five core tactics that distinguish mythic historiography from other rhetorical methodologies. In explaining how each tactic works, I outline its unstated assumptions, track affiliated concepts, and observe how Burke models its application in *A Rhetoric of Motives* and *The War of Words*.

In the "Epilegomena," I highlight new opportunities for research that both applies and extends Burke's best insights. Specifically, I argue for a clearer definition of what Burke means by human motives, underscore the importance of determining why critics appealed to myth when responding to political crises in the twentieth century, and discuss whether general theories of rhetoric can be created without reference to an origin myth.

1

Mythic Palingenesis

And the origin has to be expressed through myth, not because it is inaccessible to "direct observation," but because everything begins with myth.
       —MIKKEL BORCH-JACOBSEN, *The Freudian Subject*, 116

Reassessing Burke's philosophy of modern rhetoric from the standpoint of myth is unconventional, I know. There are few explicit references to myth in *A Rhetoric of Motives*, and even when myth peeks through the clouds, Burke's attention seems otherwise directed. In one of his more elaborate references to myth, Burke invites readers to "imagine a myth . . . built around the hierarchic principle of 'higher' and 'lower' beings." Because a direct hit on the hierarchic principle was "not likely," Burke creates this myth to provide a "different approach toward the center" (*RM* 137). Although this strategy clarifies the argument, the passage suggests that myth is an adjunct pedagogical device. Why pay it much attention?

 In *The War of Words*, Burke is somewhat more direct about the function of myth in postwar news media. When discussing the "say anything" device, for example, Burke cites the prevalence of myth in historically polarized disagreements. "Take the myth for what it is, a way of using quasi-historical words to designate a universal motive in the War of Words," he explains, "and you realize why the charge 'they did it first' is so appealing" (*WW* 126). Still, Burke is not theorizing myth so much as he is explaining how rhetorical devices can be exploited for political ends. As a result, myth again seems to be an adjunct pedagogical device. Where does the deeper significance lie?

 Even if we accept that myth functions as a pedagogical device in Burke's argument, it is still not clear why he chooses it from the stack of available options.[1] What does myth offer to a discussion of the hierarchic principle that could not be attained by another concept or form? Did the prevalence of myth in postwar political and scholarly discourse connect with audiences more effectively?[2] It was, after all, the "fashionable term" in academic circles (Cowley to Burke, 3 March 1947, KBP, Burke-3). Or is there something more to the story, as Burke's drafting process seems to suggest? What, for example, do we make of Burke's notes on Virgil's *Aeneid*, where he writes, "But I'm afraid (I mean afraid, literally, terrified) that it's all there. The whole hopeless turmoil of human motives. the drive towards imperialist war (which means, now, drive towards universal wretchedness)" ("on myth"). How can a myth contain "the whole hopeless turmoil of human motives," and what would it mean that a myth written centuries ago could explain the contours of postwar capitalist expansion?

Myth shows up variously in scholarly articles and books that engage Burke's work.[3] Generally, scholars agree that myth provides Burke with an "imaginative structure that makes social institutions meaningful" (Coupe, *Burke on Myth* 22). And yet no scholar has explained how myth functions in *A Rhetoric of Motives*. If the goal of this book is to identify coherence in Burke's philosophy of modern rhetoric, we need to shift the terms and begin to think of myth as a formal conceit Burke *thinks through* rather than a formal object he *thinks about*.[4] By conceptualizing myth as Burke's formal conceit, we can observe how, at crucial moments in *A Rhetoric of Motives* and *The War of Words*, he invokes mythic images and terms such as *Edenic unity* and *Babylonic split* to establish a universal scene of linguistic conflict. As we noted in Part I, these mythic images draw together local acts of rhetoric, allowing them to transcend their immediate circumstances and participate in a broader philosophy of rhetorical action.[5] In subsequent chapters, I explain how Burke selects representative examples that extend the range of rhetoric via an appeal to the universal. In this chapter, I explain how Burke uses mythic forms and images to establish the universal grounds for such an extension.

Burke conceptualized myth as a poetic form that was constitutively oriented toward the universal. Remember, Burke's typology of criticism defined poetic criticism as "thoroughly timeless" because it focused on how art could be interpreted without reference to context.[6] Burke conceptualized universals as the *logical priorities* that grounded philosophies of human action. In *A Grammar of Motives*, Burke claims that logical priorities are often "translated into a temporal or narrative equivalent by statement in terms of the thing's source of beginnings" (*GM* 13). For example, Freud explained the genesis of human subjectivity by drawing on myths.[7]

In *A Rhetoric of Motives*, Burke expands this claim, arguing that logical priorities may also be revealed in terms of "an ultimate of *endings*" (GM 13). For example, Milton exposes the logical priorities of division, identification, and transformation by committing symbolic suicide via an appropriation of the Samson and Delilah myth. Because myth narrates *both* ultimate beginnings and endings, it is ideal for disclosing the logical priorities that organize social philosophies.[8]

Whether creating or appropriating mythic images and terms, Burke is trying to explain how humans manage conflict across history via the dialectic principle. This purpose is apparent in Burke's definition of rhetoric, which he connects to core functions in human language: "*For rhetoric as such is not rooted in any past condition of human society. It is rooted in an essential function of language itself, a function that is wholly realistic, and is continually born anew; the use of language as a symbolic means of inducing cooperation in beings that by nature respond to symbols*" (RM 43).

Mythic images and terms do not argue for a particular outcome, engage in a debate, or explain how to achieve understanding.[9] As origin stories, they simply "invit[e] our involvement" via dramatization (Miller and Slote 101).[10] If, Burke reasoned, the problems of human conflict emanated from a single source (e.g., a logical priority that mythic images render), then a critic could collect resources from different historical periods to address problems characteristic of his contemporary moment. The mythic images that Burke appropriates and creates demonstrate the perennial nature of verbal conflict and thus encourage the accumulation of resources to redress them. By accumulating such resources, Burke would alter the public's tendency to accept war in the name of peace.

The reason why myth appears in this chapter's title should now be clear. But why *palingenesis*? The term appears in the work of Roger Griffin, who defines it as a distinctively modern form of rebirth oriented toward the "revolutionary ... transformation of society" (Griffin 6). For Griffin—and for Burke as well—transformation is the characteristic feature of all mythic appeals; it exposes logical priorities with new and often greater perspective.[11] Transformation signifies a transcendence (perennial form) beyond existing ideas or ideals vis-à-vis death (temporal form), in metapolitical myths oriented toward "collective redemption, a new national community, a new society, a new man" (Griffin 8).[12] In Part I, we observed how Burke came up with rules for creating a redemptive metapolitical myth. In this chapter, I am arguing that Burke theorizes a metapolitical myth that defines redemption in terms of the rhetorical education of public audiences.

Mythic palingenesis has been tied to totalitarian regimes that seek justification for their tactics of governance. Burke indicates as much in "The Rhetoric of Hitler's Battle," an essay in *The Philosophy of Literary Form*.[13] But palingenesis is not peculiar to violent political groups. *A Rhetoric of Motives* and *The War of Words* demonstrate that palingenesis can yield a new philosophy of modern rhetoric capable of counteracting "the torrents of ill will" characteristic of the early postwar period and, indeed, our own (*RM* xv). By studying the relationship between myth and rhetoric—and myth *in* rhetoric—Burke tried to curb the tendency toward nationalistic aggression that plagues human interactions. Mythic palingenesis thus functions as a mechanism for organizing a new philosophy of modern rhetoric that invites citizens to participate more fully in the local scenes of action where rhetoric unfolds. In *A Rhetoric of Motives*, Burke presents his modern philosophy of rhetoric; in *The War of Words*, he demonstrates how to apply his philosophy in everyday life.

The best starting point for analyzing mythic images and terms in the published *Rhetoric of Motives* and *The War of Words* is defining how the war of words functions as a mythic image in Burke's philosophy of modern rhetoric. As mythic image, the war of words:

1. Renders visible naturalized language capacities and tendencies
2. Helps audiences conceptualize how such tendencies connect to the past, present, and future of human conflict
3. Establishes a scene where such conflict unfolds
4. Creates an infrastructure for studying such a scene, and
5. Facilitates the continued study of human conflict via rhetorical devices.

These five features of the war of words highlight the philosophical coherence in *A Rhetoric of Motives* where there was presumed to be none.

In the pages that follow, I reassess Burke's analysis of Milton's *Samson Agonistes*, characterizing it as a representative anecdote that discloses how mythic images render the dialectic principle visible.[14] I then track the curve of history that Burke builds from this representative anecdote, which draws into conversation the contributions of Milton, classical Greek and Roman rhetoricians, Marx, Gourmont, Mannheim, Castiglione, Machiavelli, Shakespeare, and others. Having established a new level of coherence in Burke's argument, I close by explaining why, in the light of my analysis, the concepts of *identification* and *rhetorical devices* demand reassessment. I take up each task in the next two chapters, respectively.

The War of Words as Mythic Image

Burke's philosophy of modern rhetoric is organized around a mythic image he calls the war of words. The primary function of the war of words is to render visible the dialectic principle, which acts as the logical priority of Burke's philosophy of modern rhetoric. Burke defines the dialectic principle as the capacity of language to set terms into differential relationships, transcend the differential pair through abstraction, and transform perspectives associated with the pair through hierarchic reversal.[15] As a mythic image, the war of words posits an irrecoverable point in time when human beings were not at war with words. Because this moment in time cannot be recovered, the war of words can only indicate its existence via a failure of representation.

Burke focuses on the interplay between identification and division in order to theorize the dialectic principle at a specific and a general level. As compensation for an original division, identification prevents a strict separation between objects, people, and spaces by assigning to them common properties (e.g., consubstantiality) via linguistic symbols. Because the paradox of substance ensures that all acts of identification are ambiguous, new divisions will emerge and thus demand more and sometimes greater compensations. Identification can thus respond to but never overcome the problem of division. Division is written into the constitution of our language systems.[16]

Because the need to establish consubstantiality between different terms, ideas, and objects emanates from an originating division, all acts of identification can be organized under one heading irrespective of the historical circumstances that call them into being. In Burke's argument, the war of words provides such a heading, allowing historical examples to be read "like successive positions or moments in a single process" (*RM* 187). The war of words accomplishes this task by translating "a pure idea" into a universal truth (RM 200). In this case, the pure idea is pre-linguistic unity; the universal truth is the perennial fact of linguistic conflict.

Mythic images may function as a precept for social governance. If, for example, a mythic image indicates a "fall" from a unified state, it suggests the impossibility of recovery and thus encourages the acceptance of conflict in language (*RM* 62). Accepting the inevitability of conflict can reorient an audience's attitude about the functional value of verbal conflict. Specifically, it can motivate efforts to work through conflict rather than seeking to overcome it via the creation of a utopian state.

Because mythic images are language-based, one shouldn't seek in them a "literal interpretation" of the pure idea they represent (*RM* 202). Pure ideas, Burke explains, "[do] not lend [themselves] to statements in ideas" because they are beyond ideas; having only "fallen" tools at our disposal, we can only indicate pure ideas' existence through a failure of representation (202). Each time we assign properties to a prelinguistic period, we fall victim to the dialectic principle, since the identification of a property compensates for an original division. The best we can do, as the phrase *Edenic unity* suggests, is tell an origin story that explains why we are divided in language.

If conflict is written into the constitution of language, then we must be creative in our efforts to mediate it. Burke underscores this point when he argues that "there is a difference between an abstract term naming the 'idea' of, say, security, and a concrete image designed to stand for this idea, and to 'place it before our very eyes'" (*RM* 86). "For one thing," he explains, "it will not represent merely one idea, but will contain a whole bundle of principles, even ones that would be mutually contradictory if reduced to their purely ideational equivalents" (86–87). Even if a utopia is rendered via a mythic image, it will inevitably contain a "bundle of principles" that spur conflict (86). In order to navigate this "bundle of principles," critics must first accept the inevitability of linguistic conflict and then mediate it with attention to the material circumstances that called it into being.

One reason why Burke uses the war of words to "body forth" the dialectic principle is that it helps audiences visualize a linguistic phenomenon that is otherwise difficult to observe (*RM* 86). Burke never explains why linguistic conflict is difficult to visualize. But we can infer from his drafted and published works that humans have a tendency to naturalize their language habits in order to rationalize their value judgments. As a mythic image, the war of words thus functions as an *argumentative heuristic* for helping audiences denaturalize their linguistic habits.

Drawing the hidden aspects of human language into view requires a mythic image that can "figure a motive beyond sociological knowledge" toward "a real and universal ground" (*RM* 203). As we learned in Part I, failing to establish such a ground would limit the explanatory reach of Burke's argument. To avoid this outcome, Burke used the war of words to draw a "body of positive terms" underneath "a titular term which represents the principle or idea behind the positive terminology" (189). The war of words thus disclosed a creative, universal "design" that located episodes in rhetorical history as "moments in a single process" (187).

Burke's history of rhetoric in *A Rhetoric of Motives* and *The War of Words* is thus a story about how human conflict emanates from the dialectic principle. Although the "ultimate ground of motives" that organizes this story is not "available for empirical inspection," Burke's mythic image provides a framework for visualizing universal functions of human language as they appear in history (*RM* 203). The war of words helps with this task by supporting a "new vision" of human conflict that refigures our "commerce with the world" (205, 95). Burke's vision centers on a conscious study of how rhetorical devices incite war in the name of peace. The war of words thereby functions as a *narrative heuristic* for conceptualizing the past, present, and future of human conflict.

By reconceiving the history of human conflict in terms of the dialectic principle, the war of words constitutes a *scenic heuristic* where such conflict unfolds. In *The War of Words*, Burke presents the war of words as a scene of human conflict when he argues that "the essential rhetorical situation in the *constancy of the invitation to war*" (WW 242). Burke is clear that conflict emanates from the dialectic principle. Because it is difficult to visualize the dialectic principle without reference to time and space, Burke enlists the war of words to help audiences identify its manifestations. As a mythic image, the war of words aggregates examples of human conflict under one heading while honoring the material differences among them. Though the material circumstances change, the rhetorical situation, according to Burke, remains essentially the same.

Burke claims that a number of principles emanate from the dialectic principle. Chief among them is *the hierarchic principle*, which explains how a developmental series organizes objects, people, spaces, and properties. To create a developmental series, one must have the capacity to transcend a thesis-antithesis pair; without this capacity, there is no way to determine which example is "better" or "worse." For this reason, Burke argues that the dialectic principle "is 'prior' to any particular kind of development" (*RM* 138). Noting this priority, critics may study "the possibilities of classification in its *partisan* aspects" and consider "the ways in which individuals are at odds with one another, or become identified with groups more or less at odds with one another" (22).

As we will observe in the next chapter, Burke adds to the hierarchic principle the principles of persuasion, courtship, autonomy, oxymoron, ultimate identification, and pure persuasion (among others). By drawing together principles and historical episodes beneath one heading, the war of words provides *an infrastructure* to the study of language as Burke conceives it.

Burke's mythic infrastructure relies on poetry's capacity for self-reference. A poem, mythic or otherwise, can be read "*in itself*, without even considering" its author; to render the poem intelligible, a reader would simply need to focus on its "internally related parts" (*RM* 4).[17] The relationships between the parts of the poem form its "structure," thus enabling a context-independent interpretation (4). By using the war of words to organize rhetorical history, Burke advances a poetic interpretation of rhetoric that is organized around the dialectic principle. When critics recognize the war of words as the organizational heading of *A Rhetoric of Motives*, Burke's history of rhetoric functions as a systematic study of how the dialectic principle sponsors and redresses conflict across rhetorical history.

Because Burke used the war of words to establish infrastructural integrity for his philosophy of modern rhetoric, it may be characterized as *a rhetorical device*. In *A Rhetoric of Motives*, Burke argues that mythic images represent the final stage of a dialectical inquiry; as such, they figure "a motive that transcends reason" in order to render intelligible the developmental series that led to its production (*RM* 203). If we define the war of words as a rhetorical device, then its primary function is to render intelligible the qualities of language that produce conflict. Because *A Rhetoric of Motives* is a work of rhetoric seeking a particular outcome—the avoidance of a universal holocaust (332)—Burke must have determined that his postwar contemporaries would recognize and be persuaded by a mythic terminology. In chapter 3, "Devices Old and New," I discuss this possibility as it relates to Burke's seeking more tolerant and contemplative forms of public deliberation.

Tracking the War of Words as Mythic Image

Burke often refers in passing to the war of words as he presents his philosophy of modern rhetoric. For example, in discussing Jeremy Bentham's contributions to modern rhetoric, Burke writes, "Since the point he is considering is the primary weapon in the war of words, we should dwell on it here" (*RM* 92). Because Burke's stylistic strategy has not yet yielded a comprehensive understanding of *A Rhetoric of Motives*, it is important to pause and explain how the war of words functions in his argument. This approach should draw the constituent parts of each volume of *A Rhetoric of Motives* together and thus reveal the coherence of each as a philosophy of modern rhetoric.

The first explicit reference to the war of words appears just after Burke defines identification and consubstantiality in the chapter titled "The Range of Rhetoric." Because the reference is embedded in an explanation of the sources of human conflict, it is well positioned to explain the argumentative function of the war of words in Burke's philosophy of modern rhetoric. "The *Rhetoric* must lead us through the Scramble, the Wrangle of the

Market Place," Burke writes, "the flurries and flare-ups of the Human Barnyard, the Give and Take, the wavering line of pressure and counterpressure, the Logomachy, the onus of ownership, the Wars of Nerves, the War" (*RM* 23). This passage in Burke's opening presentation of identification and consubstantiality indicates that human conflict emanates from a problem (division) that identification attempts to solve (via consubstantiality). "If men were not apart from one another," he argues, "there would be no need for the rhetorician to proclaim their unity" (22). Therefore, Burke designed *A Rhetoric of Motives* to help audiences mediate conflict between identification and division with greater precision, purpose, and scope.

Burke's study of identification provides both a narrative arc (a curve of history) and an argumentative outcome (there will be a denouement). His references to "specialized disciplines such as esthetics, anthropology, psychoanalysis, and sociology" in *A Rhetoric of Motives* are thus not idiosyncratic but are representative contributions to the study of human conflict. As we will discover in the pages that follow, the disciplines to which Burke refers expose core principles of rhetoric that emanate from the dialectic principle. Each principle, in turn, helps audiences cope with their immediate historical moment by situating it within the long history of human conflict. Again, the tie that draws the episodes together is the interplay between *identification* and *division*. Identification and division could serve this narrative function only if Burke could explain why humans identify (and divide) in the first place. As a mythic image, the war of words furnishes this explanation and, in so doing, provides *A Rhetoric of Motives* and *The War of Words* with infrastructural integrity.

Starting Again with the War of Words: Milton's *Samson Agonistes*

Having established a baseline definition of the war of words as a mythic image, we can now determine why Burke viewed Milton's *Samson Agonistes* as an ideal opening for the book. As a poet, Milton, in "sullen warlike verse" (poetic form), celebrates Samson (a mythic figure) in order to oppose "the Royalists" (identification and division rooted in history), who have created an untenable political position that requires rhetorical counteraction (*RM* 3–5). Milton's identification with Samson produces "a notable transformation" (logical priority) wherein, through "a kind of witchcraft, a wonder-working spell by a cantankerous old fighter-priest," he translates "political controversy into high theologic terms" (ultimate or universal order) and thus "sanction[s] the ill-tempered obstinacy of his resistance" (rhetorical counteraction) (5).

Milton did not write *Samson Agonistes* because a motive for war raged deep inside him; he wrote to achieve some semblance of peace via a transformation of his "self" (via symbolic self-immolation) and political circumstances (palingenesis). The symbolic resources made available by the dialectic principle allow him to carry out such a transformation in poetic verse: "For the poet could define the essence of a motive narratively or dramatically (in terms of *history*) by showing how that motive *ended*: the maturity or fulfillment of a motive, its 'perfection' or 'finishedness,' if translated into the terms of tragic outcome, would entail the identifying of that motive with a narrative figure whose acts led to some fitting form of *death*" (14). By putting himself to death in poetic verse via identification with Samson, Milton reveals "the essence of a motive," which, Burke suggests, is manifested in the effort to transform one's immediate historical moment via an appeal to the universal. For Burke, Milton's method is a representative anecdote because it pursues political transformation without enacting direct violence against the enemy (e.g., Milton slays the enemy via poetic form).

Burke could have chosen any number of examples to set the terms for his argument. He chose poetry, specifically *mythic poetry*, to disclose the capacity for war that resides in the dialectic principle.[18] To the extent that Milton's poem accomplishes this task, it authorizes Burke to plot a curve of history that discloses additional episodes in the history of human conflict. As Burke explains in the opening pages of the published version of "The Range of Rhetoric," poems "can be studied and appreciated as a structure of internally related parts" (*RM* 4). Plotting a historical curve that rendered the functions of the dialectic principle required Burke to define structural relationships among the various points along the curve. Together, these points disclose corollary principles that expose how deep the militaristic ingredient in human vocabulary goes and thus show how complicated living in the war of words can be.

Myth as a Second-Order Reality

Burke presents concepts in the chapter "Traditional Principles of Rhetoric" to draw "manifestations of the logomachy" into clear view (*RM* 45). Specifically, he shows how concepts such as *eulogistic coverings*, *mystification*, and *hierarchy* are extensions of the original division that called the dialectical principle into being. The first point in Burke's curve of history begins in ancient Greece, where the relationship between classical rhetoric and identification first emerged. "Besides the *extension* of rhetoric through the concept of identification," Burke explains, "we have noted these purely traditional evidences of the rhetorical motive: persuasion, exploitation of opinion (the 'timely' topic is a variant), a work's nature as addressed, literature for use (applied art, inducing to an act beyond the area of verbal expression considered in and for itself), verbal deception (hence, rhetoric as an instrument in the war of words), the 'agonistic' generally, words used 'sweetly' (eloquence, ingratiation, for its own sake), formal devices, the art of proving opposites (as 'counterpart' to dialectic)" (64). In this passage, the war of words is not a distinctly modern phenomenon. Instead, there is a direct connection between traditional definitions of rhetoric and the existence of the war of words; identification is (in part) a type of *conscious persuasion* that has defined rhetorical studies from the beginning. But that is not the primary upshot of this passage.

The primary upshot is that the war of words is not reducible to rhetoric. Notice, for example, Burke's claim that rhetoric is *an instrument* in the war of words. The indefinite article "an" implies that there are other instruments available *besides* rhetoric. Burke could have written *the* instrument to emphasize rhetoric's primacy. However, his grammatical choice allows for a much more capacious study of how the rhetorical motive is manifested in the war of words. Not only can we choose from a number of different types of linguistic forms—whether poetic, anthropological, philosophical, or economic. We can also read such forms generously, noting where the study of rhetoric is relevant and explaining how such forms ultimately exceed its scope.

By positioning the war of words as the scenic backdrop for rhetorical and nonrhetorical action alike, Burke creates a *second-order reality*. In the context of his engagement with mythic form, the term *second-order reality* first appears in his speech "Revolutionary Symbolism in America," in which he explains how groups of people use symbol systems to cooperate with one another (or not). Burke focuses on myth in this talk because it is one of "our basic psychological tools for working together" (i.e., myth facilitates identification within a community). Although myths can be "wrong" or produce "bad" outcomes, they "cannot be dispensed with"; as orientational devices, they are "as real as food, tools, and shelter," except that they "deal with a *secondary* order of reality" that exceeds material objects and situations ("Revolutionary" 267).

Burke does not define what he means by the phrase "*secondary* order of reality."[19] But we can deduce his meaning by studying positive, dialectical, and ultimate terms in *A Rhetoric of Motives*. A positive term, Burke explains, is "most unambiguously itself when it names a visible and tangible thing which can be located in time and place" (*RM* 183). Terms such as *tree*, *apple*, and *basketball* function as positive terms provided that they refer to a *specific* tree, apple, or basketball (e.g., *that* tree, *this* apple, *my* basketball). By contrast, dialectical terms "have no such strict location as can be assigned to the objects in the world of the first order" (*RM* 184). A good example of a dialectical term might be *freedom* or *justice*, because each term refers to different types of social relationships that obtain across different times and places (e.g., oppressor/oppressed, crime/virtue). Thus dialectical terms "refer to *ideas* rather than to *things*" and "are more concerned with *action* and *attitude*" (*RM* 185).

Myths do not name a first-order reality; they shape attitudes toward objects in the first-order reality by assigning values and properties that make them more or less visible. They do so by narrating where the oppressor/oppressed relationship first emerged. The process of narration creates a second-order reality of ideas that implies universal or ultimate outcomes (e.g., oppression will always occur, but it may be resisted).

Sometimes, the second-order realities created by myth will seem illusory when "they survive as fossils from the situations for which they were adapted into changed situations for which they are not adapted" ("Revolutionary" 268). For the most part, though, we don't think about the myths that orient our perspectives. As origin stories that explain the basics of human motives, myths naturalize attitudes or actions associated with them. We therefore tend to think *through* myths rather than *about* them. For this reason, Burke places a strong emphasis on studying and reconfiguring mythic images and terms.

Burke Imagines a New Myth

Burke's characterization of myth as a "second-order reality" adds new meaning to what is arguably the most important and admittedly perplexing section on myth in *A Rhetoric of Motives*. Approximately halfway through "Traditional Principles of Rhetoric," Burke interrupts his march through rhetorical history to discuss the hierarchic principle in greater detail. As before, he underscores the difficulty of identifying principles that orient our perspectives. "A direct hit" on the hierarchic principle "is not likely here," Burke explains; "the best one can do is to try different approaches towards the same center" (*RM* 137). To clarify his argument, Burke creates a myth that dramatizes why the hierarchic principle is important to the study of rhetoric.

Burke tells his readers to "imagine a myth built around the hierarchic principle of 'higher' and 'lower' beings" (*RM* 137). He then asks them to assume that such beings originated in the sea, as this will set off a chain reaction that demands that these beings explain why they preferred specific habitats and forms of nourishment. By tracking such preferences, readers will encounter the "doubly regressive" quality of myth; a yearning for the womb is in fact a yearning for the original sea home, which cannot be attained because of "biological interference." Thus Burke's imaginary beings live in frustrated division from the sea, always trying to identify themselves as "sea beings" but never fully succeeding because it is impossible to "live on the level of principle" (138).

Burke's myth suggests that biological conflict is partially responsible for calling the hierarchic principle into being: there are better and worse responses to the urge of returning to the sea home environment. Those who come closer to it are, by definition, living nearer the level of principle, whereas those who stray from it live farther away. And yet the biological conflict must be mediated with symbols in order to be meaningful. On the level of principle (not conflict), each member of the sea group can accept his or her "gradation" (i.e., the capacity to be ordered relative to principles; proximity to the sea home). Their acceptance allows a reversal of the prevailing order, which, Burke argues, is "just as meaningful as [the] actual material arrangement" because it creates the conditions for transformation.

Burke's emphasis on transformation is significant because it indicates that the "sea myth" is an iteration of the Samson myth. When placed under the heading of the war of words, these episodes locate the capacity for transformation not in material contingencies but in linguistic conditions that enable us to interpret such myths as *episodic*. As members in a series, they disclose a universal principle that is "'prior' to any kind of development." Burke underscores this point when he discusses the Christian doctrine "the first shall be last and the last shall be first," arguing that such a "rhetorical appeal" must be interpreted "as a dialectic more roundabout" (*RM* 138).

In the state of principle, which Burke characterizes as "a mythical term for the *logically prior*," we encounter both the "'Edenic' world of universal principle" and "the state of the 'fall,' the communicative disorder that goes with the building of the technological Tower of Babel" (*RM* 139). Burke references Judeo-Christian creation myths because they establish a familiar commonplace. The inability to return to the sea in Burke's imagined myth—like the Tower of Babel or the fall from grace in the Garden of Eden—is a proxy for the inability to return to a pre-linguistic unity.[20] There are better and worse approximations of returning to such a state; Burke's hierarchy, as we will see in subsequent chapters, is designed to reduce the threat of intense violence. But there is no getting around the problem of division, which is the constitutive feature of the dialectic principle.

Burke's myth is not meant to be taken literally, of course. Not more than a page after introducing his sea myth, Burke suggests—with no small tinge of irony—that he might have "started in the middle of things," since "the sea itself [is] a jungle of divisiveness." Is it not plausible that the living beings left the sea because "their sea-home had already become a wrangle"? And couldn't the abandonment of their home be rationalized as a step toward enlightenment? Burke does not raise such questions in order to answer them. He raises them to indicate there are no secure answers in the war of words. In the absence of secure answers, readers must pay attention to how myths function in language, not fashion or settle on an all-encompassing myth that guarantees peace. By focusing on how myths function in language, readers may come to terms with "the 'rhetorical situation,'" as Burke defines it, "wherein division may be idealistically buried beneath a terminology of love" (RM 139). We come to terms, that is, with *the* war of words, which is launched, sustained, and perpetually renewed by the dialectic principle.

We know that Burke is referring to the war of words in this passage for several reasons. In Part I, we tracked Burke's interest in the terms *love*, *war*, and *work*, focusing specifically on his analysis of the French poet Aragon as well as fourth-century desert anchorites. These writers discovered a way to modify war by reconfiguring its relationship to love and work. In the passage cited above, there is no modification. The living beings who emerged from the sea jungle toward enlightenment move, unaware, toward "the speed-up of a Detroit factory, and thence towards atomic and bacteriological war." Burke's references to a Detroit factory and atomic and bacteriological war indicate that his sea creatures are his immediate contemporaries. But any person can be a contemporary of this argument, provided he or she is subject to divisions "idealistically buried beneath a terminology of love" (RM 139). The moral of Burke's myth is that universal holocaust will seem inevitable unless rhetorical critics conduct a conscious and systematic study of the dialectic principle.

We also know that Burke is referencing the war of words because the function of this passage is to locate human conflict in the dialectic principle. Notice, for example, the frequency with which Burke refers to division, divisiveness, and compensatory deference in these passages. His purpose in doing so is to point toward "a myth still farther back, the myth of a power prior to all parturition," when "divided things were not yet proud in the private property of their divisiveness." This myth "reminds us how far back the unrest of *Homo Dialecticus* really goes" and signals a general scene of human conflict wherein various episodes emerged as meaningful (*RM* 140). Because this passage is not the only one that refers to the unrest of *Homo dialecticus*—not *Homo rhetoricus*—we can deduce that Burke's focus is the dialectic principle.

Obviously, this passage allows Burke to address the inevitability of nationalistic warfare. In the chapter "A Metaphorical View of Hierarchy," which clarifies the relationship between myth and war, he asks, "Are we proposing that men cannot resolve their local fights over property until they have undergone the most radical revolution of all, a return to their source? Are we saying that because the warlike divisiveness of property is inherent in our very nature, such mythic design justifies the *status quo* or can properly serve as an argument for the 'inevitability' of some particular war?" Burke answers "no" to each question, and in doing so emphasizes the importance of addressing the dialectic sources of human conflict. The dialectic principle's capacity for conflict does not make nationalistic war (or any *type* of war) inevitable. Burke's myth is designed to identify a *capacity* for war in the dialectic principle that is manifested via the interplay between identification and division. A return to our origins will not solve this problem; we don't need a political or religious myth that promises unity. In fact, Burke makes a grammatical point to qualify his assertions about hierarchy through the use of quotation marks (e.g., "top," "culmination stage," "image," "idea," "mystifications," and, most important, "universal"). The only way to solve the problem or, to be more precise, redirect its most dangerous capacities is to accept unrest as the "universal" condition of our existence as language. Doing so will allow us to be more "thorough" and "shrewd" when analyzing our linguistic inheritance (*RM* 140).

Burke's hope, as he makes clear in subsequent paragraphs, is that more civilized forms of conflict will disrupt "the entelechial tendency" characteristic of nationalistic warfare. "To say that hierarchy," and thus conflict, "is inevitable," Burke explains, "is not to say that any particular hierarchy is inevitable." Hierarchies can be scrutinized, reverse course, and crumble; sometimes hierarchies dissolve on their own accord. But Burke suggests that a conscious and systematic study of the dialectic principle can foster more deliberative conditions that address material inequities even when— or *especially* when—they are cloaked in altruistic appeals. Critics can identify mythic images that "cloak the state of division" and thus produce mystifications that "the most distinguished rank in the hierarchy enjoys" (*RM* 141). They may then explain how such enjoyment relates to "ill will" via denial, suppression, and excision of "the elements it shares with other classes" (142). Carried to its logical conclusion, ill will produces "the scapegoat," who purifies the hierarchy of its imperfections and promises a more unified people. Learning to become conscious of such entelechial tendencies can prevent the violence that accompanies acts of purification. There is, in short, more than one way to fight in the war of words. As we will discover in subsequent chapters, Burke proposes two methods to carry out such work: rhetorical counteraction and mythic historiography.

Mythic Revelations: Special and General Mystification

Burke spends the remainder of "Traditional Principles of Rhetoric" analyzing how mystifications emerge in the war of words. Specifically, he explains how readers may identify and counterbalance the "mysteries" that underwrite organizing images (e.g., a national flag) and ideas (e.g., freedom) that conceal the threat of violence (*RM* 180). Mythic references abound in his discussion; he asks readers to consider Diderot "from the standpoint of our myth" (142); claims that a culture's appeal to unity produces ideas best understood in terms of a "theologian's concerns with Eden and the 'fall'" (146); and makes consistent appeals to a "'universal' rhetorical situation" created by "the ultimate division, prior to the community of status" (146, 149). Each citation builds on his earlier claim that the dialectic principle is best stated in mythic terms (138).

As Burke develops his claims about the function of mystification in the war of words, he defines rhetoric's relationship to the dialectic principle with greater precision. The benefits of Burke's approach are on clearest display when he engages Remy de Gourmont, whose essay on dissociation "is almost sadistically concerned with the breaking of identifications" (*RM* 150). Burke values Gourmont's work because, in characterizing ideas as "but a worn-out image," Gourmont "discovers that the pattern of the god incarnate lurks in every single commonplace, which links some particular image, or set of worldly conditions, with some abstract principle or idea" (151). Gourmont's discovery helps Burke explain how mythic images underwrite mundane identifications: "For instance, if the topic identifies a particular kind of economic structure with 'freedom,' then 'freedom' is the god-term, the pure abstraction; and the particular kind of economic structure is the 'fact' to which it is topically tied, quite as though it were a pure divinity that came down to earth and took this particular economic structure as its bodily form" (151). Burke's observations are reminiscent of the work of his contemporary Mircea

Eliade, who argues in *The Myth of the Eternal Return*, "Among primitives, not only do rituals have their mythical model but any act whatever acquires effectiveness to the extent to which it repeats an act performed at the beginning of time by a god, a hero, or an ancestor" (22). Like Eliade, Burke advances a philosophy of history that explains why certain actions obtain across different groups of people despite differences in their material circumstances and cultural assumptions. Unlike Eliade, however, Burke locates the tendency toward mythic explanation in the dialectic principle, whereas Eliade is committed to excavating universal archetypes.[21] Emphasizing the linguistic roots of division allows Burke to study the specific ways in which humans use language to mediate division. At this point, rhetoric enters the picture.

In characterizing ideas as worn-out images, Gourmont "describes the rhetorical commonplaces as associations which resist dissociations because of the part that special interests play in human thinking." In most instances, we accept associations between ideas and things as "truth" because they seem to correspond with our sense of reality; our sense of "goodness," Burke explains, is felicitous with "some conditional matter, some time, place, persons, operations and the like" (*RM* 150). However, Gourmont shows that no necessary link exists between an idea and its corresponding object, time, place, operation, etc. Drawing associational linkages between ideas and objects, time, place, and so on is thus an exercise in *rhetorical* identification—assuming that such identifications are designed to persuade an audience to view the world in a particular way. One can draw from Gourmont's insights a "method for helping the initiate experimentally to break free from all topical assumptions, and thereby to cease being the victim of his own naive rhetoric" (153). To drive the point home, Burke calls for the dissociation of naive identifications between patriotism and militarism, which, he argues, have given rise to a particularly violent form of aggression. This approach to dissociation would not liberate a person from the demands of the dialectic principle (to bridge division via identification), of course. But it would allow him to create new associations that are less violent in their assumptions (154).

We must therefore pay careful attention to Burke's use of the phrase *quite as though it were* in the sentence "and the particular kind of economic structure is the 'fact' to which it is topically tied, quite as though it were a pure divinity that came down to earth and took this particular economic structure as its bodily form" (*RM* 151). Burke's phrase underscores how cultures use rhetorical devices to characterize "a particular kind of economic structure" (for example) in terms of "a pure divinity." Such devices enact a mystification by characterizing the ritual act as *the* truth (which, by definition, transcends historical contingencies). Burke calls this type of mystification "special" (179).

There is a "general kind" of mystification as well, which Burke defines as an idea's capacity to transcend its object (*RM* 179). Such transcendence is tied to a "theological principle of language" wherein any device can appeal to an ultimate or universal order (155). Such theological principles link Gourmont's observations about symbolic dissociation to Milton's and Burke's observations about myth, along with every other episode in the published *Rhetoric of Motives*. What distinguishes special mystification from general mystification is the appeal to a local audience in the former case.

Burke's discussion of general mystification explains why mythic references often populate his discussions of rhetoric. Burke is not appealing to specific myths as truth, but rather characterizing them as indicative of the linguistic conditions whereby truth is established. If the dialectic principle creates the capacity to associate or dissociate (via identification) and one can only replace associations with associations, then the distinction between different types of identification lies in the vertical scope of the abstraction. Burke makes this point explicitly in the opening pages of the third section, "Order," which creates the groundwork for understanding the creation of myth as a form of rhetorical counteraction.

The Ups of Myth

To create a myth, one must differentiate between three different types of language that emanate from the dialectic principle: positive, dialectic, and ultimate terms. As noted earlier in the chapter, positive terms are characterized by their descriptive specificity and thus occupy the world of the first order. Dialectical terms transcend the first world order by creating ideas about things; they exploit the dialectic principle's capacity to transcend first-order reality distinctions by placing them under a common heading. For example, one can refer to an orange and an apple as "fruit" in order to transcend the differences between the two.

According to Burke, most philosophies of human motives stay at the level of dialectical terms. For example, after a close reading of Karl Mannheim's sociology of knowledge (a form of criticism that discounts the false promises of utopias as ideological), Burke suggests that Mannheim could have claimed a deeper insight. "Such appears to be the nostalgic problem which Mannheim, in the thoroughness of his scrambled 'Platonic dialogue,' finally confronts," Burke observes, "for he explicitly asks himself where the zeal of human effort would come from if it were not for the false promises of our Utopias." Myths can function as ideologies, so that's not the problem. The problem is that Mannheim's sociology of knowledge has to function as an ideology in order to operate in the way that he proposes. "If you apply the same sociological methods to eliminate the bias from both ideologies and myth," Burke argues, "the success of your method would necessarily transcend sociological motivation." In other words, Mannheim's readers, in order to trust his method as capable of discounting all sociological bias, would have to transcend the differential fray; otherwise, Mannheim's approach "could not survive" its own critique (*RM* 201).

Rather than dismiss Mannheim, Burke demonstrates how ultimate terms saturate his philosophy of motives. To explain why societies are capable of being persuaded by one ideology or another (or simply to explain how ideologies form in and across time), "myth may become necessary for figuring motives not sociological at all, hence not grounded in either sociological error or sociological knowledge" (*RM* 201). The problem is not that Mannheim was misguided. He simply did not go far enough up the chain of dialectical abstraction. When Mannheim arrived at a rival "ideology," he overlooked how his position exposed a higher order of abstraction. According to Burke, Mannheim needed not just to look down from the standpoint of an ideology to gauge its material effects; he needed to look at how such an ideology is organized by a mythic image that moves beyond the material consequences that give it infrastructural coherence (203).

Ideologies never simply appeal to the immediate historical moment. To justify their existence, they move "from and toward a real and ultimate universal ground" (*RM* 203). A critique of ideology must therefore factor in an ultimate universal ground not simply to explain how the ideology frames its value to audiences, but also to examine the conditions that allow such a move to be made. Burke characterizes his approach to myth as "the upward way" and claims that its primary function is to yield a "New Vision," which is both dialectical and rhetorical in its approach to human motives (207). This approach is dialectical in the sense that it figures "a motive beyond the realm of the empirical," and rhetorical in the sense that it is a device designed to persuade audiences of the new vision's merits (203).

The Downs of Myth

Whenever justifications for a new vision appear, the critic has transitioned from the "upward" to the "downward" way; the critic has resumed "commerce with the world," which now appears "in a new light, in terms of the vision" (*RM* 95).[22] When this "new light" appears, "a rebirth, a transformation" has taken place (244). Characterizing such transformation as a mythic palingenesis is appropriate because, as Burke explains, the furthest one can go in the dialectic method is mythic image: "Only by going from *sensory* images to ideas, then through ideas to the end of ideas, is one free to come upon the *mythic image*. True, such an ultimate motive would not be correctly stated in terms of an image. But men have only idea and image to choose from" (202).

By establishing a new order or refiguring an old one, mythic images add a new element to the analysis of motives. "We start this on its Upward Way," Burke explains, "until it reaches the realm of Oneness in Infinite Being. After it has been thus purified, we start it on its Downward Way, back to the world of business and gossip. When it has thus returned, we find that in its purified form it now requires a totally different vocabulary to chart its motivations" (*RM* 245). Burke does not italicize the term *motivations* in this passage, but the weight of his argument clearly falls on this term. Burke's analysis of Mannheim shows that he is not simply explaining what motivates certain ideologies; he is also identifying the linguistic conditions that allow ideologies to exist. By establishing an ultimate order, critics may furnish a vocabulary to explain both sides of the coin. Nowhere is this process more obvious than in Burke's discussion of the principle of courtship.

The principle of courtship is a feature of rhetoric that responds to the mysteries created by the hierarchic principle. As Burke explained earlier in the published version of *A Rhetoric of Motives*, hierarchies form as a result of an original division that separates people, objects, places, etc. Such division, in turn, produces mysteries between people, which may be bridged via identification. "Suasive devices" help individuals transcend the social estrangement (mysteries) produced by this division (*RM* 208). For this reason, rhetoric is fundamental to negotiating divisions between people, objects, places, etc.

The "suasive devices" of courtship are generic to all historical periods (*RM* 208). By using the term "devices" to describe them, Burke implements a commonplace vocabulary in rhetorical studies for tracking how the principle of courtship mediates local conflicts. A rhetorical device, as we will discuss in greater detail later in the book, is a linguistic tool adapted for a particular purpose. As such, it is time-bound and must be evaluated according to the material conditions that called it into existence. While devices may vary depending on circumstances, the fact of their existence reveals a general truth about rhetoric when framed by the war of words. Notice, for example, how Burke characterizes the relationship between courtliness and the early postwar scene: "But can we think of the hierarchic (bureaucratic) structure necessary for teaching scientific method and managing a scientific society, without finding there the conditions for a 'rhetorical situation' that requires some 'bourgeois,' 'socialist,' or 'technocratic' variant of courtliness" (211)? By "conditions for a 'rhetorical situation,'" Burke is referring to the war of words. Bourgeois, socialist, or technocratic devices are thus not simple referents to a material-historical order; as devices, they all work within the "rhetorical situation" to indicate that the principle of courtship obtains across history. If we want to counteract the dangers of such devices, we cannot simply unmask them at the level of ideological critique. Instead, we need a new or revised myth that explains how such devices function across history.

As we noted in Part I, Burke believed that prominent myths in the early postwar period stoked nationalistic aggressions. To redirect such tendencies, he studied Virgil's *Aeneid*. As Burke explains in his lecture and eventual essay "Ideology and Myth," Virgil was a contemporary of the early postwar scene in the sense that "there was [a] very pronounced *archaeological* or *museum* approach" in both classical Roman and midcentury American cultures ("Ideology" 201). In his drafting notes, Burke explains that a museum civilization is distinguished by a form of "modern imperialism" that has "assembled trophies from all over the world" ("myth" 1). A museum approach to culture is dangerous because it prevents citizens from addressing the violence of imperialism. "Go to the Museum of Natural history," Burke advises, "and you'll get, in this scientific 'mausoleum' of culture, an experience with totems such as never was before. A thanatopsis, a 'convenient view of death'" (ibid.). This *convenient view of death* constitutes "the *real conditions* that invite us to contemplate a step from 'myths' to 'the myth,' that call for a 'higher level of generalization' to encompass the cluster" (ibid.). In other words, prevailing myths did not allow audiences to contemplate the violent underpinnings of so-called civilized progress. So Burke imagined "new principles of *organization* and development" to revitalize "this new level" of generalization (ibid.). The outcome would be a new myth that "could build a whole human society about the critique of ambition" (*RM* 140). Burke's critique of ambition centered on the study of rhetorical devices that incited war in the name of peace.

Courting the Abyss

To organize a systematic study of rhetorical devices, Burke adapted a method he called *socioanagogic interpretation*. Building from his analysis of social courtship, Burke argues that ultimate orders mediate how social classes interact via rhetorical devices. He uses the terms *temptation* and *strong tendency* to underscore how such orders orient perspective on a nonconscious level.

In Part I, we noted that Burke developed socioanagogic interpretation in response to feedback from Watson, who was concerned that Burke's theory of identification did not represent a strong enough counterpoint to psychoanalysis. Watson recommended that Burke emphasize the logical priorities latent in the dialectic principle, which would add *gravitas* to his analyses of contemporary devices by couching them in the universal. Again, the prefix *socio-* in *socioanagogic* interpretation signifies that all social orders—spiritual and otherwise—grow out of the dialectic principle. Although all social groups are united by their susceptibility to the dialectic principle, each group is differentiated by the rhetorical devices it uses to mediate its estrangement.

Disclosing the immediate and universal scope of rhetorical devices is best achieved (at least initially) via the analysis of mythic poems—in this case, William Shakespeare's *Venus and Adonis*. Like Milton's *Samson Agonistes*, *Venus and Adonis* addresses how different classes of people (or beings) transform the male character via sexual reversals. The transformation of Adonis, like the transformation of Samson, makes material a social hierarchy that places gods at the top and mortals at the bottom. Burke's interpretation of Adonis's transformation underscores the reversibility of social hierarchies; in this case, a god (Venus) may be seen as begging favors from a mortal (Adonis) because he is mysterious to her. The reversibility of the hierarchy is a function of the dialectic principle that signals that new arrangements can be made. "When this poem is viewed 'socioanagogically,'" Burke explains, "it will be seen to disclose, in enigmatically roundabout form, a variant of revolutionary challenge. By proxy it demeans the old order, saying remotely, in sexual imagery, what no courtly poet could have wanted to say, or even have thought of saying, in social or political terms" (*RM* 217).

Myths dramatize how courtly devices mediate inadmissible motives and disclose the ultimate order that social hierarchies rely upon. In doing so, they reveal logical priorities (e.g., the dialectic principle) that connect acts of identification across history. Identification, within the framework of the war of words, does not simply involve assigning properties to people, objects, places, etc. It also places and replaces people, objects, places, and so on within social hierarchies. Socioanagogic interpretation thus becomes the "search for . . . implicit identifications" within an ultimate order (*RM* 219).

Descending into the Street

The themes of social courtship, ultimate order, and the dialectic principle continue for the remaining pages of the published version of *A Rhetoric of Motives*, laying the groundwork for Burke's concentrated study of rhetorical devices in *The War of Words*. I discuss Burke's devices at length in subsequent chapters. For now, it is important to demonstrate how his presentation of rhetorical devices is mediated by the war of words as mythic image.

Burke makes a clear transition to rhetorical devices in the "original" conclusion of *A Rhetoric of Motives* when he explains—after an extended discussion of pure persuasion—that it is time to "descend into the street" (294). In a footnote, Burke writes that his proposed descent into the street was "originally intended as a transition into our section on The War of Words" (294). However, as noted in Part I, Burke suspended the completion of this second volume and wrestled with whether to tell his editors about its existence. Why, then, insert the footnote?

If what I have argued about the function of myth in *A Rhetoric of Motives* is true, then this footnote is Burke's way of indicating that he had completed the upward way. As we noted in Part I, the upward way is defined by a period of exile that allows the critic to transcend historical time and space. We know that Burke has reached the highest levels of abstraction in rhetoric when he defines pure persuasion as "'the dead center' of motives," characterizing it as a "biologically unfeasible" moment where the "irresistible force meets the immovable body" (*RM* 294). In claiming that "no material world could be run on such a motive," Burke implies that pure persuasion can exist only in abstraction. True, he uses the example of standoffishness to explain how pure persuasion is manifested in everyday life. But, more commonly, he characterizes it as "wraithlike" and connects it to an ultimate order that demands reverence (291). When he does so, he makes a familiar turn to mythic images, this time referring to the biblical Apocalypse bodied forth by the Whore of Babylon.

Again, Burke is not privileging one myth over another. "Though our discussion of 'pure persuasion' has brought us to the rhetoric of theology," he explains, "we must again emphasize that 'pure persuasion' in itself is not to be equated with 'religious' persuasion" (*RM* 291). Instead, the purpose of a mythic reference is to underscore the capacities of the dialectic principle, which make new orders possible via transformation and reversal—in this case, eschatological reversal. Set in this context, Burke's turn toward rhetorical devices in the war of words makes more sense. The war of words, as I have argued in this chapter, underscores the linguistic roots of human conflict; it shows how identification mediates division across human history, yielding linguistic principles (e.g., the principle of hierarchy, the principle of courtship, special and general mystification, pure persuasion, etc.) that naturalize our tendency to wage war over material and figurative properties.

Rhetorical Devices in the War of Words

Given that the title of Burke's planned second volume was to be *The War of Words*, the entirety of his argument implicitly references his eponymous myth. However, Burke makes explicit references to the war of words throughout the second volume to emphasize the continuation of his argumentative framework. Perhaps the most suggestive reference to the war of words (mythic image) appears when Burke reengages Machiavelli in the first chapter, "Of the Devices."

Burke had discussed Machiavelli at length in the published *Rhetoric of Motives* when analyzing how administrative rhetoric relates to the formation of national identity. Notably, his analysis appears shortly after his discussion of the hierarchic principle and tracks Machiavelli's study of rhetorical devices in sixteenth-century Florence. So Burke's presentation extends the argument about myth and the war of words even if he does not make explicit reference to it. This extension is felt clearly when Burke outlines the nationalistic imperatives that distinguish Machiavelli's *The Prince*. In the first four chapters of *The Prince*, Machiavelli speaks of nationalistic power in "acquisitive terms," which Burke defines as "the ways of getting and keeping political power" (*RM* 165). In the final chapter, Machiavelli uses "sacrificial tonalities" to facilitate "the redemption of Italy as a nation" (165–66). Burke argues that this shift in tone "led Ernst Cassirer to treat the last chapter as incongruous with the earlier portions" (166). Burke's citation of Cassirer is not incidental.[23]

In *The Myth of the State*, Cassirer writes that the last chapter of *The Prince* "shakes off the burden of [Machiavelli's] logical method," adopting a "style that is no longer analytical but rhetorical" (144). The shift to exhortation, Burke observes, adapts "the universal, sacrificial motives . . . to a competitive end" by transforming "the Christian vision of mankind's oneness in the suffering Christ" into "the vision of Italians' oneness with the suffering Italy" (*RM* 166). The passage that Burke cites from *The Prince* is worth quoting at length:

> Although lately, some spark may have been shown by one, which made us think he was ordained by God for our redemption, nevertheless it

> was afterward seen, in the height of his career, that fortune rejected him; so that Italy, left as without life, waits for him who shall yet heal her wounds and put an end to the ravaging and plundering of Lombardy, to the swindling and taxing of the kingdom and of Tuscany, and cleanse those sores that for long have festered. It is seen how she entreats God to send someone who shall deliver her from these wrongs and barbarous insolencies. It is seen also that she is ready and willing to follow a banner if only someone will raise it. (Machiavelli, quoted in *RM* 134–35)

The most important phrase in this passage is "that fortune rejected him," because it exposes the mythic quality of Machiavelli's political philosophy. According to Cassirer, fortune is a "half-mythical power" in Machiavelli's work that serves as "an indispensable element in political life" (*Myth* 157). Though fortune "seems to be the ruler of things," in fact, "whatever Fortune does she does not in her own name but in that of a higher power" (*Myth* 157, 160). Machiavelli's passage asserts that God (the top of the hierarchy) used fortune (a step below) to ordain a leader (a step below) of Italy (a step below) who, by virtue of his career choices, was rejected by fortune, thus leaving Italy permanently wounded. To restore national (via ultimate) order, God must send another leader (via fortune) who may "deliver her from these wrongs and barbarous insolencies" (Machiavelli, quoted in *RM* 165–66). In other words, national restoration may be attained only by establishing and maintaining an ultimate order.

According to Burke, Machiavelli's appeal to an ultimate order creates "the possibility of identification between ruler and ruled" (*RM* 166). At the conjunction between national and universal, the prince may "present privately acquisitive motives publicly in sacrificial terms" that draw a nation together (e.g., the ruler wishes to acquire political power privately but uses terms that express deference toward a higher, nonpolitical power in order to render such acquisition palatable). Administrative rhetoric will accordingly possess a "conspiratorial strain" that "student[s] of rhetoric" must consider as they evaluate the diffusion of rhetorical devices; specifically, they must consider how "attempt[s] to transcend the disorders of [one's] times" can involve "seeking to scrutinize them as accurately and calmly as [one] could" (166). Through such scrutiny, they may attempt to reestablish order and thus move a nation toward a patently different outcome. Insofar as such restoration involves an ultimate appeal, it will require a new vocabulary. Hence the need to track rhetorical devices.

Burke picks up the trail in *The War of Words* when discussing the "say anything" device. According to Machiavelli, a ruler may "break faith" with an existing political order by claiming (via the "say anything" device) that his competitors "did it first" (WW 126). "They did it first" is an example of the "say anything" device when it is enacted for "hit and run purposes" and "where the opposition is at a disadvantage in answering" (119). This appeal works, according to Burke, only because "everybody did it first" (126); "trace the matter [of they did it first] back far enough, and you get to the Tower of Babel," Burke explains, and "you come upon the *essence* of the conspiratorial situation, the *essence* of wrangling alliances, a *universal* 'priority' that, in the story of the Tower, is expressed *mythically* as an event actually occurring at some particular time and place in the past" (126). Again, Burke's point is not that the Tower of Babel myth is correct. Instead, he is arguing that rhetorical devices (such as the "say anything" device) are underwritten by an appeal to an originating division (bodied forth in a mythic image like the Tower of Babel) that explains why conflict in language obtains across history (126).

The "they did it first" device is persuasive because of the quasi-historical framework (e.g., the capacity to transform an "all" or *universal* into an "us" versus "them"). But it gains force from its connection to the hierarchic principle, which is a function of the dialectic principle. The capacity to say "they did it first" is possible only if the dialectic principle allows differential terms to separate historical from universal beings. The myth thereby renders the universality of the rhetorical situation (the constant mediation of verbal conflict) intelligible by indicating its existence across time. On these grounds, Burke can characterize the war of words as "inevitable" (WW 167). The task is not to eliminate verbal conflict but to imagine "civilized forms" of verbal competition that lessen the need for "those burlesques of primitive substance-thinking we find in modern nationalism" (167). With this claim, Burke gives the most precise definition of what he means by "the purification of war" (167). One counteracts the "ultimate *disease* of cooperation: *war*" not by developing a stance outside language but rather by creating alternatives *within* language—devices, which are inevitably connected to myths that posit an ultimate order—that, while spurring conflict, do so in order to "break into a new cascade of song" that heralds the arrival of a new spring (167). Burke's approach is advantageous because it implicates all language users in the war of words, calling them to account for how their appeals to order, however mundane they seem to be, identify them with catastrophic violence.

Conclusion

I have argued in this chapter that the war of words myth helps Burke counteract the nationalistic aggression that was characteristic of the early postwar period. I draw the term *counteraction* from *A Rhetoric of Motives,* in which Burke claims that his argument should facilitate "tolerance and contemplation" in the face of "strident . . . journalists, politicians, and alas! even many" churchmen (xv). Although I discuss what Burke means by rhetorical counteraction in later chapters, it is worth asking now how such an outcome may be attained. There are, after all, different ways of pursuing tolerance and contemplation.

In *The War of Words*, Burke furnishes an answer. One of the important features of the war of words is that although the dialectic principle is an unavoidable fact for language users, the outcomes it produces are not. Burke makes this point explicitly in *A Rhetoric of Motives* when he writes, "To say that hierarchy is inevitable is not to say that any particular hierarchy is inevitable; the crumbling of hierarchies is as true a fact about them as their formation" (141). We could argue similarly that the principle of perfection in language (e.g., the capacity for something to realize its ideal symbolic end) is inevitable, but how such an endpoint may be pursued or achieved remains open (300). Burke makes this point when he claims that it is possible to replace myths that offer a convenient view of death with "the Myth" that makes such convenience a source of contemplation ("Museum" 1). By attaining a higher order of abstraction—one might be tempted to say a *grammatical* myth—we may reconfigure the ideal ends of our capacities as language users.

Burke's tolerant and contemplative orientation accepts what is and is not inevitable. "We take the War of Words to be inevitable," Burke argues at the end of "Of the Devices." "A project that looks 'towards the purification of war' should hope for not less of such battles, but many many more." One can hope for more battles because verbal conflict will obtain across human history. However, such conflict need not be perfected in "nationalistic 'total war.'" By coming to terms with our linguistic inheritance, we can imagine a new order wherein imperialistic forms of nationalistic war become an "outmoded burlesque" of "primitive substance thinking." Once this barrier is removed, we may advance a form of war that is characterized by "conflict and competition" suffused with civility and vitality (WW 167).

This civil approach to war would not eradicate the convenience of nationalistic wars. Instead, it would make the need for such violence seem less urgent. If nationalistic warfare abated, then "tempests could be tempests in a teapot" and turmoil could be seen as the turmoil of wrens who, "interrupting their song to scold, . . . break into a new cascade of song" (WW 167). Accepting the inevitability of the war of words would, in short, foster the constant renewal of terms that are satisfied with neither pure critique nor pure invention. Such terms would value both critique and invention equally, allowing one to reinforce the other. Palingenesis, according to this view, is not a one-time affair but an ongoing act of civic duty.[24]

2

Identification's Dimensions

Yesterday's sneeze is gone forever? The "principles" of that sneeze are eternal.
—KENNETH BURKE, *The War of Words*, 46

Although critics have written about Kenneth Burke's concept of identification for the better part of seven decades, the systematic coherence in Burke's philosophy of modern rhetoric has remained perennially out of reach.[1] For many critics, the source of the problem is Burke's tendency toward accumulation. According to critic Tim Crusius, Burke "draws so much into it [*RM*] that the seams of the inherited category begin to creak under the strain, bulge, and finally burst. By the time one finishes the concluding section, called simply 'Order,' one is so far beyond what preceded it, 'Traditional Principles of Rhetoric,' which itself ranged far beyond the traditional principles it purportedly explicates, that one can only say that the gentle accessory is actually perhaps the most violent appropriation of standard lore we have. There is a deconstructing after all—by slow-motion explosion" (*Kenneth* 120). This type of observation is not critical per se, but its metaphors are less than flattering.[2] If *A Rhetoric of Motives* is "deconstructive," it is also—and perhaps more so—*destructive*. Indeed, Burke's proclivity toward argumentative compression pushes rhetoric beyond its breaking point, leaving critics the unenviable task of picking through the wreckage.[3]

When critics take this interpretive route, they make claims about identification that are mostly but not entirely correct.[4] For example, in an essay dedicated to Burke's "theories" of identification, Mark Wright emphasizes the benefit of returning to Freud's original definition of the concept (301). Wright argues that Burke's concept of identification moves beyond Freud's intrapsychic theories to include "the success and failure of communication"

(308). In a footnote, Wright asserts that Burke "divides identification into three types" that do not correspond with Freud's "threesome of condensation, displacement, and identification and/or introjection." Wright then claims that Burke introduces "other types of identification" that are "differentiated according to the amount of self-deception that is involved in identification" (309).

Wright is correct; there are different types of identification. But these types of identification are neither tethered to self-deception nor limited to the passages Wright cites from "The Range of Rhetoric." In *A Rhetoric of Motives*, Burke defines identification in the context of traditional principles of rhetoric and thus does not seek simply to "overcome classical rhetoric's bias toward explicit design" (309). We also know from Burke's drafting materials and correspondence that concepts such as "'hierarchy,' 'order,' 'courtship,' etc. are all variants of the identification business" (Burke to Watson, 9 April 1948, JWP). Clearly, there is more to the story.[5]

Taking our cue from the drafting history in Part I, this chapter takes another look at identification.[6] If the war of words is a "universal" scene that makes visible the functions and capacities of the dialectic principle, then recognizing its infrastructural role in Burke's argument should yield a more dimensional view of his concept of identification (*RM* xiii). Specifically, it should reveal different types of identification working at different temporal, formal, and contextual scales. To help readers keep track of the dimensions of identification, I offer the diagram in figure 3.

In the pages that follow, I explain how each component of identification relates to the others.[7] I begin at the top of the diagram with *pre-linguistic unity* and, moving left to right down the page, conclude at the bottom right corner with *rhetorical devices*. "Pre-linguistic unity" comes first because it is the theoretical limit of Burke's philosophy of motives. As I argued in the previous chapter, the war of words makes visible this theoretical limit. In the process of doing so, it discloses the "characteristic invitation to rhetoric" that Burke defines as the irreparable linguistic division between individuals and communities (*RM* 25).

Although the war of words discloses the characteristic invitation to rhetoric, this invitation is not exclusively rhetorical. Linguistic division incites all forms of symbolic action, which includes, but ultimately exceeds, rhetoric. The upshot, as we will discover, is that the conflict between rhetorical identification and poetic identification is mediated by a broader *principle of identification*. Acknowledging this principle helps critics explain how linguistic forms structure human consciousness, imagine methods for political

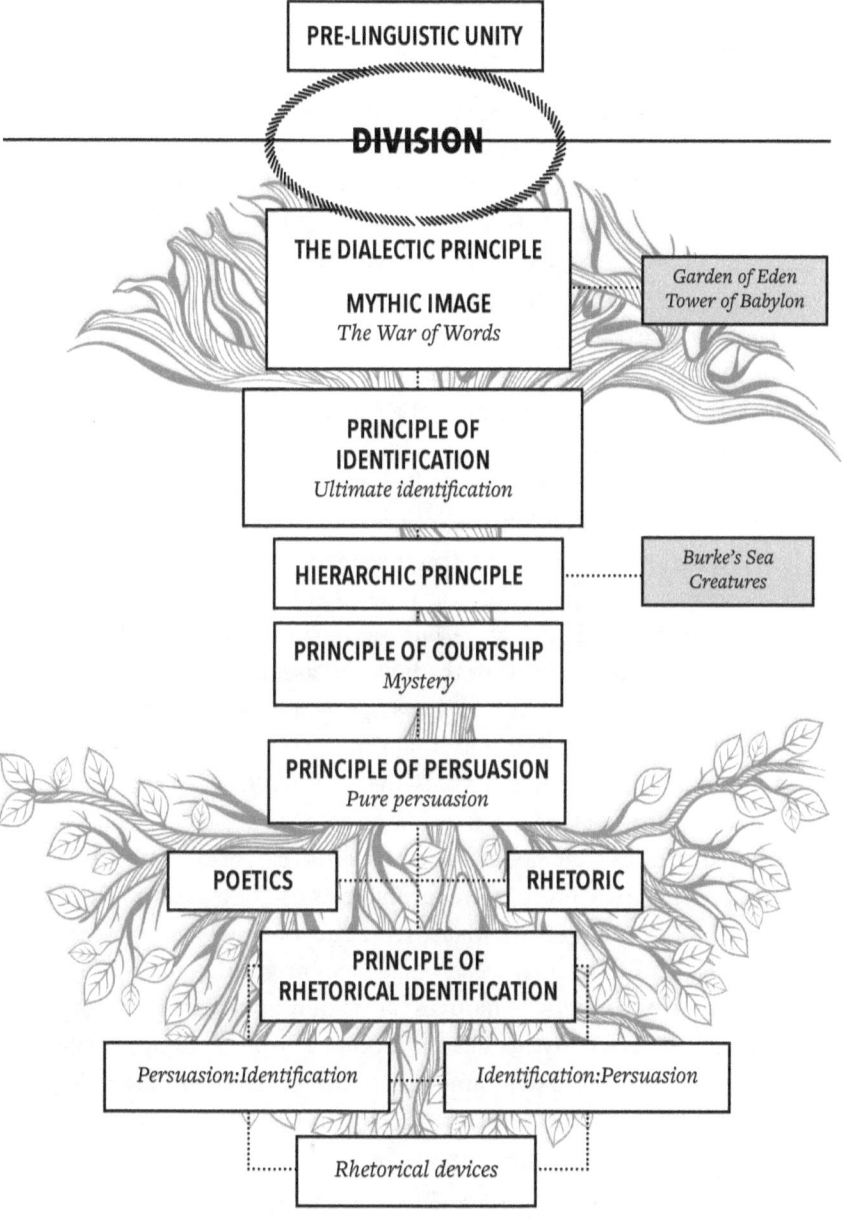

Fig. 3 The dimension of identification

counteraction that address verbal warfare in the contemporary moment, and develop new methods of historiographical research in rhetorical studies.[8]

Pre-Linguistic Unity/ Division/ Mythic Image

To briefly summarize the argument from the previous chapter, Burke argues that the dialectic principle "can be stated mythically either in terms of a heavenly before the world began, or one after the world has ended, or one outside of time" (*RM* 138). Although Burke uses eschatological images in *A Rhetoric of Motives*, the majority of his mythic images refer to origin stories that explain the causes of human conflict.

The war of words is Burke's most provocative mythic image, but it is not the only one. For example, in *The War of Words*, Burke cites the Tower of Babel and its corresponding mythology to identify the origin point of linguistic conflict.[9] "Trace the matter [of human conflict] back far enough," he writes, "and you get to the Tower of Babel. That is, you come upon the *essence* of the conspiratorial situation, the *essence* of wrangling alliances, a *universal* 'priority' that, in the story of the Tower, is expressed *mythically* as an event actually occurring at some particular time and place in the past" (126).

According to biblical literature, humans built the Tower of Babel in order to reach the heavens. To prevent the builders' ascent to heaven, the Jewish god Yahweh/Elohim confuses their language. Humans have not been able to fully understand one another since that time.[10]

When Burke cites the war of words, the Tower of Babel, or another mythic image to discuss the dialectic principle, he posits an irrecoverable point in time when human beings were not at war with words (e.g., pre-linguistic unity).[11] Because pre-linguistic unity is irrecoverable, it can only exist in theory via the negative. For example, the visual rendering of a deity is representative only to the extent that icons are *not* capable of presenting its full complexity; the "ultimate ground[s] of motives" are simply unavailable "for empirical inspection" (*RM* 203). Mythic images address this problem by establishing an "absolute . . . non-existent, limit" that differentiates "modes of expression that are 'impure,' and seek advantage" (268–69). Insofar as rhetoric both studies and develops "impure" modes of expression to mediate conflict, it is "concerned with the state of Babel after the Fall" (23).

Burke differentiates impure modes of expression according to their proximity to the pure idea. For example, *pure persuasion*, which "involves the saying of something, not for an extra-verbal advantage to be got by the saying, but because of a satisfaction intrinsic to the saying," is different from Machiavelli's "acquisitive" rhetoric (*RM* 269).[12] The former is an act of persuasion for its own sake and thus resides closer to the pure idea—hence *pure* persuasion. The latter uses persuasion to acquire political power via factionalization. The basis for differentiation is the quality of acquisition, since acquisition implies a greater or lesser need to redress division. The fall from pre-linguistic unity makes *absolute separateness* impossible. Absolute separation would count as no separation at all, since all would share equally in separateness (i.e., there is no "other" ground upon which to mediate). Such equality would, in turn, make the need to communicate unnecessary, since symbol systems would have no mediatory function. Since we do not enjoy this existence, we must take a step down toward the principle of identification.

Principle of Identification

Burke defines the principle of identification as language's capacity to bridge divisions among people, objects, and situations via claims to consubstantiality (*RM* 215). The metaphor of *bridging* implies not only that material and/or symbolic chasms exist between people, objects, and situations, etc., but also that such chasms may be symbolically traversed via claims to shared substance. The ambiguities inherent in property assignments ensure that claims to consubstantiality are never totalizing. Every congregation will produce segregation, which in turn initiates or sustains conflict ("Rhetorical" 268). Burke's approach to rhetorical criticism takes its cue from the inevitability of conflict, focusing specifically on how partisans mediate conflicts in the war of words.

There are several explicit references to the principle of identification in *A Rhetoric of Motives*. The most notable appears early in "The Range of Rhetoric," in which Burke formally introduces the concept of *identification*. Building from his discussion on Milton's *Samson Agonistes*, Burke argues that poetic transformations that involve killing or death may be categorized under the *principle of identification*. "We need never deny the presence of strife, enmity, faction as a characteristic motive of rhetorical expression," Burke explains; "we can be on the alert always to see how temptations to strife are implicit in the institutions that condition human relationships." "Yet," Burke asserts, "we can at the same time always look beyond this order, to the principle of identification in general, a terministic choice justified by the fact that identifications in the order of love are also characteristic of rhetorical expression" (20). The key to this passage is Burke's claim that identifications in the order of love are *also* characteristic of rhetorical expression. The implication of this "also" is that love-based identifications are not *exclusively* rhetorical; they may also be poetic, per Burke's analysis. Whether identifications in the order of love appear in rhetoric or in poetic works, the principle of identification functions as a general heading that organizes different species of identification. By expanding identification along these lines, Burke may collect examples of transformation across different histories, cultures, and genres (20).

The principle of identification is a "dialectical device" that allows critics to "shift to a higher level of generalization" (*RM* 20). "Invective, eristic, polemic, and logomachy" are all valuable starting points for rhetorical criticism, of course (19). But the failure to abstract beyond local conflict leaves critics with only the resources of the present. Using identification as a dialectical device, critics may extend the range of rhetoric and, in so doing, identify new resources. For example, they may discover that rhetorical devices used by Machiavelli or Marx are relevant to present conflicts, even though the local audience and context are radically different. For Burke, the capacity to identify relevant episodes in the history of rhetoric is predicated on the perennial quality of linguistic conflict. Such perennial conflict assumes that war is a "'*special case of peace*'—not . . . a primary motive in itself, not as *essentially* real, but purely as a *derivative* condition, a *perversion*" (20).

Burke's early references to the principle of identification explain why both *A Grammar of Motives* and *A Symbolic of Motives* make cameos in his subsequent argument. The passage on identification that receives the most attention is Burke's claim that "to identify A with B is to make A 'consubstantial' with B" (*RM* 21). Again, this argument explains how divided individuals form communities via common property assignments. Having established this point, Burke shifts his attention (curiously) to the place of substance in his motives trilogy. "Accordingly, since our *Grammar of Motives* was constructed about 'substance' as [the] key term," he says, "the related rhetoric selects its near equivalent in the areas of persuasion and dissuasion, communication and polemic. And our third volume, *Symbolic of Motives*, should be built about *identity* as [the] titular or ancestral term, the 'first' to which all other terms could be reduced and from which they could then be derived or generated, as from a common spirit" (21). It is tempting to see in this passage Burke connecting the dots among the three volumes. But such an interpretation does not explain why Burke provides detailed explanations of *grammar* and *symbolic* in the next breath. Why, for example, is it necessary for readers to note substance's "long history of quandaries and puzzlements" as an "abstruse philosophic term"? What do readers gain by learning about an as yet unwritten book focused on "unique individuals, each its own peculiarly constructed act, or form," who are "capable of treatment in isolation" (*RM* 21)?

To answer these questions, we need to explain what Burke means when he argues that "the related rhetoric selects its near equivalent in the areas of persuasion and dissuasion, communication and polemic." The weight of Burke's argument falls on the terms "related" and "near equivalent" because each term indicates that *rhetorical* identification is "related" to a more general type of identification. According to this logic, identification is related to the principle of identification as a child is related to its parent; it is a *"near equivalent"* of the principle of identification because the principle of identification is not reducible to rhetoric. There are other "near equivalents" of the principle of identification that exceed the areas of persuasion and dissuasion, communication and polemic (*RM* 21). Burke introduces *A Symbolic of Motives* in this section to demonstrate this point via an appeal to poetry.

The differences between rhetoric and poetic identification highlight "the universal paradoxes of substance" outlined in *A Grammar of Motives* (*RM* 21). For partisanship to exist, rhetorical identification must occur "in a work written with a definite audience in mind, and for a definite purpose"; otherwise, it would only be at odds with itself (*RM* 4). *A Symbolic of Motives*, by contrast, focuses on poetic identifications that form identity "as a self-subsistent unit proclaiming its peculiar nature" (*RM* 23). Any conflict that exists within the poem proper would thus indicate that it is at odds only with itself. Remember that a poet could establish internal unity only if such unity does not naturally exist. Burke calls this phenomenon poetic identification.

Burke introduces the principle of identification to emphasize that division exists not in a *related* or *near equivalent* genre or language but in language broadly defined. By framing the problem this way, Burke establishes the dialectic principle as the sine qua non of all language use. The war of words, in turn, draws the functions and capacities of the dialectic principle into clear view. Scholars such as Tim Crusius and Jim Zappen are thus quite correct to emphasize the importance of dialectic to Burke's argument.[13] However, Burke's argument about dialectic is not a supplement to his theory of rhetorical identification. Dialectic is its core.[14]

The Hierarchic Principle

The hierarchic principle may be defined simply as the capacity of language to set objects, genders, classes, and so on into a series of "levels, or developments, or unfoldings" (RM 138). An outgrowth of the principle of identification, the hierarchic principle allows systems to capture growth and signify progress via property assignments. Although hierarchic gradation signifies a system's development, more often it naturalizes "rigid social classifications" (141). For this reason, Burke analyzes the "actual material arrangement[s]" that hierarchies create (138).

In the preceding chapter, we noted how Burke used myth to explain the hierarchic principle. You'll recall that Burke creates a myth about sea creatures to demonstrate how one may respond to homesickness in better or worse ways. On the level of principle, each member of the sea group is graded according to its response. Burke refers to the war of words in this section when he locates verbal conflict in the dialectic principle. The frequency with which Burke refers to division, divisiveness, and compensatory deference all remind "us how far back the unrest of *Homo Dialecticus* really goes," and thus signals a general scene of human conflict wherein various episodes count as meaningful (RM 140).[15] Burke's sea creature myth is thus more than an example used to illustrate a point; it is a representative anecdote that clarifies the functions and capacities of the dialectic principle.

The hierarchic principle allows the "highest and lowest" members of a hierarchy to be reversed via the identification of a scapegoat (RM 140). According to Mircea Eliade, scapegoats enact "a new birth" of the individual and community by restoring, "if only momentarily—mythical and primordial time, 'pure' time, the time of the 'instant' of the Creation" (54). The scapegoat thus repeats a mythical moment in time when chaos passed into order. A scapegoat may reverse the prevailing order per Burke's analysis, but mostly it reaffirms a hierarchy's organizing structure. A hierarchic reversal does not introduce new elements into a hierarchy so much as it reconfigures existing elements in a familiar manner. True, the highest and lowest exchange places. But the meaning of the exchange relies on the continuation of the hierarchy, which governs the relationships between highest and lowest.

Burke claims that one may pray "to the *hierarchic principle* itself," meaning one may attempt to preserve the existing form of a hierarchy (via reversal) in order to maintain the rhythms it has established. In such cases, the audience of the prayer is not an object or a god but the dialectic principle's capacity for *symmetry*, which courts its audience (RM 276).[16] The upshot of Burke's argument is that a person may be persuaded by the form of an argument over and sometimes against its content. Consequently, one may become identified with the formal unfolding of corporate operations more generally. Burke is clear that these "bureaucratic" identifications may render one complicit in the expense of "financial, industrial, diplomatic, and military resources" that are "unprofitable to the nation as a whole" (*WW* 226).

Given our tendency to be persuaded by form over content, we must "watch for the goadings of the hierarchic principle" (*WW* 161). According to this view, the hierarchic principle is persuasive irrespective of the content it grades. The basis of its appeal, Burke argues, is the *mystery* it creates between divided classes, which produces a sense of *estrangement* and thus gives rise to *courtship rituals* to close the distance.

The Principle of Courtship/ Mystery

Burke defines the principle of courtship as a function of the hierarchic principle whereby different classes of people mediate their "social estrangement" via rhetorical devices (*RM* 208). He argues that social estrangement is a by-product of both biological division (e.g., existing in separate bodies) and linguistic division.[17] Social estrangement is thus not specific to any particular hierarchy; it obtains across history and may be studied through rhetorical devices. On these grounds, Burke differentiates the principle of courtship (general phenomenon) from the rhetoric of courtship (specific devices).

When Burke defines mystery in *A Rhetoric of Motives*, he cites Thomas Carlyle's "philosophy of clothes" in the novel *Sartor Resartus*, which illustrates how different classes use sartorial strategies to mediate their social estrangement. Carlyle's study of clothes is suggestive of how "pronounced social distinctions" manifest themselves in individual interactions between, say, a clerk and a manager, or a nobleperson and a commoner (*RM* 115). Burke makes this point explicitly when he claims that each class is *identified* "with and by different social *principles*" (115). In the war of words, classes are associated with properties based on their proximity to the mythic ideal. These properties are in turn rendered via rhetorical devices that are more or less characteristic of the class as such. To explain how certain classes maintain their identifications with one another, critics may characterize the habituated use of devices as "the rhetoric of . . ."—as in, the *rhetoric of commoners* or the *rhetoric of administrators*.

As we noted in Part I and again in the preceding chapter, the principle of courtship is easiest to identify in poetic works because, unlike rhetoric, they appeal to the universal. As such, they are at a greater remove from the material conditions that naturalize their operations. By locating the principle of courtship within literary works, Burke places poetics under the dialectic principle, which, as we have shown, reveals the "ultimate stage" (the war of words as mythic image) in his philosophy of modern rhetoric. In doing so, Burke denaturalizes courtship rituals and thus makes them available for conscious evaluation.

Poetics/ Poetic Identification

Poetic identification refers specifically to the internal relationships between elements in a poetic work. Unlike rhetoric, poetry "can be read simply *in itself*, without even considering the fact that it was written by" a specific person (*RM* 4). In this way, "poetic language is a kind of symbolic action, for itself and in itself," and thus has "no overt, practical outcome" (42, 50). As I explained in Part I, Burke uses this definition of poetry as a point of contrast with rhetoric, which always has an identifiable audience and purpose.

Burke makes clear that poetic identifications exist under the banner of the principle of identification. For example, when discussing Matthew Arnold's poetry, he writes, "the poet . . . imagines that the figure with whom he identifies himself is *being killed*" (*RM* 8). In the next paragraph, he explains, "by putting Empedocles and Sohrab together, as variants of one attitude in the one poetic agent who had identified himself with both figures, we tried to establish the common character of both a suicide and a warlike death" (9). Like Milton, Arnold creates poetic images to transform himself through self-immolation. That Arnold's death is "warlike" compels readers to imagine what war Arnold finds himself in (9). Arnold cannot identify with the specific war that frames the Sohrab and Rustum epic; he is not a soldier, nor does he belong to the historical period or cultural group depicted in the poem. Instead, he participates in the common war of words that unites all language users and thus places him in identification with Sohrab and Rustum and numerous others.[18]

Poetic identifications can be dangerous. If, for example, a corporation can posit an ultimate identity that its members can share in via poetic identification, then such members can become caught in the internal operations of the corporation irrespective of its outside effects. We can read the corporation as if there were no author, which dissociates corporate action from material reality, just as a shepherd might dissociate his care of sheep from the marketplace. To correct this problem, critics must address the formal overlap between rhetoric and poetics. Attending to this overlap helps them remember "the possible bad effects of the many devices whereby such brutality is made 'virtuous,' through dramatic pretexts that justify it in terms of retaliation and righteous indication" (*RM* 18). In other words, critics can observe how the ultimate appeals of corporate identities conceal material violence in the name of peace. It is possible to overlook such violence in the name of ultimate appeals such as "Make America Great" and "Don't Be Evil"; Burke argues as much in the section titled "Spiritualization" in *The War of Words* (92–108). However, it is also possible to measure ultimate appeals against the material conditions they create. Rhetoric helps us accomplish the latter task.

Rhetorics / The Principle of Persuasion

Burke defines the principle of persuasion as the capacity of language to produce persuasive appeals that target a specific audience to attain a specific purpose.

Burke's first explicit reference to the principle of persuasion appears shortly after he discusses Aristotle's study of commonplaces and topics in "Traditional Principles of Rhetoric." After providing a brief synopsis of Aristotle's approach, Burke argues that "the important thing . . . is to note that such types are derived from the principle of persuasion, in that they are but a survey of the things that people generally consider persuasive, and of methods that have persuasive effects" (*RM* 56). By arguing that persuasive acts fall into a category *type* that is *derivative* of a more general principle, Burke advances a definition of rhetoric that is not tethered to classical Greek culture. In the preceding section, Burke defined rhetoric in terms that exceed classical Greece. "Rhetoric," Burke argues, *"is not rooted in any past condition of human society. It is rooted in an essential function of language itself, a function that is wholly realistic, and is continually born anew; the use of language as a symbolic means of inducing cooperation in beings that by nature respond to symbols"* (43). So, at this point in the book, he is merely doubling down on his claim.

By claiming that Aristotle's topics and commonplaces are *"rooted in an essential function of language,"* Burke signals the existence of higher-order linguistic principles that organize all forms of human cooperation. Burke's claim that rhetoric is *rooted* in such a linguistic function means that rhetoric is not the only *"means of inducing cooperation in beings that by nature respond to symbols."* There are other forms that adhere to language's general functions. The result is that identification, though it is fundamental to rhetoric and characteristic of the principle of persuasion, exceeds rhetoric.

As a special application of the principle of identification, the principle of persuasion is distinguished by "its use of *identification* and its nature as *addressed*" (*RM* 45). If identification can be *used* for such purposes, it is most accurately characterized as a *resource* or *device*. Burke emphasizes this point in the second reference to the principle of persuasion, which appears at the conclusion of "Traditional Principles of Rhetoric." Summarizing his argument about the temporization of essence, Burke writes, "If this were so, if the ultimate reaches in the principle of persuasion are implicit in even the trivial uses of persuasion, people could not escape the ultimates of language merely by using language trivially (as with some mothers who seem to think that they can make their children 'wholesome' merely by keeping them stupid)" (179). Burke's analogy identifies "*superficial* uses of persuasion" with wholesome but stupid children who are protected from social complexity. By referring to the ultimate reaches of language, Burke's analogy implies that critics may treat rhetoric as a trivial category of human communication that is divorced from universal orders of existence. Burke uses this argument to extend the range of rhetoric, "showing how a rhetorical motive is often present where it is not usually recognized, or thought to belong" (xiii). Burke's argumentative tactic encourages critics to expect a definition of the ultimate order of language, which appears later in the book. For our purposes, the key insight is that the principle of persuasion articulates with the higher-order principles of language that precede it (fig. 3), indicating that trivial acts of persuasion, even if they are made by naive children, respond to the invitation to rhetoric initiated by the dialectic principle.

The Principle of Rhetorical Identification

The principle of rhetorical identification is the capacity to assign common properties among people, objects, and situations. Such property assignments may be drawn consciously or nonconsciously, but they always seek to attain a particular purpose.

Burke refers to the principle of rhetorical identification early in "The Range of Rhetoric" when he introduces identification and autonomous action. "As regards 'autonomous' activities," he writes, "the principle of Rhetorical identification may be summed up thus: The fact that an activity is capable of reduction to intrinsic, autonomous principles does not argue that it is free from identification with other orders of motivation extrinsic to it" (*RM* 27). Here, Burke is concerned with the scope of human motives, or the capacity of rhetorical identifications to radiate outside themselves. Burke introduced the concepts of scope and reduction in *A Grammar of Motives*, as they are key to any study of symbolic action: "Men seek for vocabularies that will be faithful *reflections* of reality. To this end, they must develop vocabularies that are *selections* of reality. And any selection of reality must, in certain circumstances, function as a *deflection* of reality" (GM 59). The concepts of scope and reduction address the limits of representation by claiming that, within a certain scope, vocabularies may represent an object or situation with fidelity. But increasing the scope of an analysis will cause the vocabulary to appear selective in its representational capacity.

In *A Rhetoric of Motives*, Burke's claim that an activity *may be* reduced to autonomous principles harks back to his argument in *Grammar*, adding to it the claim that identifications are connected to broader social operations and outcomes.

Burke's argument in *A Rhetoric of Motives* is, in part, critical in nature. His reference to the militarization of scientific research during World War II is clearly an indictment of nuclear armaments. But his argument is also pedagogical. Notice, for instance, his famous claim about identification in the subsequent passage: "The shepherd, *qua* shepherd, acts for the good of the sheep, to protect them from discomfiture and harm. But he may be 'identified' with a project that is raising the sheep for market" (RM 27). Whereas Burke characterizes scientific researchers as "conspirators," in the shepherd example he asserts that one's rhetorical identifications may be principled and even designed to protect those who are exposed to danger (26). The shepherd, in other words, may just as easily not be identified with the marketplace.

By introducing such qualifications, Burke emphasizes the value of tracking the consequences of rhetorical identifications. Doing so allows identifications held nonconsciously to become the objects of conscious attention. One may begin to differentiate between types of identifications that yield more or less positive outcomes and locate within them characteristic rhetorical devices that may or may not carry out nationalistic aggression in the war of words. Either way, the capacity to attribute or analyze such identifications is a function of this principle.

Persuasion:Identification

Burke presents two categories of rhetorical identification in *A Rhetoric of Motives* and *The War of Words*. Parsing each category is challenging because he does not systematically differentiate them. Still, Burke's analysis clearly marks the difference between each category via an appeal to conscious awareness.

The first category, which consciously consumes and deploys rhetorical devices to persuade an audience, might be characterized as *persuasion:*

identification. The second, which does the same, but nonconsciously, might be characterized as *identification:persuasion*. Burke claims that the former category is more characteristic of classical rhetoric, whereas the latter is more characteristically modern. Both draw on the resources of the principle of rhetorical identification in order to persuade audiences to adopt an attitude or take an action and are thus fundamentally connected to the war of words.

Persuasion:identification is the conscious act of identifying with an audience to achieve a particular purpose. In the penultimate paragraph of "The Range of Rhetoric," Burke explains this concept, writing, "a speaker persuades an audience by the use of stylistic identifications; his act of persuasion may be for the purpose of causing the audience to identify with the speaker's interests; between himself and his audience" (*RM* 46). Notice how Burke characterizes identification as a stylistic device. His point is that there is an element of identification and persuasion in all acts of rhetoric because rhetoric, by definition, addresses an audience via claims to consubstantiality. The distinguishing marker is not whether a rhetor uses identification but to what degree he is consciously aware of establishing an identification with his audience.

Burke picks up the trail in the opening sentence of a section in "Traditional Principles of Rhetoric" titled "Identification," arguing that identifying with one's audience is "perhaps the simplest case of persuasion." "You persuade a man," Burke explains, "only insofar as you can talk his language by speech, gesture, tonality, order, image, attitude, idea, *identifying* your ways with his." Although persuasion via conscious identification, or "persuasion by flattery," is simple, it indicates "a paradigm" of rhetoric "if we systematically widen its meaning, to see behind it the conditions of identification or consubstantiality in general" (*RM* 55).

Burke's discussion of conscious acts of *persuasion:identification* encourages readers to track the circulation of rhetorical devices. In subsequent paragraphs, Burke argues that "though the translation of one's wishes into terms of an audience's opinions would clearly be an instance of identification, [Aristotle's] list of purely formal devices for rhetorical invention takes us farther afield" (*RM* 57). Burke claims here that devices are designed "to be *functional*, and not mere 'embellishments'"; when it comes to matters of form, framing the problem in terms of *rhetorical invention* is unnecessarily restrictive. Though the classical emphasis may fall on the conscious deployment of rhetorical devices, such deployment inevitably produces nonconscious identifications with forms of argument that move people to action. To explore the complexities of such motivational dynamics, Burke asks us to differentiate tactics of argument from one another, noting how, "in given instances, one or another of these elements may serve best for extending a line of analysis in some particular direction" (46). While consciously appealing to audience sympathies may be a simple form of *identification:persuasion*, it indicates how simple patterns of argumentation yield more complex forms of action.

Burke argues this point explicitly in the subsequent pages of "Traditional Principles of Rhetoric," claiming that efforts to gain advantage in an argument involve more than "cunning or aggrandizement." If seeking advantage is "reasonable and [even] ethical," rhetoric comments on "psychology and sociology," as well as on a number of other "doctrines" of human communication, which all agree "that human effort aims at 'advantage' of one sort or another" (*RM* 61). Since intellectual domain is characterized by vocabularies, concepts, and forms that explain why humans seek advantage, they are relevant but not reducible to rhetoric as Burke defines it.

Having established these grounds, Burke may argue that textual forms such as *epideictic rhetoric* have "modern variants in 'human interest' stories depicting the sacrificial life of war heroes in war times, or Soviet works . . . that celebrate the accomplishments of individuals and groups who triumph over adversity in carrying out the government's plans for exploitation of the nation's resources" (*RM* 70). Burke is not simply arguing that classical forms persist throughout history. He is arguing that conscious forms of *advantage seeking* exist in human communication because human beings are fundamentally divided from one another. The perennial problem of human division will continue to appear in the conscious use of rhetorical devices and forms (e.g., epideictic rhetoric). As a result, audiences may reasonably expect to encounter familiar devices and forms in recurring situations. Characterizing the conscious use of naturalized argumentative forms, *persuasion:identification* emphasizes the long history of such formal usage and underscores the need to bring such usage into conscious awareness.

Identification:Persuasion

Identification:persuasion is the nonconscious act of identifying with a person, situation, object, or corporation. Such identifications may be based on a common property assignment (e.g., "we work at this nonprofit because we both value social justice"), or they may be based on the formal rhythms of a particular argument (e.g., "the way my corporation operates makes me feel confident"). Either way, *identification/persuasion* motivates symbolic actions associated with specific value systems.

To explain how *identification:persuasion* works, Burke describes how individual employees may identify with argumentative forms associated with larger corporations. In the published edition of *The War of Words*, Burke writes at length about a phenomenon he calls corporate boasting, a practice in which one vicariously shares "in the dignity (or supposed dignity) of the 'substantial body' with which one feels oneself consubstantial" (WW 224–25). Burke cites a number of class-based examples to track the dynamics of corporate boasting; the most notable is "the rhetoric of public relations counsels" who are "hired to build up a sense of 'company loyalty' by so channelizing men's pious 'loyalty to the sources of their being' that they may be encouraged to take delight in the company's powers vicariously, being moved by the magic of obedience to superiors and accepting *insignia* of reward rather [than] in partial substitution for monetary terms" (225).

In *The War of Words*, Burke argues that "the consubstantiality of corporate identity can serve as [the] Edenic ground for all rhetorical devices assisting in the 'socialization of losses,' as with fictions that identify nations with their nationals, whereby the financial, industrial, diplomatic, and military sources belonging to the people as a whole are expended to the special profit of capital invested abroad in ways unprofitable to the nation as a whole" (WW 226). Burke's appeal to Eden seems to be about the war of words. But in fact it is tied to his observations about rhetorical devices associated with corporate boasting. Corporate identification acts as the *ur*-device that responds to the inevitable "socialization of losses" created by the original division that inaugurated the war of words. To cope with national losses, corporations leverage rhetorical identifications as "fictions" in order to obscure the uneven distribution of wealth created by global investment—at least in this example (226). In this section, Burke consciously exposes the inequitable distribution of national resources that should belong to everyone. According to this argument, our consent to inequality exists on the level of form. We consent because the fiction is familiar to us; we know its ending, deduce the values that drive the narrative forward, and so on. Consenting to the use of such a device implicates us in the process of economic disenfranchisement even if it does not attain the results of the promised "fiction" (i.e., equitable distribution of financial resources). A national identity may thus be built on the *formal rhythms* established by such fictions.

Burke's frame for *identification/persuasion* curbs the impulse to scapegoat others. For example, a person who consents to a certain political argument may do so not because she agrees with its content but because the rhythms of the formal delivery seem more or less secure with a sense of personal, corporate, or national selfhood when compared to other options. Again, such identifications/identities are formed around a mythic image that motivates action, even as that image lies just beyond the horizon of awareness. Burke makes clear that there is nothing inherently nefarious in competing for resources in the war of words. Problems emerge when a person unwittingly uses a device without consciously assessing its potential pitfalls. Accepting that dangerous devices may be a problem of conscious awareness rather than evil design leads to rhetorical education rather than polemical conflict.

Conclusion

If Burke is correct that political, professional, and even familial situations demand renewed attention to form, then we need a precise definition of how identification functions in order to become more responsible, accountable, and civically engaged. Knowing that we use symbol systems to create consubstantiality with one another is important, of course. But we must factor into our analysis how argumentative forms encourage the nonconscious consumption of public arguments.[19] To engage such problems with the appropriate scope, Burke recommends that we consciously track the functions and capacities of the dialectic principle. Obviously, the war of words helps us with this task because it provides a setting in which such analysis can take place.

Building on Part I, I argue in the next chapter that rhetorical counteraction is the pedagogical undercurrent of Burke's two-volume work. As we noted in Part I, Burke's audience was not fellow academics but the postwar public at large. Though valuable historical research has been conducted on *A Rhetoric of Motives*, the fact that it was written as a work of public criticism seems to have been forgotten, if it was ever fully acknowledged.[20] Of course, whether Burke's prose connects with public audiences is an open question. If, for example, scholars trained in rhetoric have had difficulty making sense of his system over the past three-quarters of a century, then it is reasonable to be concerned that Burke missed the mark with his larger audience. But this is not to say that he missed the mark entirely. The drafting history in Part I allows us to step back and recognize that Burke's final delivery may not square well with his purpose or intention for the work. However, by plodding through the details of his system, we can succeed where he may have failed—if one is so bold as to call one of the most influential works of rhetorical philosophy a "failure." Treating Burke as a writer engaged in an ongoing process not only helps us understand the problems he was trying to solve; it also allows us to pick up where he left off as a scholar of rhetoric. The work of *A Rhetoric of Motives* may yet evolve in our hands. We remain, after all, enmeshed in the war of words.

3

Devices Old and New

It has always been the prime function of mythology and rite to supply the symbols that carry the human spirit forward, in counteraction to those other constant human fantasies that tend to tie it back.

—JOSEPH CAMPBELL, *The Hero with a Thousand Faces*, 7

In the previous two chapters, we've examined how the war of words myth breathes infrastructural coherence into Burke's philosophy of modern rhetoric. As we turn now to Burke's engagement with the war of words in the early postwar period, we will examine its relationship to modern rhetorical devices.[1] As we noted in Part I, Burke was preoccupied with modern rhetorical devices because he felt that they incited nationalistic violence. To counteract this threat, Burke scoured popular news media to identify the argumentative tactics that politicians, religious leaders, and reporters used to motivate or justify aggressive political and economic policies. At first, Burke catalogued modern rhetorical devices as an exercise in "self-cure"; the goal was simply to get comfortable in an increasingly fraught sociopolitical situation (WW 265). Over time, his work evolved into a public-facing form of civic engagement that I am calling rhetorical counteraction.[2]

Rhetorical counteraction is a method of criticism that identifies the devices of everyday argument in order to assess the implications of leaving nationalistic aggressions unchecked.[3] Within Burke's modern philosophy of rhetoric, rhetorical devices are temporized manifestations of the war of words. As temporal expressions of a logical priority (division in language), they signify essential conditions of human existence and thus participate in a broader scene of linguistic conflict across history.

According to Burke, rhetorical counteraction is "useful in the sense that an attitude towards life might be called useful: useful not as a device for throwing an enemy, but for purposes of solace and placement, and for the cultivation of mental states that make one less likely to be hurt by enemies" (*WW* 159). If Burke's insights about identification are correct, then the threat of harm lurks in all forms of human communication; each time we establish, or seek to establish, consubstantiality, we participate in a steady march toward culminating acts of nationalistic aggression. Of course, identification is not inherently directed toward nationalistic warfare; nationalistic warfare is a "disease of cooperation," not its inevitability (*RM* 22).[4] The antidote to this disease, Burke argues, is identifying how rhetorical devices incite violence in the name of peace. By learning this form of rhetorical criticism, audiences may find a different, more contemplative stance relative to their historical moment and thereby build strategies for counteracting the threat of war that exists in seemingly innocuous acts of community organization.

Given that so much of *The War of Words* is dedicated to cataloguing modern rhetorical devices, and in light of the fact that so little has been written about it, it is tempting to focus our attention exclusively on that work.[5] However, as Part I demonstrated, *A Rhetoric of Motives* anticipates the completion of *The War of Words* and thus establishes the necessary groundwork for what would have appeared in published form. Recognizing this fact not only allows critics to observe the frequency with which rhetorical devices feature in the published version of *A Rhetoric of Motives*; it also places Burke's discussion within the broader mythic framework that organizes his two-volume work.

The distinction between *persuasion:identification* and *identification:persuasion* guides my analysis in this chapter. Again, *persuasion:identification* is characteristic of the classical tradition and focuses on conscious acts of persuasion associated with sustained deliberation. Under this heading, rhetorical devices are components of invention and formal argumentation. By contrast, *identification:persuasion* is allied primarily with the modern tradition and focuses on nonconscious acts of identification. Under this heading, rhetorical devices are components of *style* and *personality*.

In what follows, I set the parameters for Burke's general theory of rhetorical devices, focusing specifically on why the war of words is fundamental to his discussion. After defining Burke's general theory of devices, I explain how cataloguing devices can function as a form of rhetorical education. Burke's philosophy of modern rhetoric is not a purely intellectual exercise but rather an orientation toward public conflict that "descends into the street" (*RM* 294).

With this argument in hand, I turn to *A Rhetoric of Motives* and *The War of Words* to differentiate classical and modern devices. For reasons that should now be obvious, my analysis focuses on the relationship between form and consciousness as it relates to identification and myth. I close the chapter by explaining how the study of rhetorical devices relates directly to public rhetorical counteraction.

What Is a Rhetorical Device?

Rhetorical devices are patterns of argument that may be used in different and sometimes divergent contexts to motivate specific attitudes, actions, or outcomes in response to specific material exigencies.

As patterns of argument that may be used in different and sometimes divergent contexts, rhetorical devices may be "abstracted and named without reference to any particular subject matter, [and] hence can be looked upon as capable of 'reindividuation' in a great variety of subject matters" (*RM* 65). In other words, they can travel to any context. A device's capacity to travel across time, space, and topic is made possible by the dialectic principle, which allows critics to identify properties with, or dissociate them from, objects, people, situations, cultures, etc. For example, one could use *amplification* today because the dialectic principle allows patterns in language to be abstracted from and subsequently redeployed in material circumstances that depart significantly from classical usage.[6]

With regard to their capacity to motivate specific attitudes, actions, or outcomes in response to specific material exigencies, although classical rhetorical devices "can become obtrusive, sheer decadent decoration," there is reason to believe that "even the most ostentatious of them arose out of great functional urgency" (*RM* 66). This definition assumes that rhetoric addresses specific audiences with a specific purpose and thus emphasizes the inextricable connection between argument and measurable outcomes.

The war of words frames Burke's analysis of rhetorical devices in each published work. Notice, for example, how Burke's analysis of Jeremy Bentham in *A Rhetoric of Motives* draws on his eponymous mythic image: "Since the point [Bentham] is considering is unquestionably the primary weapon in the war of words, we should dwell on it here. The 'question-begging-appellative,' he says, is a 'fallacy of confusion' that is used 'for the designation of objects belonging to the field of moral science.' If we include the 'political' in his term 'moral,' we have here a name for a basic rhetorical device of modern journalism" (*RM* 92).

We know that Burke is referencing the war of words because, like every other reference in *A Rhetoric of Motives*, he uses the definite article. In doing so, Burke assumes either a specific or already established reference point in his argument. This reference point allows Burke to make sweeping claims such as "the 'question-begging-appellative' ... is ... unquestionably the primary weapon in the war of words." Obviously, there is a need to explain why "the question-begging-appellative" is the primary weapon in the war of words. I will attempt an answer in this chapter's conclusion. For now, we can simply note how Burke uses the war of words to link eighteenth- and twentieth-century media communications.

The temporal framework of the war of words allows Burke to place into identification seemingly divergent contributions to the rhetorical tradition. Again, Burke is not collapsing distinctions between different material contexts; instead, he is emphasizing the sources of human conflict by tracking the recurrence of argumentative patterns. By tracking such patterns via the study of rhetorical devices, critics not only become conscious of the argumentative tendencies that are characteristic of, say, political reporting in the twenty-first century. We also find solace and contemplation in knowing that the problem is not unique to our present conditions.[7]

Identifying Devices as Rhetorical Education

As *patterns* of argumentation, rhetorical devices establish order over chaotic exchanges that are otherwise difficult to assess. Burke makes this point explicitly when he claims that public debate in the war of words operates somewhere between the scripted positions "of formal dancing" and "the everyday world in which no holds are barred" (*WW* 131). In *The War of Words*, Burke emphasizes Aristotle's investment in this work, arguing that the link between devices and real-time negotiation is a perennial feature of rhetorical education. In the *Topics*, for example, Aristotle admonishes students against arguing with everyone in the street because such arguments are "bound to degenerate" (131).[8] Because informal arguments are inevitable, one must learn to use "any means ... to bring about [their] conclusion." Although Aristotle admits that this strategy is "not good form," we must be prepared to deploy it (131).[9]

Burke's claim about the nature of public debate is noteworthy. According to this definition, public debate resides in an "intermediate area of expression that is not wholly deliberate, yet not wholly unconscious. It lies midway between aimless utterance and speech directly purposive" (*RM* xiii). The deployment of a rhetorical device is thus no simple thing. However *time-bound* the device may seem to be, it is also *timeless* because of its connection to the war of words. The principle of identification helps us recognize this fact.

Remember that Burke dedicates a majority of *A Rhetoric of Motives* to defining the capacities of the dialectic principle via the study of identification. An extension of *A Rhetoric of Motives*, *The War of Words* explains how critics may use their knowledge of identification to negotiate social change in real time. As both volumes are dedicated to the purification of war, they attempt to transform this intermediate area of expression by making consciousness "a matter of conscience" (*WW* 143). Such transformation requires a definition of social action as *willed*, meaning that we must assume that individuals and groups have motives that move them to specific actions.[10] Though we may have no choice about whether to become a language user, we do have a choice about how we use language. Making our language the subject of conscious attention, Burke suggests, exposes our greatest source of freedom and hope.

As the capacities of persuasion become a matter of conscience, public audiences may achieve a proper focus on the current state of device-based argument, which, in Burke's view, demanded methods for achieving greater levels of linguistic accountability. The first step toward linguistic accountability is the dissociation of identification from "the imagining of villanies" that rely on the vocabulary of "'projection' or 'sublimation' of a 'suppressed desire'" (*WW* 143).[11] As long as such myths remain in place, we will lean on individual pathologies, which, in Burke's estimation, are inadequate to address the problem of linguistic warfare. To counteract this tendency, Burke created the concept of the war of words to account for language's capacities to sponsor or redress violence through rhetorical devices. Burke recognized that "symbol-guided resources [may] be invented, modified, and accumulated, including devices for 'implementing' the accountancy" (*Attitudes* 425). The goal was not to excavate personal history to address the symptoms of a pathology. Instead, the goal was to establish the conditions for shared accountability by accepting verbal conflict as the baseline expectation for all human conduct.

Classical Devices

Burke engages Aristotle in the chapter "Traditional Principles of Rhetoric" to differentiate classical and modern devices. In classical argument, devices are characterized primarily by their *quality*, whereas modern devices are distinguished primarily by their *quantity*.

Burke explains that Aristotle's classical devices are forged from "the materials of opinion" and for this reason are often characterized as topics (*RM* 57). Aristotle's characterization involves "abstracting some formal or procedural element as [the device's] distinguishing mark" and then pairing it with a particular situation where its use is probable (57). Topical abstraction thus conceptualizes rhetorical devices in terms of context. If, for example, one wished to *turn* "an adversary's words against himself," one would need to recognize the *situations* in which such turns were possible, to understand how certain devices allowed combatants to *switch spots*, and to implement such a device in order to attain a desired outcome. Regardless of the topical specificities, classical devices refer to situations characterized by *formal* acts of persuasion. Hence the need to view them in terms of *persuasion:identification*.[12]

Burke introduces the concept of *collaborative expectancy* to explain how form persuades audiences to act. "A passage built about a set of oppositions," Burke argues, may encourage an audience to swing "along with the succession of antitheses, even though [one] may not agree with the proposition that is being presented in this form." The appeal of form is not located in one's "capacity as a partisan." Instead, the persuasive element exists in "some 'universal' appeal" that is subsequently "transferred to the matter which happens to be associated with the form" (*RM* 58).[13] In light of what we have observed in the previous two chapters, the universal appeal Burke references in this passage is the *symmetry* between the rhetorical situation and the dialectic principle.

Recognizing this point underscores how devices can obtain across history in the war of words. For example, Burke argues that a "formal device like climax (*gradatio*)" appears in Demetrius's *On Style* and in Shakespeare's *As You Like It*, which are classical (rather than modern) in their formal orientation. But *gradatio* also appears in popular news reports, such as those that were published during the "'Berlin Crisis' of 1948," as in the headline "Who controls Berlin controls Germany; who controls Germany controls Europe; who controls Europe controls the world" (*RM* 58).[14] With regard to the distinction between classical and modern rhetorical devices, there are three points to make.

First, the distinction is a matter of degree, not of kind. In the previous chapter, we noted that Burke locates identification in classical rhetoric even though he also defines the concept in distinctly modern terms. He is able to do this because the principle of identification is not unique to either the classical or the modern period. Burke's point is that identifications will manifest themselves differently in different contexts. Because rhetorical devices emanate from the same overarching principles, they follow the same logic.

Second, classical devices appear in public debate even when modern devices predominate. When Burke argues that modern devices are characterized by the speed and quantity of their profusion, he is making an argument about delivery and context: "We are not greatly concerned here with rhetoric as argument," he explains, because argument "usually involves sustained attack.... The characteristic rhetoric of today is done in quick raids, as with Indian warfare, guerrilla tactics, commando operations. It is neither good argument nor bad; it is not argument at all. For argument it substitutes *identification* and *dramatization*" (WW 134). Remember that Burke defined his project in contradistinction to Aristotle's approach to rhetoric so that he could prepare audiences to address the rhetorical devices that characterized the early postwar period. Burke is not claiming that classical devices no longer exist; he is simply arguing that they are not as relevant to his project as modern devices because a focus on sustained deliberation is incommensurate with the problem he is attempting to solve. Being stuck in the weeds, he needed an approach to rhetoric that yielded greater solace and contemplation than classical devices could provide.

Third, we can establish order over public debate by cataloguing patterns as devices, focusing specifically on how they move audiences to action by appealing to form. Burke makes this point explicitly when he argues that devices "must be *functional*, and not mere embellishments" (RM 57). Their primary function, as we noted in the previous paragraph, is to address context-specific exigencies. For example, a critic could use the rhetorical device of *repetitio* to draw attention to a concerning turn of phrase that threatened violence against a subgroup of the national population; alternatively, a critic could use it to naturalize new or old expectations for governance built upon such violence. Either way, the use of rhetorical devices can be defined as an act of invention that induces audiences to "participate in the form" through argument (sustained deliberation), identification, and/or dramatization (59).

Why, then, does Burke engage classical devices? As I have argued in the previous two chapters, Burke outlined the functions and capacities of the dialectic principle to make them useful for rhetorical criticism. The war of words helps with this task by dramatizing an originating conflict that obtains across all historical periods. A major implication of Burke's argument is that there is no necessary link between a historical period and the presence of rhetorical devices. Instead, devices appear throughout human history because human societies need to develop and track patterned responses to perennial problems. The distinction between classical devices (persuasion/identification) and modern devices (identification/persuasion) helps audiences recognize the change amid the permanence and thus tailor arguments to achieve specific outcomes.

Modern Devices

To mark the distinction between classical and modern devices, Burke compares Aristotle's discussion of amplification with one of his modern devices, "say anything." "Say anything" may be defined as using any means to negate the validity of an opposing stance. For example, if a political figure was accused of using corrupt political tactics, he could say anything to cast aspersions on the credibility of his accuser.[15] The goal of "say anything" is not to achieve a mutually agreeable outcome via reasoned deliberation but to inflict as much damage as possible (*WW* 19). By contrast, amplification draws attention to a premise "by extension, by intensification, and by dignification" with an overriding commitment to quality—meaning that the quality of an argument, or a premise within an argument, is the primary source of attention (*RM* 69).

In order to inflict the largest amount of damage possible, the "say anything" device must be repeated ad infinitum "through the great bureaucracies (of government, of press and radio chains: the Rhetoric Trusts)." Such repetitions act as "tiny droplets of persuasion, until in their mere number and persistence they overwhelm their audience *physically*" (*WW* 130). By dissociating material from spirit, the device encourages a "semi-comatose state" in which "the same advertised Spirit [appears] everywhere, and it is no less than God Himself" (*WW* 130). Accordingly, the "say anything" device is oriented toward *quantitative saturation*.

In addition to the "say anything" device, Burke lists ten other modern devices. He defines each device in *The War of Words* using topical, personal, and mythic examples to explain how they work (see fig. 4).

When defining his list of modern devices, Burke draws upon mythic examples to explain their topical relevance to the early postwar period—"Swiftian allusion," as he called it. Because "Swiftian allusion" is a poetic device, it is important to pause and consider again the relationship that Burke establishes between rhetoric and poetics.

As we noted in Part I, Burke uses Swiftian allusion to solve the stylistic problems that Hyman had identified in his argument; Hyman, we will recall,

THE BLAND STRATEGY

"Says one thing to imply the opposite (exclaiming 'Spendid!' when meaning 'Abominable!') Blandness is a practical application of this principle." (WW46)

SHREWD SIMPLICITY

"Rhetorical devices that equate the simpleton with the lovable, the stupid with the wholesome. Obviously, we are still on the subject of Blandness. 'Blandness' refers to the looks from the outside; 'shrewd simplicity' names from within." (WW 51)

UNDO BY OVERDOING

"Formula: Since a buildup prepares for a letdown, assure the letdown by making the buildup vulnerable. . . . It reverses the process of damning with faint praise, as with the man who 'confessed' about himself that he was 'too sincere.'" (WW 57-62)

YIELDING AGGRESSIVELY

"Becomes merely the rush for the bandwagon, or the politician's haste to identify his measures with any cause that happens to be in popular favor at the moment. . . . The device is clearly like excess of consistency when it says, 'Very well, if you would have it so, let's have it thoroughly so.'" (WW 64)

DEFLECTION

"Deflection is got by a changing of the terms in which a question is considered. . . . Deflection can become indirection, or roundabout allusion." (WW 71-73)

MAKING THE CONNECTION

"The device of putting two and two together by saying the word at the appropriate moment." (WW 110)

Fig. 4 Burke's modern rhetorical devices

SPOKESMAN

"The Spokesman, as a rhetorical device of deflection, enters when, under the guise of speaking *for* another, we in reality speak *to* him. The spokesman device, in this sense, is designed to *induce in* an audience an attitude which the audience is supposed to have already, and which the rhetorician is ostensibly but expressing in their behalf." (WW 77)

REVERSAL

"A device that uses langauge's capacity to 'prove opposites.' . . . Rhetoricians can so readily reverse apparent meanings because real meanings are so reversible." (WW 80)

SAY THE OPPOSITE

"For every hold, a counterhold; for every thrust, a parry—but to Say the Opposite in the sense we mean here is more than that, it gives to defense a positive assertiveness." (WW 88)

SPIRITUALIZATION

"Of all opposites, all reversals, rhetorically the most resonant, characteristic, and far-reaching is polemic translating back and forth between materialist and idealist terms for motives. Are things disunited in the 'body'? Then unite them 'in spirit.' Would a nation extend its physical dominion? Let it talk of spreading its 'ideals.' . . . Sanction the manifest (the incarnate) in terms of the invisible and intangible (the divine)." (WW 92)

SAY ANYTHING

"Whenever they make a concession, greet it by announcing that they show signs of weakness. Or warn that it is a mere ruse for lulling Perfectos into a false security. In any case, Say anything that prevents it from being seen as a reasonable move in exchange." (WW 120)

Fig. 4 Burke's modern rhetorical devices

was concerned that Burke's claims would imperil his standing as both critic and citizen. But Burke's literary allusions signify more than just a stylistic revision. As the previous two chapters have shown, Burke used the tension between rhetoric and poetics to identify an array of linguistic resources for his philosophy of modern rhetoric. So our explanation needs to address the practical and theoretical benefits of this tactic.

Practically speaking, Burke's tactic explained the commingling of rhetorical and poetic forms that appeared in the historical record, sharpened his explanation of the differences between classical and modern devices and forms, and thus exposed novel ways to counteract nationalistic aggression in the early postwar period. For example, in *A Rhetoric of Motives*, Burke cites Longinus's theory of imagination, which argues that *phantasia* could be used in poetry to "show a strongly mythic exaggeration, far beyond the limits of literal belief," and in rhetoric "to convince the audience of the speaker's assertions" (*RM* 79). *Phantasia* could be distinguished in terms of poetics and rhetoric only if it emanated from a common source—in this case, imagination. Whereas *phantasia* in poetics moves audiences far beyond the limits of literal belief, in rhetoric it convinces them to seek a particular outcome.[16] At this point in the book, Burke has already shown how poetic appeals can have a rhetorical function (e.g., Milton), provided that such appeals are oriented toward a specific purpose. So Burke claims this capacity of imagination on behalf of the rhetorical tradition in order to counteract the nationalistic aggression characteristic of the postwar period. Imagination could accordingly function as a "suasive device" (78).

Theoretically speaking, Burke's tactic provided internal consistency to his philosophy of modern rhetoric and endowed his insights with a "universal" scope. Insofar as poetic and rhetorical devices respond to the same problem of linguistic division, they fall into perennial patterns that address specific material exigencies. Specifically, they (perennially) assign properties to individuals, objects, situations, events, and so on in order to bridge their separation—hence the need for references to both poetic and rhetorical identification. In doing so, they allow critics to plot a curve of history that connects different episodes in rhetorical history without collapsing them. Burke's decision to use a poetic device from the eighteenth century (Swiftian allusion) to address problems specific to the early postwar period demonstrates this fact, although, as we have seen in previous chapters, examples such as these populate each published volume.

According to Burke, critics can employ rhetorical and poetic devices for specific purposes by using their imagination. We find this argument in the opening pages of *A Rhetoric of Motives*, where Burke shows how poets such as John Milton use the resources of rhetoric in their poetic works. The implication is that poetic works often contain rhetorical devices and vice versa.

Distinctions between rhetorical and poetic uses of imagination therefore hinge on their *reducibility* to each other. Although Burke used poetic devices for rhetorical purposes, his work did not count as poetry because it was written for a particular audience and purpose. As a result, it could not be reduced to an act of poetic imagination. Still, the commingling of form allowed him to argue for the timeless quality of the war of words. By this measure, Burke might have been a contemporary of Swift, who used poetic allusion to address certain ideological struggles. In Burke's hands, Swiftian allusion becomes a tactic for addressing exigent problems.

By appropriating the imaginative devices of poetry, Burke expands the terrain of available resources—even into the supersensible. In doing so, he helps audiences develop a more complex understanding of human motives. According to the war of words, images (including Burke's mythic image, the war of words) will always lead to conflict because they cannot represent pre-linguistic unity. Any attempt to make them do so will always fail, and, in the process of failing, will spur conflict. At the same time, if an "image employs the full resources of imagination, it will not represent merely one idea, but will contain a whole bundle of principles, even ones that will be mutually contradictory if reduced to their purely ideational equivalents" (*RM* 87). Burke embraces this internal conflict because it leads to the generation of more imaginative outcomes.

Leveling the Ground for Modern Rhetorical Devices

Recognizing the poetic undertones of Burke's argument helps explain why references to, say, the Perfectists and Loathesomites appear alongside examples from his personal life. If every device points to the war of words via the temporization of essence, then one manifestation can never exert privilege over another. As Burke explained in the letter to Cowley of 3 April 1946 (Jay 274–75), the first draft of *A Rhetoric of Motives* was full of anecdotes that treated "everything as of equal importance," whether the pronouncements of international diplomats or his young sons' chatter in the sandbox.

If the devices that young Michael and Butchie Burke used in the sandbox were no different from diplomatic pronouncements, then all devices responded equally to the problem of linguistic division and thus shared equally in the state of the fall. Our instinct may be to question Burke's assertion that his sons could not use rhetorical devices with the same level of sophistication. But raising that question would confirm Burke's fundamental point: *nobody knows what they're doing*. Without knowledge of how language works via the dialectic principle, public audiences will continue to assume either that rhetoric was duplicitous or that the news media could be trusted. This assumption creates a pedagogical exigency to recover the tradition and reverse its ignominious reputation, expand the tradition so that it addresses how argument has evolved in response to shifting material conditions, and explain how various strands in the tradition connect to one another, so that public audiences may consciously accumulate resources capable of counteracting dangerous political threats.

The heartbeat of Burke's rhetorical education is that audiences must learn to identify the war of words in themselves—to connect what is happening in their everyday conflicts with what is happening on the geopolitical scale. Burke makes this point explicitly in his famous argument regarding the shepherd's relationship to his flock: "Any specialized activity participates in a larger unit of action. 'Identification' is a word for the autonomous activity's place in this wider context, a place with which the agent may be unconcerned. The shepherd *qua* shepherd acts for the good of the sheep, to protect them from discomfiture and harm. But he may be 'identified' with a project that is raising the sheep for market" (*RM* 27). The shepherd is not unconcerned with the wider context of his actions because he is negligent or reckless; Burke indicates as much when he explains that within the capacity of his station, he is consciously invested in the protection and care of his flock. However, the shepherd's protection and care *may become* appropriated by material processes in excess of the shepherd's station.

Were this to occur, his labors might become less about caring for the sheep *qua* sheep and more about caring about the market for sheep. The absence of an agent in Burke's argument (e.g., "a project that is raising the sheep for market") warrants our attention, particularly in light of what he has argued about form. Grammatically, his argument implies that the formal unfolding of the project identifies the shepherd with its operations. Perhaps the shepherd is tacitly aware of market realities; he may be protecting "an interest merely by using terms not incisive enough to criticize [his actions] properly" (*RM* 36). But the tone of Burke's argument is more gracious than such an interpretation allows. If the shepherd has freedom in language, he has an opportunity to dissociate himself from the market's projects by paying attention to the scope of his identifications. He can, in other words, make his consciousness a matter of conscience.

Burke's "Swiftian allusion" demonstrates that modern devices are "primarily matters of *style*" and thus "readily bring us to confront matters of *personality*" and ethics (WW 135). As he explains in "Foreword (to end on)" in the published *War of Words*, "The originating impulse behind [studying modern devices] was an effort at self-cure. Since I seemed to be seeing more signs of plotting, deviousness, and duplicity than were good for me, I tried to work out 'comic' ways whereby, as far as possible, a measure of fun might be derived from such observations" (265). For Burke, *satire* was the poetic form that best articulated his approach to curing the disease. Having been exposed to worrisome acts of aggression, he looked for moments of mutual stupidity that might expiate nationalist aggression. If he was successful, he could recalibrate formal imbalances that unwittingly encouraged further aggression. Of course, learning to laugh meant accepting the inevitability of our stupidity; expiation was possible only if everyone shared in the formal imbalances. Hence the need for the war of words myth. Hence Burke's references to the human barnyard.

Blandness is the modern rhetorical device most consistent with satire. Burke defines blandness as saying "one thing to imply the opposite." A functional manifestation of irony, it exploits the linguistic resources of ambiguity without ever "quite showing its hand" (WW 46). By allowing a "surface meaning [to be] the true" meaning, blandness forces audiences to choose between two options: either that the claim is honest in its critique or that it is a joke. Once the audience has made a decision, the critic may respond to the interpretation with, "Your inference is correct" or "I was just joking." Making a choice requires that audiences accept that they share "the weaknesses and temptations" the satirist has exposed. For example, if readers understood a satirical narrative depicting the reinstitution of racial segregation in education, they would necessarily recognize their own lack of investment in correcting such an arrangement.[17] In this case, the exposed weakness or temptation would be the willingness to accept that public education is defined, whether implicitly or explicitly, along racial lines. The sins of direct application fall on the audience.

Critics familiar with Burke's published works will immediately notice echoes of *hypochondriasis* and *the comic corrective*. Hypochondriasis is an exercise in adjusting "to one's conditions" via the connection between individual symptoms and group orientations (Hawhee, *Moving* 105; Burke, *Permanence* 245). By accepting that prevailing definitions of health may in fact be unhealthy, it embraces "neurotic" qualities in order to "reorganize the national or racial pieties to new ways of classification" (*Permanence* 246). "Comedy," Burke explains, similarly "warns against the dangers of pride, but its emphasis shifts from *crime* to *stupidity*." In doing so, it "accepts that *every* insight contains its own special kind of blindness" and thus returns "again to the lesson of humility that underlies great tragedy" (*Attitudes* 41).

The synthesis of these methods yields key insights into Burke's orientation to modern rhetorical devices. Using satire and blandness, he figured acts of nationalistic pride in terms of comic foolishness rather than criminality. Per the war of words, Burke's argument emphasizes that "*all* people are exposed to situations in which they must act as fools, that *every* insight contains its own special blindness" (*Attitudes* 43). Again, such blindness emanates from our fall into language, which, ironically, demands that every identification yield division. By recognizing this fact, our individual and collective pride may become chastened, causing us to observe our own stupidity in the stupidity of others. The need to render equivalent devices used in the sandbox and in diplomatic hearings becomes even more necessary.

The recognition of our own foolishness in language transforms language into a source of pain and creativity. With regard to pain, "the sense of guilt can quicken the sense of style by intensifying a retributive attitude." Burke characterizes this approach as an act of ingratiation insofar as it exposes the "the integral relationship between conflict, consciousness, conscientiousness, and conscience" (*Permanence* 246). Recall that in *The War of Words*, Burke argues that dramatizing injustice makes the audience's consciousness a matter of *conscience*, thus creating the conditions for accountability (143). It does so by "compelling [people] to make a choice between [their] conscientiousness as [professionals] and [their] conscientiousness as humanitarian[s]" (144). A choice like this may transform pain into counteraction and thus curtail the threat of nationalistic aggression.

It is tempting to conclude that the choice is simple, once it has been brought to our attention. But Burke's subsequent analysis makes clear that the problem is more complicated than we might hope or assume. "The positions in a given bureaucratic order," he explains, "have a nature of their own; hence persons who uncritically adapt themselves to the genius of these positions can then 'spontaneously' respond to the conditions of their office." As a result, there is "a [reasonable] modicum of deliberate mental blindness" that may be called simply "a loyal dislike of biting the hand that feeds them" (*WW* 148). Burke's point is not simply that "official" conditions encourage us to behave unfairly. He is also arguing that expressing fidelity to our way of life is a reasonable stance: "There is one notable virtue in the rhetorical stress upon the purposive. Such concern with the ways in which men are moved by their interests makes human conduct seem much more rational than do attempts to treat ritualistic motives as primary" (146).

By focusing on purpose over ritual, Burke adds dimension to the study of motives. Not every motive is symptomatic of a buried sexual desire or a deeply held economic drive. Purpose can be defined simply as a desire to acquire without being aware of one's capacity for broader influence. The keys to Burke's argument are *capacity* and *awareness*. Butchie and Michael's acquisitive efforts in the sandbox become symptomatic of diplomatic relations only if Burke draws them into equivalence via the war of words. In this respect, all symbolic acts may be drawn together for a particular purpose. The job of the rhetorical critic is to carry out such work.

In light of Burke's argument, we need to define motives in terms of different and sometimes overlapping hierarchical exigencies. "Although the devices can be considered pretty much in isolation of one another," he explains, "one should watch for the ways in which the artificer is goaded by the motives of hierarchy. For as we have said, the desire for 'order' is rational, but a given order is a 'ladder,' and the maintaining of a ladder of fixed discriminations involves 'injustice,' which is *irrational*" (WW 166). What we are watching for, in other words, is how our (rational) desire for order is built on (irrationally) fixed discriminations that oppress some for the benefit of others. Devices, when they become a matter of conscious deliberation, expose the irony of such desire, asking us to consider whether we wish to be implicated in an unjust and irrational arrangement. Although the war of words guarantees our implication in division as language users, our orientation toward linguistic use needn't be fixed. By observing how devices unwittingly place us in identification with projects we would otherwise consciously oppose, we create opportunities to renegotiate the terms of our motivation, placing certain priorities above others in the hope of finding solace amid the tumult. Framing this opportunity in terms of comedy rather than tragedy increases the probability that audiences will not be alienated by the identification with a scapegoat. Instead, they may learn to laugh at themselves with the sincerity that fosters a new perspective and purpose.[18]

Burke's Final Act: Scene 1

However promising Burke's approach to rhetorical counteraction may seem, we must address its viability as a method of education and criticism. If tracking and deploying devices such as *blandness* provided solace and contemplation amid the rhetorical tumult, then why couldn't Burke complete the project as planned? Wouldn't he be the perfect case study to demonstrate the success of the method, given his own emotional turmoil?

Let's make the negative case first.

Recall from Part I that Burke wrote a letter to Watson after he had finished revising *A Rhetoric of Motives*. In that letter, he enclosed a poem titled "A Prelude and a Prayer" that signaled the hopelessness of his situation. Again, Burke wasn't sleeping well at the time, and the fact that he had been unable to finish *The War of Words* as planned must have weighed heavily on him. Yet the quality of his lines is so consistent with the tone of his drafts and letters that one cannot help but speculate that Burke's attitude had become a familiar companion. Here, again, is the poem in full:

> Were everybody to spit in the ocean at once
> It would make little difference. Hence our hero
> Though siclied o'er with the pale thought of caste
> and ailing physically, found no good ground
> For public bellyaching.
>
> Assailed by radio
> Blasting vug-music for brigs and gunds to blank by,
> He said: It stinniks. Noting the free press's
> Indoctrination towards greater global frenzy,
> He but felt a dull pain in the pain-receiver. Confronting
> Professional pronouncements, he glumly edsay itshay.
>
> He knew the country was so God-damned rich,
> The rest of the world would sit up all night trying
> To keep its politicos from making monkeys of themselves.
> He knew there was less religion in a carload of cigarettes
> Than in Cardinal Francis Pukeman's spiritual mug,
> And wondered if they had a pissant for President.
>
> (Burke to Watson, 9 August 1949, JWP)

The sense of despair in these stanzas does not appear to be tied to Burke's inability to find ground for "public bellyaching." Of greater concern is the momentum of an argumentative form that, like the ocean, subsumes individual efforts at counteraction. The radio, the free press, organized religion, the office of the US president, and even governments across the world all contributed to the persuasiveness of the form, fostering a sense of belonging for those who participate and a corresponding sense of isolation in anyone who dared deviate from it. The form, in turn, produced such wealth ("The country was so God-damned rich") that imagining an alternative, more dynamic approach to love, war, or work was unthinkable.

If there were a smoking gun that explains why Burke chose not to publish *The War of Words* in his lifetime, this might be it. Although he lectured and published short works on the devices, he never delivered anything so sustained or detailed as what appears in the posthumously published *War of Words*.

Given what we know about the cultural climate of the early 1950s, it is reasonable to conclude that Burke heeded Watson's advice and lived, however despairingly, to fight another day. But I believe that there is a more complicated explanation. Remember, self-cure was Burke's original motive for analyzing modern rhetorical devices. By using a comic device such as satire to track "signs of plotting, deviousness, and duplicity," Burke discovered the fun in a dire situation. However, as we saw in Part I, the fun of lassoing opponents quickly gave way to anger and despair. In the foreword to *The War of Words*, he explains how observing the argumentative tactics of his contemporaries caused him to feel "downright mean" (266).

Interpreting Burke's reflections in terms of rhetorical devices helps us see that the grounds for criticism may have been more *formal* than *topical*. His decision to employ "Swiftian allusion," though it had clear stylistic and temporal advantages, was not *bland* enough to deliver an evenhanded analysis. There was simply no humor to be found, and whatever cure self-conscious laughter promised was perpetually chased by an urgent demand to do something. As Burke's letters and drafts demonstrate, the emotional tenor of such work was far angrier than he had hoped or intended, which threatened the intellectual integrity of the published volume *A Rhetoric of Motives*.

Would another device have worked better as a guiding framework? It is difficult to say. The remaining devices on Burke's list have as many pitfalls as promises. For example, the devices of *undo by overdoing* and *yielding aggressively*, though they present a deferential stance toward the opposing view, do so only to unravel it. The potential for antagonistic aggression thus hovers around their edges.

In spite of himself and, it seems, at his own expense, Burke proved the thesis of his philosophy of modern rhetoric: there are no clean hands in the war of words. From studying its vicissitudes Burke learned to "hope for not less of such battles, but many many more" (*WW* 167). But the fact remains that such work requires perseverance. Over time, we become battle weary, which transforms hope into faith. In order to believe that the purification of war is possible, one must assume that forms can be found, that devices can be figured and even refigured to attain more equitable terms of deliberation.

The problem is that forms and devices do not clear the ground as easily as Putt-Putt could. Our rhetorical purposes, no matter how faithful to purification, are compromised by inequitable interests. And so weeds continue to proliferate and threaten to take over. What's worse, we even plant some of them. It is a wonder that Burke's "Prelude and a Prayer" is not even more despairing.

Burke's Final Act: Scene 2

Let us now make the positive case.

To conclude his opening chapter of the published *War of Words*, Burke presented a poem titled "The Wrens Are Back," which highlights the benefits of a device-based approach to rhetorical counteraction. "We propose," Burke explains, "to think of wrens, interrupting their song to scold; then in the very midst of scolding, they break into a new cascade of song" that holds open the promise not only of personal transformation but of societal transformation as well (*WW* 167).

> The wrens are back.
> Their liquid song, pouring across the lawn—
> (Or, if the sunlight pours, the wren's song glitters)
> Up from the porch, into the bedroom where
> It is the play of light across a pond,
> Sounding as small waves look: new copper coins
> Between the seer and the sun. Therewith
> Is made the contract between the brightly waked
> Sleeper and his wren, neither the wren's
> Nor his, but differently owned by both.
> Behind the giving-forth, wren-history;
> Man-history behind the taking-in.
> (Define the city as a place where no
> Wrens sing, as though April were seas of sand,
> With spring not the burial of lilac,
> The funeral of rebirth, the floral wreaths
> For pollen, but heat quaking above stone.)

> After magnetic storms that made all men
> Uneasy, but those the most who feared the loss
> Of salary or love—
> The wrens are back.
>
> (WW 167–68)

Like "A Prelude and a Prayer," this poem employs nature tropes to emphasize the dangerous scope of linguistic conflict. In the former case, Burke compares the torrent of political ill will to an ocean that simply overwhelms efforts at counteraction (e.g., spitting in the ocean). Here, Burke appeals to magnetic storms, seas of sand, and heat quaking above stone—all of which threaten the economic and political security that human history seeks. We can also observe in both poems a concern with the calcification of language. In "Prelude," Burke emphasizes the tendency of the free press to indoctrinate us "towards greater global frenzy" for the sake of economic gain, and to conceal such gain for the love of one's country (WW 167). The city is a place where no wrens sing and where a recognition of the perennial cycles of nature simply does not occur.

Despite these similarities, there is a hopeful quality to the "The Wrens Are Back" that distinguishes it from "A Prelude and a Prayer." Burke's hope hinges on the capacity of the sleeper to be awakened to the transformative capacities of language. This capacity is available even when language has become calcified. In order to draw this capacity of language into clear relief, Burke counterposes nature's abundance with the city's barrenness. Noting such abundance, which cannot be owned entirely by the wren or the recently awakened sleeper, one may observe the entanglement of human and natural history.

Human history and wren history are simultaneously connected and divided by humanity's use of symbol systems, which takes more than it gives. And yet, the abundance of nature, which may be defined as the overwhelming complexity of natural life, can overwhelm humanity's acquisitive tendencies—unless, that is, humanity's "taking-in" destroys natural life altogether.[19] And so the "brightly waked sleeper" must listen for the wren's song. Upon hearing it, the sleeper must hold up his end of the contractual bargain, which demands reconfigured notions of ownership and agency so that neither is perfected in violence.

In "The Wrens Are Back," Burke does not identify the sleeper as a hero in the same way that he does in "A Prelude and a Prayer." In "Prelude," the hero, who is explicitly identified as such, cannot return to his society because he can find no grounds for linguistic transformation. In "Wrens," Burke shifts the burden of transformation from the hero to the wrens. Whereas in "Prelude" the hero needs to find grounds for transformation, in "Wrens" the sleeper must simply recognize the recurring song that heralds the birds' return. In both cases, "he and/or the world in which he finds himself suffers from a symbolical deficiency," as Joseph Campbell puts it (*Hero* 37); this deficiency leads him on a quest to achieve both "a domestic, microscopic triumph" and a "world-historical, macrocosmic triumph" (38). But the sleeper's agency in "Wrens" is bound to his contract with the wrens; this contract "brings back from his adventure the means for regeneration of his society as a whole" (38). This argument allows Burke to write wistfully, "Would that the Theory of the Devices could be thus under the Sign of the Wren," by which he seems to mean that "a theory of the devices must be used to preserve natural life, which can always be counted upon to lay bare language's limits" (*WW* 168).

The permanence of natural patterns allows us to look forward to more conflicts in the war of words. Accepting that our devices, our symbolic identifications, our narrative forms, our mythic images will fall prey to the complexity of the natural world, we may enact a constitutive humility that accepts the need for linguistic and perspectival transformation. The need for transformation, in turn, connects us to other language users from the past, the immediate present, and the future, revealing an abundance of resources, inventions, and consolations. Knowing that we are all susceptible to linguistic calcification, to the "hierarchic yearnings" cultivated by "rhetorical trusts," we may learn to tolerate our failures, which fuel the need to contemplate the capacities of linguistic transformations with greater purpose and scope (*WW* 137).

Begging the Question

It is tempting to privilege "The Wrens Are Back" as a more representative example of Burke's perspective on device-based rhetorical counteraction than "Prelude" is. On the one hand, it appears within a larger, more polished work that underwent multiple stages of revision. On the other, it appears to be more consistent with his long-standing political, social, and ecological commitments. Laurence Coupe has argued that one of Burke's most important contributions to literary and rhetorical criticism consists "in his foregrounding of earth itself as the ultimate setting of critical activity" (*Burke on Myth* 418).[20]

And yet I think it would be a mistake to prioritize "Wrens" over "Prelude." Never mind that the rhetorical counteraction presented in "Prelude" may explain why Burke abandoned his draft of *The War of Words*. And never mind that the poem indicates how early postwar politicians scapegoated acts of national dissent—both past and present.[21] It would be a mistake, rather, because "Prelude" helps us understand the emotional costs of investing in the form of rhetorical counteraction that Burke created. No matter the level of expertise, it is difficult, if not impossible, to find adequate grounds on which to counteract the torrents of ill will that typify our rhetorical situation. In spite of our personal and collective actions, the weeds proliferate at an overwhelming rate, and there is rarely a clear path toward a hopeful future. Burke, an experienced critic and student of modern rhetorical devices, bodies forth this difficulty.

By locating the source of transformation in both language and nature, we can imagine a future where our failures are not totalizing. As Burke argues a few lines before "Wrens," "It is only that grim disease of cooperation, nationalistic 'total war,' that must be outmoded, unless the human race itself is to become outmoded" (WW 167). A retreat from society may be as simple as finding a quiet post in nature, where the wrens' song, along with water and trees and sun, exposes our tendencies toward linguistic calcification and offers opportunities for invention. We may then return to our cities of sand and acquisitively count the grains, contemplating our place within them and seeking some semblance of order. Whenever our yearning for ownership becomes too strong, we can return to our post, knowing that the wrens will sing again.

Earlier in this chapter, we noted Burke's observation that the question-begging appellative may be the primary weapon in the war of words. A fallacy of logic, question begging assumes the truth of a conclusion without presenting evidence to support it. A good example of such a fallacy can be seen in the statement "Burke's approach to rhetorical devices is a failure because he abandoned it as a failed project." This kind of conclusion is a weapon because it assumes, as a point of departure, that complexity does not exist.

As I have argued throughout this book, a more complex account of Burke's argument is needed if we are to judge it adequately. Krista Ratcliffe has shown that granting an argument a hearing does not mean that one must be persuaded by it. After reading this chapter, some may conclude that Burke's mythic orientation to rhetorical devices is worrisome. Of course, the goal of rhetorical counteraction is not to be persuaded by one claim or another but to affirm the limits and possibilities of language, so that our judgments may be suspended and transformed. For such suspension and transformation to occur, we need multiple accounts and complicated stories. We need wrens and shepherds, rhetorical trusts and the threat of destruction. But mostly we need a stance that is willing to accept, as a grounding principle, that we all tend toward linguistic failure. Affirming such failure allows us to imagine ways to counteract it, to invent vocabularies for explaining failure, and to invent devices that stem the tide, if only for a moment. "Would that all wars could be the turmoil of wrens," Burke laments (*WW* 167). But they are not. There will be inevitable hope and despair in the war of words. Embracing this fact allows rhetorical transformation to take place.[22]

4

Mythic Historiography

The enunciation of any mythic variant opens up an arena of struggle and maneuver that can be pursued by those who produce other variants of the myth and other interpretations of the variant.

—BRUCE LINCOLN, *Theorizing Myth, 151*

As far as I can tell, Kenneth Burke never defined a methodology for *A Rhetoric of Motives*. The drafting history laid out in Part I indicates that he was still "finding his way as he wrote," which made it difficult to "explain and argue for his methodology in a sustained way" (George and Selzer 160). And yet the drafting history also shows that he systematically collected both *historical texts* "that had become obscured when rhetoric as a term fell into disuse" and *"rhetorical forms* [that were] employed in the struggle for advantage" (RM xiii; WW 43, emphasis added). It is no coincidence that nearly every example relies on mythic images and terms to stake its claims. As I have argued in previous chapters, Burke selected examples for *A Rhetoric of Motives* because their use of mythic images and terms exposed core functions of the dialectic principle. By studying how Burke engages these mythic images and terms in *A Rhetoric of Motives* and *The War of Words*, we can identify the tactics he used to locate, analyze, evaluate, and denaturalize them. In the process, we may discover methodological clarity where there was presumed to be none.[1]

I am calling Burke's methodology *mythic historiography*.[2] Mythic historiography identifies, analyzes, evaluates, and denaturalizes mythic images and terms that organize modern rhetorical philosophies. The identification, analysis, evaluation, and denaturalization of mythic images and terms redefine rhetorical history so that rhetoric can be theorized with greater depth and scope. In this way, mythic historiography helps critics address unstated assumptions about how language functions and imagine new directions for rhetorical criticism.³

There are five core tactics that distinguish mythic historiography as a rhetorical methodology:

1. Identify Mythic Images and Terms in Works of Rhetoric
2. Invent Mythic Images to Extend Works of Rhetoric
3. Track Manifestations of the Hierarchic Principle via Mythic Images and Terms
4. Investigate the Limits of Rhetoric via Mythic Images and Terms
5. Catalogue Rhetorical Devices That Grow Out of Mythic Images and Terms

In the pages that follow, I define each tactic by identifying its unstated assumptions, tracking affiliated concepts, and observing how Burke models its application in *A Rhetoric of Motives* and *The War of Words*. Generally, I focus on Burke's engagements with Marx because they provide the best context for understanding the nuances of each tactic. I have sequenced the presentation of each tactic according to its appearance in *A Rhetoric of Motives* and *The War of Words*. However, critics may employ these tactics in a different order depending on the nature of their inquiry.

An Overview of Mythic Historiography

Mythic historiography is a methodology that "mark[s] off the areas of rhetoric . . . where it is not usually recognized or thought to belong" (RM xv). In the process, it expands rhetoric's historical scope, enhances its theoretical precision, and adds focus to its material practices. Mythic historiography accomplishes these tasks by identifying, analyzing, evaluating, and denaturalizing mythic images and terms that organize rhetorical works. For Burke, this process involves *reclaiming* what was left unattended when "esthetics sought to outlaw rhetoric" and *developing* the "subject beyond the traditional bounds of rhetoric." Each task involves collecting historical examples that reveal "an intermediate area of expression that is not wholly deliberate, yet not wholly unconscious" (xiii). As I have argued in previous chapters, this intermediate area of expression is the defining characteristic of Burke's modern theory of identification, which tracks the functions and capacities of the dialectic principle.

The war of words underscores the constitutive role that the dialectic principle plays in creating and mediating human conflict. According to Burke, rhetoric is not rooted "*in any past condition of human society*" but "*in an essential function of language itself, a function that is wholly realistic, and is continually born anew; the use of language as a symbolic means of inducing cooperation in beings that by nature respond to symbols*" (*RM* 43).[4] This definition of rhetoric emphasizes the value of tracking manifestations of the dialectic principle in historical texts, focusing specifically on how identification and division interanimate each other to productive and sometimes dangerous ends.

Burke begins using mythic historiography in the early pages of "The Range of Rhetoric," when he claims that Milton's identification with the mythic figure Samson functions as a "ritualistic kind of historiography in which the poet could, by allusion to a Biblical story, 'substantially' foretell the triumph of his vanquished faction" (*RM* 19). By claiming Milton's *Samson Agonistes* as an ideal opening for his modern philosophy of rhetoric, Burke defines his project as a historiographical search for the universal dialectic in the local rhetorical.

Burke expands mythic historiography in "Traditional Principles of Rhetoric," in his discussion of Cicero's definition of general and particular cases. Burke argues that because "any one particular era in history ... will be unlike any other in its exact combination of cultural factors, historiography seems naturally vowed to a measure of rhetorical casuistry" (*RM* 73). If rhetorical casuistry involves "the application of abstract principles to particular conditions," then the relationship between abstract principles and particular conditions "is essentially like that of mind and body, spirit and matter, God and God's descent into Nature" (155). As a form of rhetorical casuistry, mythic historiography tracks temporized manifestations of universal principles via mythic images and terms (e.g., God and God's descent into nature) and emphasizes how general principles cannot subsume the unique material traits of local contexts (73).

Burke extends mythic historiography even further in "Order," in which he argues that Karl Mannheim's sociology of knowledge—a "neutralization and liberalization of Marxism" (*RM* 197)—rejects utopias as ideological but nevertheless depends on mythic images and terms to authorize its claims. Burke's analysis of Mannheim tills the ground for *socioanagogic interpretation*, which, again, employs the mythic terms and images from Shakespeare's *Venus and Adonis* to demonstrate how the hierarchic principle is manifested in local rhetorical acts. Although this section presents the most abstract philosophical reflections in *A Rhetoric of Motives*, Burke's analysis, as we will see, demonstrates how writers such as Mannheim and Marx sought to transform their local situations via appeals to mythic terms and images.

Each of the aforementioned examples—to say nothing of those not mentioned—is marked by the subtle tactics that distinguish mythic historiography as a rhetorical methodology. It is important to note how Burke models the identification, analysis, evaluation, and denaturalization of each mythic image and term as we move on to the discussion of these tactics. By observing how he engages mythic images and terms, critics may apply or evolve mythic historiography with greater precision and scope.

Tactic No. 1: Identify Mythic Images and Terms in Works of Rhetoric

The first methodological tactic of mythic historiography is to locate mythic images and terms in works of rhetoric. This tactic assumes that works of rhetoric not only contain mythic images and terms but implicitly or explicitly employ them to transcend their local circumstances. Burke is most interested in examples that draw on literary forms for their appeal. As I have argued in previous chapters, this is because Burke viewed literary art as a close approximation of the universal.

The first tactic of mythic historiography helps critics explain how mythic images assign meaning to rhetorical actions. For example, by recognizing how rhetorical vocabularies draw on mythic images, critics may explain how a rhetorical appeal offers "the fullest kind of understanding, wherein one gets the immediacy of participation in a local act, yet sees in and through this act an over-all design, sees and *feels* the local act itself as but the partial expression of the total development" (*RM* 195). Burke's emphasis on *feeling* in this passage indicates that mythic images and terms are most persuasive when they structure the *attitude* of an audience. By providing a "series of [principled] steps" that signal a pathway beyond "parliamentary 'conflict,'" they correlate mind and body in rhetorical action (197). Burke calls this phenomenon dialectical symmetry.

The first tactic of mythic historiography appears throughout *A Rhetoric of Motives*, though it is perhaps easiest to spot in the subsection "Ultimate Elements in Marxist Persuasion" in the section "Order." Here, Burke claims that "much of the *rhetorical* strength in Marx's work stems from the ultimate order it creates" (101, 190). Burke's phrase "ultimate order" suggests that Marx relies on a mythic image to place local acts of class struggle within a universal framework. According to Burke, *the proletariat* is the mythic image that accomplishes this task, allowing audiences to believe that their immediate class struggles are connected to previous class struggles and will eventually coalesce in an economic revolution that will result in a new kind of society in which class distinctions no longer exist. As a result, "a spokesman for the proletariat can think of himself as representing not only the interests of that class alone, but the grand design of the entire historical sequence, its final outcome for all mankind" (190–91). The realization of this outcome would be significant because, in Burke's parlance, it would obviate the need for identifications that bridge divisions (e.g., there would be no such thing as private property).

Burke uses Marx to illustrate his modern philosophy of rhetoric because Marx shows how all vocabularies "are concerned with advantage, not only in analyzing the hidden advantage in other terminologies (or 'ideologies'), but also in [themselves] inducing advantages of a special sort" (*RM* 103). Insofar as Marx relies on the proletariat to gain economic advantage, his vocabulary would count as interested. And yet, according to Burke's analysis, Marx resisted the idea of a "red rhetoric," claiming that his work was scientific rather than discursive in nature. Knowing that he consciously identified with the working class, why did Marx stress the scientific veracity of his work? Certainly not because he held a *concealed* motive that sought advantage in the form of economic justice. Instead, the mythic images and terms Marx used to universalize his insights *naturalized* the ultimate order he presented as true. To demonstrate this point, Burke outlines the rhetorical quality of Marx's intervention; through a concentrated analysis of Marx's core concepts as *mystification, hierarchy*, and *courtship*, Burke analyzes, evaluates, and denaturalizes Marx's allegedly scientific claims. He does not expose Marx as misguided but claims Marx's insights into the dialectic principle for modern rhetorical studies.

If Burke's argument about Marx is correct, then mythic images and terms organize all vocabularies that seek material advantage. Often, these images and terms present "an inverted genealogy of culture, that makes for 'illusion' and 'mystification' by treating ideas as *primary* where they should have been treated as *derivative*" (*RM* 104). As *origin* stories, they obscure the local conditions that called them into being, and in the process they naturalize unstated assumptions about our shared linguistic inheritance. In order to denaturalize such images and terms, critics may return to the local conditions that called them into being and historiographically reconstruct how they gained the status of primary truths via dialectical abstraction.

Tactic No. 2: Invent Mythic Images to Extend Works of Rhetoric

This tactic assumes that invented mythic images and terms are sometimes best equipped to help critics identify, analyze, evaluate, or denaturalize the unstated assumptions of rhetorical works. Burke employs this tactic when he appropriates and revises existing mythic images and terms such as the *Babylonic split*. He also employs this tactic when he creates new mythic images and terms such as the war of words, which extend his philosophy of modern rhetoric. I characterize each approach as invention because these mythic images and terms establish new argumentative frameworks for rhetorical action and counteraction.

This second tactic of mythic historiography helps critics define rhetorical problems in ways that exceed local contexts. Recall from the first chapter of Part II that Burke invented a "sea creature" myth to explain why the hierarchic principle is fundamental to rhetorical studies. Observing how the hierarchic principle organizes rhetorical action is difficult, according to Burke, because hierarchical thinking is as familiar to us as breathing. By inventing a sea creature myth, Burke denaturalizes our relationship to the hierarchic principle and shows, once again, how human conflict emanates from the dialectic principle.

Although Burke's sea creature myth is the most prominent example of the second tactic of mythic historiography, it is by no means the only one. A second, less obvious example appears roughly thirty pages earlier in the section "Marx on Mystification." There, Burke invites his audience to imagine what ideological analysis might look like independent of anti-Communist sentiments (*RM* 105). As with the "sea creature" myth, Burke encourages his readers to reevaluate Marx's place in rhetorical history by denaturalizing their unstated assumptions about the value of Marxist philosophy to rhetoric.

Burke initiates this process when he invents a mythic image that transcends the boundaries of the early postwar period: "Of course, in the War of Words, there is nothing to prevent contestants from hitting one another with anything they can lay hands on" (*RM* 104). The "of course" in this passage may feel like a throwaway phrase, but it actually assumes that linguistic conflict can *always* be unpredictable and unwieldy. Assenting to this proposition creates the need for an organizing terminology, which the war of words, as an invented mythic image and term, furnishes. As an invented mythic image, the war of words defines verbal combat as a constitutive quality of human communication. This explanation establishes a new framework for ordering what, on the surface, seems only to be a local struggle. Specifically, it connects the most seemingly mundane spats between children with UN debates about the state of global warfare.

With this framework in place, Burke argues that Marx is relevant to his philosophy of modern rhetoric because he "isolate[s] a principle which can even be applied beyond the purposes" of Marxist philosophy (*RM* 105). This principle in Marx's work is, of course, the dialectic principle. To help readers connect the dots between Marx and the dialectic principle, Burke invites his audience to "imagine, now, an 'ideologist' who, with the documents of many centuries to work from, inspects a whole developmental series of such successive 'ruling' ideas." The ideologist's series of documents transcend their local circumstances, allowing her to see the "ideas 'in themselves.'" The ideologist may then assign an "over-all title, a word for ideas in general," which allows her to "look upon the succession of 'ruling' ideas as though each were an expression of the one Universal Idea." The overall title functions "not just as a summarizing word, but as a 'sub-ject' in the strict philosophic sense, that is, an underlying basis, a sub-stance, of which any step along the entire series can be considered as a property, or expression" (106). In other words, it acts as the ground upon which both Marx's and Burke's modern philosophies may be built.

As the overall title of Burke's universal idea, the war of words establishes the scene where ideas, properties, and expressions relevant to a modern study of human motives find order. If human motives manifest themselves in conflict, and if conflict emanates from the linguistic interplay between divided subjects and material properties, then all human motives may be collected under the war of words heading. To help Marx find a place under this heading, or title, Burke encourages his audience to imagine Marx's contribution as a landmark contribution to the study of the dialectic principle.

When placed under the heading of the war of words, Marx's contributions are transformed into a methodological indicator of how to observe the dialectic principle. The difference between Marx and Burke—between their engagement with the dialectic principle—is that Burke underscores the importance of imagination to his methodology. In this way, Burke does not offer a science of motivational analysis but a rhetoric that consciously acknowledges its limits and potential.

Tactic No. 3: Track Manifestations of the Hierarchic Principle via Mythic Images and Terms

This tactic assumes that the hierarchic principle is a core function of the dialectic principle and may be identified in mythic images and terms that constitute ultimate orders. Burke defines the hierarchic principle as language's capacity to classify people or things in terms of higher or lower ranks. According to Burke, the hierarchic principle is "inevitable in systematic thought," appearing anytime there is reference to the "process of growth" (e.g., "class divisions of youth and age, stronger and weaker, male and female, or the stages of learning, from apprentice to journeyman to master") (*RM* 141). Burke is particularly concerned with mythic images and terms that naturalize class privileges as inevitable (140).

The third tactic of mythic historiography helps critics explain how mythic images and terms structure rhetorical action between different types of people. If Burke is correct that all language users sit at the hierarchic table, then critics may track how individuals closer to the culminating stage of a hierarchy benefit materially from their position. For example, those closer to the ideal (e.g., economic wealth) serve as representatives of a culture or group, whereas those further away from the ideal do not. Such idealizations tend to obscure the material consequences of the hierarchical arrangement, making it seem as if those closer to the ideal are naturally—as opposed to *structurally*—endowed with certain privileges. To recalibrate the arrangement, critics must identify and denaturalize mythic images and terms "that cloak the [original] state of division" (*RM* 141).

To identify the ideal (or mythic image) that props up an ultimate order, critics would simply study the "differences that drive [groups of people] apart" and "the *elements they share*, 'vices' and 'virtues' alike" (*RM* 141). Scapegoats are a particularly useful entry point for such analysis because they "combine in one figure contrary principles of identification and alienation" (140).[5] In "The Rhetoric of Hitler's Battle," Burke argues that scapegoats are distinguished by certain appeals and devices that promise "a 'positive' view of life" once they are eradicated (*Philosophy* 203). In *A Rhetoric of Motives*, he takes this argument one step further, arguing that hierarchical divisions "idealistically buried beneath a terminology of love [e.g., rhetorical appeals and devices], or ironically revealed in combination with varying grades of compensatory deference," are not peculiar to totalitarian regimes but are symptomatic of language use in general.

Burke models the third tactic of mythic historiography throughout *A Rhetoric of Motives*, though it is arguably most visible when he studies rhetorics of courtship. Drawing initially from Thomas Carlyle's *Sartor Resartus*, Burke argues that "*social* differentiations" created by the hierarchic principle estrange different classes of people (*RM* 115). Whenever different classes mediate their estrangement, rhetorics of courtship emerge. Such rhetorics might explain, for example, why loving relationships between people of different racial or ethnic groups are worthy of protection and admiration; they might also explain why the behaviors of animals and humans are not as different from each other as most have been led to believe. Regardless, rhetorics of courtship fall under the war of words heading because they dramatize the functions and capacities of the dialectic principle.

Burke models the application of the third tactic of mythic historiography when he presents socioanagogic interpretation in "Order." Again, Burke views Shakespeare's *Venus and Adonis* as a representative case study because, as "a story of *sexual* courtship," it makes "its implicit *social* identifications more available to our scrutiny" (*RM* 212). A young, standoffish Adonis resists the sexual advances of Venus, a resistance that "demeans the old order" that Venus represents. Like Milton, Shakespeare uses this poem to say "remotely, in sexual imagery, what no courtly poet could have wanted to say, or even thought of saying, in social or political terms" (217). In doing so, Shakespeare denaturalizes a hierarchical arrangement between local and universal orders and in the process leverages the universal capacities of language to address local exigencies.

If the hierarchic principle saturates language use as much as Burke argues that it does, then critics should be able to identify it and its corresponding rhetorics in a number of historical works. The remainder of "Order" models how this work might unfold. In the presentation of each example, Burke shows that although historical circumstances change, the need to address the functions and capacities of the hierarchic principle do not. To make his case, Burke often relies on poetic forms that deal in ambiguity and irony because they help critics contemplate a myth's relevance to their immediate rhetorical situation. Noting this possibility, critics may then assess where social groups are headed on the basis of the stories that explain where they've been.

Tactic No. 4: Investigate the Limits of Rhetoric via Mythic Images and Terms

This tactic assumes that mythic images and terms place limits on rhetorical action when they install an ultimate order. When Burke locates human conflict in the dialectic principle via the war of words, he characterizes rhetorical action as primarily *acquisitive* in quality. As a result, the idea of *unmotivated* rhetorical action becomes impossible. If, per the war of words, language users are divided from one another, there must be, by virtue of the dialectic negation, a nonlinguistic ground that has no divisions and thus no motives. As there is no way to render this ground independent of symbol systems, nonlinguistic existence may be imagined but not attained. Accordingly, critics are left to differentiate between more or less acquisitive forms of rhetorical action.

The fourth tactic of mythic historiography helps critics identify aspects of rhetoric that deviate from or complicate what may be considered more normal or routine forms of rhetorical action. For example, if rhetorical action is primarily acquisitive, then the war of words helps critics identify examples that are less acquisitive. By investigating the limits of rhetoric via mythic images and terms, critics not only identify historical examples that expand the range of rhetorical studies; they also denaturalize unstated assumptions about how rhetoric functions. In doing so, critics are better able to define rhetoric's ethical promises and pitfalls.

Burke's presentation of *pure persuasion* is the strongest example of how to employ the fourth tactic of mythic historiography. As with the previous three tactics, Burke enlists textual examples from literary works to track pure persuasion's appearances in rhetorical history. However, unlike his previous examples, pure persuasion is a *less acquisitive* function of the dialectic principle that underscores both the dangers and ethical possibilities of rhetorical action.

According to Burke, pure persuasion is act of self-interference; "it summons because it likes the feel of a summons" and "would be nonplussed if the summons were answered" (*RM* 269).[6] Dangerous forms of pure persuasion occur when language users interfere with an acquisition process in order to justify delayed forms of capitalist expansion. When imperialists incorporate delayed acquisition into a system (think of protracted interest on a bank loan, for example), economic systems attain an "intellectual fullness which may then be transformed into an instrument having new possibilities of gain" (272). Less dangerous instances of pure persuasion allow language users to develop a *"symbolically grounded* distrust of acquisitiveness, a feeling that one should not just 'take things,' but should court them, show gratitude for them, or apologize for killing them." Either way, the self-interference characteristic of pure persuasion is "implicit *in* the 'transcendent' nature of symbolism itself" (271).

As an implicit function of the dialectic principle, pure persuasion offers an important lesson to rhetorical critics. "Rhetorically," Burke explains, "there can be courtship only insofar as there is division. Hence, only through interference could one court continually, thereby perpetuating a genuine 'freedom of rhetoric'" (*RM* 271). Here, Burke reiterates that division is the catalyst for all rhetorical action; it makes courtship between different classes of people possible. At the same time, interference is an important theoretical component of rhetorical action because it explains why argumentative totalization has not yet occurred. It does not matter that "pure persuasion in the absolute sense exists nowhere" (269). Full acquisition has not occurred because the division created by the dialectic principle prevents total acquisition from taking place. Consequently, language users may proceed in a genuine freedom of rhetoric because they are capable of being less acquisitive.

Burke identifies, analyzes, and denaturalizes pure persuasion via his proxy term for the war of words: "the Scramble." For example, he writes, "Persons who cannot solve their problems by victory in the Scramble can certainly 'compensate for frustration' by solving arbitrary puzzles" (*RM* 270). Two pages later, Burke writes, "This should be particularly the case when, given the conditions of the Scramble, if one did not first grab, he would not have much chance not to grab" (272). Burke refers to "the Scramble" to argue that human effort is "grounded not in the search for 'advantage,' and in the mere 'sublimating' of that search by 'rationalizations' and 'moralizations.' Rather, it [is] grounded in a *form*, in the persuasiveness of the hierarchic order itself" (276). To address the persuasiveness (indeed, *pervasiveness*) of the hierarchic order, critics may observe how mythic images and terms may be transformed from "positive things to titles, thence to an order among titles, and finally to the titles of titles" (277). For example, critics could demonstrate how mythic images such as the war of words or the Tower of Babel "arose out of a temporal ground, available to sociological description," and became constitutive explanations of linguistic division (205). Tracking the material emergence of these mythic images and terms can denaturalize teleological definitions of rhetoric that foreclose historical, theoretical, and/or material contributions. In doing so, they can identify the limits imposed by such teleologies and redefine the boundaries of rhetoric to include more diverse examples. Using this tactic, critics may question the limits of Burke's war of words in the hope that doing so will lead to new, more ethical directions for rhetorical studies.

Tactic No. 5: Catalogue Rhetorical Devices That Grow Out of Mythic Images and Terms

This tactic assumes that rhetorical devices are not incidental habits of argumentation but *rituals of argumentation* characteristic of ultimate orders to which mythic images and terms give rise.[7] This tactic identifies the material instantiations of rhetorical devices. It also analyzes how rhetorical devices travel across different time periods and historical contexts. In doing so, it offers an attitude toward life that accepts rhetoric as a constitutive feature of human communication.

The fifth tactic of mythic historiography helps critics identify the prevalence of rhetorical devices, analyze why certain rhetorical devices have staying power, and denaturalize the inevitability of the argumentative conditions they establish. As I have argued in earlier chapters, the identification, analysis, and denaturalization of rhetorical devices help audiences imagine forms of counteraction that yield more ethical results. When discussing rhetorical devices that were characteristic of the early Cold War period, Burke argues that "the characteristic rhetoric of today is done in quick raids, as with Indian warfare, guerrilla tactics." Indeed, "it offers no argument at all. It merely *identifies* X by association. And instead of sustained attack, it repeats the same thing over and over. (Indeed, our remarks on Say Anything could almost as accurately have been called Say the Same Thing—for the method aims at the constant reinforcement of one attitude" (*WW* 134). In this passage, Burke not only identifies rhetorical devices that are characteristic of his time period (e.g., "say anything / say the same thing") and analyzes how they persuade audiences (e.g., by repetition); he also denaturalizes their function both in his immediate context ("it offers no argument") and within the broader history of rhetoric ("instead of sustained attack"). As a result, Burke places these rhetorical devices in the war of words and extends the boundaries of rhetoric.

If the rhetorical devices that Burke collects are "not greatly concerned ... with rhetoric as argument," then they must occupy a different domain of rhetoric, one that is more characteristic of repeated identification (*WW* 134). This form of identification carries an implicit argument that resides in nonconscious attachments to form. Indeed, the implicit quality of such argumentation enhances the staying power of such devices. According to Burke, critics must draw implicit arguments into conscious awareness in order to counteract their dangerous effects. The entry point for such work is to note the prevalence of "the Scramble," which presents critics with increasingly complicated problems (e.g., the ubiquity of communication technologies) as the dialectic principle adapts to new material circumstances.

Burke's focus on mythic terms and images appears in the title *The War of Words*, which was originally titled "The World of Publicity" and then revised to underscore the mythic quality of his philosophy of modern rhetoric. Everything in the second volume is thus organized by the mythic image that Burke theorizes at various points in *A Rhetoric of Motives*. As we observed in the preceding chapter, *The War of Words* focuses on rhetorical devices in news media such as the *New York Times* and the *Christian Science Monitor*. In doing so, it consistently draws on mythic terms and images so that the "universal" frame is not lost on readers. Consider, as a case in point, Burke's discussion in the section "Making the Connection" in the chapter "Of the Devices." "Nothing is more spontaneous than the changing of a subject from something unpleasant to something pleasant," Burke writes. "Yet, out of such Edenic simplicity there may come the rhetorical fall, when a subject is deliberately changed as a way of calling attention to the fact that it is unpleasant" (*WW* 111). "Edenic simplicity" and "the rhetorical fall" are not the first mythic terms and images Burke uses in this section, but they are the most obvious. In referencing them, Burke argues that everyday devices such as *changing the subject* are connected to an originating division that the war of words draws into view. Accordingly, critics may argue that mundane rhetorical devices such as changing the subject are rituals of argumentation, in that "their meaning, their value, are not connected with their crude physical datum but with their property of reproducing a primordial act, of repeating a mythical example" (Eliade 4).

Mythic historiography is challenging in part because "language is a miraculously subtle instrument. And in its subtlety, miraculously devious" (*WW* 249). The fifth tactic helps manage the subtle and sometimes devious qualities of language by encouraging critics to ask how rhetorical devices grow out of mythic images and terms that posit the origins or endings of verbal conflict. By cataloguing such devices in relation to mythic images and terms, critics may observe how there is an "element of war implicit in all . . . ideals, whenever the situation is such that the ideas are used for the purposes of alignment." Although such ideals may "have the peacefulness and prayerfulness of *heavenly* intent, they are weapons in the war of words" (253, emphasis added). The good news is that the dialectic principle allows a weapon to become an agent of peace. The fifth tactic of mythic historiography not only helps recognize when a device signifies a heavenly or hellish intent; it also indicates how to direct devices toward more peaceful outcomes. It does so primarily by making our nonconscious attachment to rhetorical devices a matter of conscience (143). When the pervasiveness of rhetorical conflict comes to conscious attention, critics may "hope for not less of such battles, but many many more" (167). The goal, as we have discussed throughout this book, is not victory over an enemy but an attitude of tolerance and contemplation that allows critics to place themselves in rhetorical situations both local and universal. Failures may be personal; all language users make argumentative mistakes. But Burke stresses the importance of framing such mistakes as a consequence of linguistic existence, generally defined. By accepting this fact, we may "move in the direction of order . . . towards the satisfaction of *placement*," in which "an incident that might otherwise have been sheer desolation has been transformed into a minor acquisition" (160). In this way, language users pursue different types of properties that acquire for the sake of peace.

Where Are We, Then?

Having tracked the tactics that distinguish mythic historiography, readers may still wonder: "Is the purpose of this chapter simply to understand Burke's argument better?" Simply put, yes. By learning more about how Burke selected and analyzed textual examples in *A Rhetoric of Motives* and *The War of Words*, we learn more about his philosophy of modern rhetoric and in the process expand our knowledge of the rhetorical tradition.

We can answer the question another way by arguing that there is an implicit benefit in tracking Burke's unstated methodology that has little to do with his place in the rhetorical tradition. Whether critics agree with Burke's relevance to rhetorical studies, perhaps they will agree that his work is complicated. Understanding how he developed his argument can thus serve as valuable intellectual exercise. If this agreement is extended by the principles of identity politics, then studying mythic historiography can become an exercise in understanding how a white, heteronormative philosophy of modern rhetoric selects textual examples that privilege certain perspectives as universal and relegate others to the margins. As Kris Ratcliffe and I have shown, you have to know how mythic historiography works in order to expose marginal relegation and refigure it. Done well, such refiguration allows critics to come to terms with the misogyny and racism that guide many midcentury rhetorical theories, histories, and methodologies. Of the available options, this answer is valuable for its ability to fold methodology back on itself to restore justice and expand the rhetorical tradition along different lines.

Still another way to answer the question is that there is an implicit benefit in conceptualizing Burke as a writer who, like other writers, is engaged in a complicated problem-solving process. Cast in this light, mythic historiography loses its teeth as *the* solution to Burke's philosophy of modern rhetoric and becomes, instead, *a* solution that allowed Burke to publish *A Rhetoric of Motives* and complete a significant portion of *The War of Words*. Critics have long noted Burke's preoccupation with the dialectic principle. But the archived letters and drafting materials reveal that Burke was struggling to formalize his perspective on a consistent basis. Knowing this, critics can develop greater sensitivity to how rhetorical works are written by returning to the material constraints that affect all writers. Of the available options, this answer is valuable for contextualizing Burke's writing process and accepting the imperfect quality of his solutions. By focusing on Burke as a writer, it is easier to ask simple yet revealing questions. For example, who else was solving the problems of rising nationalistic aggression in terms of myth? To what extent was Burke's problem-solving process symptomatic of an epistemic imperative to reassert the universal in the face of such impermanence? In short, one could use the Burke-as-writer framework to complicate the tendency to stabilize his or others' arguments as an authored work. This frame exposes the array of factors that influence a writer's drafting process and thus deepens our understanding of their relationship to material history.

One final answer, at least for the purposes of this chapter, is to use Burke's core insights to reimagine rhetoric's relationship to mythic images and terms. If Burke is correct that social philosophies are organized around mythic images and terms, then we can gauge their unstated role in our field's histories, theories, and methodologies. If mythic images and terms are as pervasive as Burke claims, they can become the first point of contact for historiographical renegotiation. Of the available options, this conclusion emphasizes the relationship between rhetoric and poetic forms. In doing so, it allows us to navigate the mythic images and terms associated with works that are relevant to rhetorical criticism but that may not yet be part of the tradition. An added benefit of this answer is that we don't have to accept Burke's mythic image, the war of words, to initiate the work. We can simply take our cue from Burke and pursue directions that dramatically extend the prevailing field of vision. However, when engaging mythic images and terms, we must investigate the temporal implications of their use in rhetorical histories, theories, and methodologies. In raising this question, critics may decide that the field needs alternative theories of time that reconsider the part-to-whole relationships that mythic images and terms create between the local and the universal.

I have outlined multiple answers to this question because the quality of Burke's work demands a complicated response. One could find mythic historiography inherently interesting and conceptualize Burke's writing process as a problem-solving exercise. Or one could fold mythic historiography back on itself to expose historical injustice and chart new pathways in rhetoric's relationship to time. Regardless, we are, like Burke, evaluating the limits of our miraculous language resources not to avoid argumentative battles but to seek many, many more. It may feel strange to meet Burke on this common ground. But we have an array of coping devices to carry us through. Even if such devices do not lead us back to Burke's insights, we can appreciate the ingenuity that led to his methodological solution.

Epilegomena

The cure for digging in the dirt is an idea; the cure for any idea is more ideas; the cure for all ideas is digging in the dirt. That's the whole damn thing. Body back to body.
—KENNETH BURKE, QUOTED IN SKODNICK, "COUNTER-GRIDLOCK," 12

The title of this book had long been decided when Anthony "Butchie" Burke called my attention to the "flowerish" above. Along with Jack Selzer, Butchie and I had been invited to meet with a graduate seminar to discuss our editorial work on *The War of Words*.[1] I cannot remember what prompted Butchie to recite this small prose poem; maybe Jack and I were talking about modern rhetorical devices as weeds. But upon hearing it, I was struck with the dread that accompanies most archival research: that there is something relevant to my argument that I have not yet found.

Over the past seven years my archival dread has subsided. Part of the solution was confirming the idea that originally brought me to the Burke archives. There is, it turns out, considerable benefit to reconstructing the drafting processes of writers and conceptualizing the work as a problem-solving process that dynamically evolves over time. Another part of the solution was learning that no amount of rigor allows one to be comprehensive once and for all. In the process of writing this book, I've learned that such comprehension is undesirable, anyway. The value of the work lies in negotiating perspectives different from my own.

I say that this work confirmed the idea because the benefits of reconstructing a drafting process have been touted by critics for decades. When I speak with my medievalist colleagues about this project, for example, they often give me an incredulous look, as if to say, "What's new? We've been here for years." And yet I think they would all attest that reading about the reconstruction of textual versions is not the same thing as doing the work by hand. There is both a material and an intellectual benefit to handling fragile manuscripts that have been stowed away for posterity. Excavating a seventy-year-old cutter bar from an old shed is exciting, especially when a skunk is defending its territory. It is humbling when a family opens up old photo boxes and offers the rich oral histories behind their fading pictures. In short, one does not learn to garden by opening a book. The only way is to get one's hands dirty.

Burke uses the word *cure* ironically in the epigraph above. Colleagues who spend their time navigating archival aporias often seem more infected than cured.[2] There is something contagious in the thrill of discovery, and I find that those who dig their way into the archives never really find their way out. Maybe this is because, however taxing the work may be, more and more ideas arrive. Maybe it is because, in the most taxing moments, we can cling to the hope that ideas will arrive.

As I reflect on Burke's use of the term *cure* in this "flowerish," as he ironically called it, I am reminded of his discussion of diseases and their cures in *A Grammar of Motives*. "The method" of dramatism, he writes, "would involve the explicit study of language as the 'critical moment' at which human motives take form, since a linguistic factor at every point in human experience complicates and to some extent transcends the purely biological aspects of motivation" (318). I can't help but read the phrase "the 'critical moment' at which human motives take form" as an origin myth. I am aware that my impulse is a function of having studied Burke and myth for years. For the most part, Burke wrote *A Rhetoric of Motives* after *A Grammar of Motives*, so I may simply be grafting my own motives onto Burke's. Still, I wonder: How would one propose to identify this "critical moment" independent of myth?

To answer this question, let's consider a different general theory of rhetoric that appears in George Kennedy's essay "A Hoot in the Dark." In one of the essay's more memorable passages, Kennedy claims that the crows on his university campus are deeply invested in rhetoric; one simply needs the appropriate conceptual framework in order to notice what is happening. "In the fall," Kennedy writes, "I have witnessed vocations of crows on my university campus. To me, as an informed spectator interested in rhetoric, it looked as though they had gathered to debate some important issue. There was cawing. Some of the crows seemed to become disgusted with proceedings and flew off; some turned their backs on the center of the group as if to vote 'no'" (5).

Kennedy's claims seem merely to support the guiding premise that opens the paragraph: "There is also quite a lot of epideictic rhetoric among animals. By this I mean a kind of ritualized socializing that involves reassuring 'contact calls' within the group." But a few sentences later, Kennedy's argument receives a different inflection point when he references the origins of the rhetorical tradition: "Birds are the most vocal of all animals and vocal rhetoric is more highly developed among them than in any except human beings. It is perhaps not a coincidence Greeks gave the name Corax, or 'crow,' to the 'inventor' of rhetoric." I read Kennedy's invocation of Corax as the identification of a "'critical moment' at which human motives take form, since," as Burke says, "a linguistic factor at every point in human experience complicates and to some extent transcends the purely biological aspects of motivation." The critical moment occurs in classical antiquity when, upon noting the resemblance between animal and human persuasion, someone or something named Corax invented the discipline—at least its Western version.[3]

The fact that Corax retains his crowness suggests that perhaps there is less division between humans and animals than previously thought. Or perhaps the intimacy between human and nonhuman animals has simply been forgotten.[4] Whatever the case, in order to refigure the rhetorical tradition, it is necessary to imagine a new mythic image that fosters the identification of a different, wilder terrain. Such a terrain extends well beyond Aristotle's well-cultivated garden and Burke's weed garden, throwing into crisis the human exceptionalism that underwrites so much of the Western rhetorical tradition.[5]

With a different mythic image, Kennedy may collect examples that expand the field well beyond its current boundaries. Much of the recent research on nonhuman rhetorics relies on unstated assumptions that drive Kennedy's animal brand of mythic historiography, which might be stated as the collection of examples designed to create a general theory of rhetoric:

> I suppose rhetoric is not a "substance" in the logical sense, though it does seem to me that there is something found in nature that either resembles rhetoric or possibly constitutes the starting point from which it has culturally evolved. If we could come to some understanding of that starting point we might be able to define a 'genus' of which the various historical meanings of rhetoric are 'species,' and if we could do that we might be on the way to a more general theory of rhetoric that could be useful in studying speech, language, literature, art, religion, and other aspects of human society. ("Hoot" 2)

My point, in short, is that Burke's methods and insights extend well beyond his own arguments in *A Rhetoric of Motives*. To some, this argument will seem obvious to the point of obsolescence. But it needs to be written. Coming to terms with this premise requires that we look again at works and versions of works that seem familiar but must be made strange.[6] I've tried to accomplish this task in the preceding pages.

As a final bookend, let's consider where the strangeness of the published versions of *A Rhetoric of Motives* and *The War of Words* might lead us. To put the matter simply, there is more to mine in Burke's engagement with form, particularly as it relates to identification and human consciousness. In making this argument, I am not suggesting that existing research on Burke and form is insufficient, nor am I saying that it is misguided. I am simply arguing that there is more to the story. Remember Burke's assertion that identification lies somewhere between conscious and unconscious awareness. I believe that his most provocative argument about this intermediate space appears in his discussion of collaborative expectancy, which allows individuals to identify with the rhythms of form even if an argument violates their consciously held values. I am less interested in what form can do than in what Burke had in mind when he tethered formal awareness to an alternate domain of consciousness that is difficult to know but may nevertheless become the site of critical awareness. What are the characteristic features of this domain of consciousness? Why is it receptive to formal rhythms? And what is it about this area of consciousness that allows for consciousness to fold back on and correct itself, however modestly?

These questions are particularly important in light of the connection Burke draws between the dialectic principle and human motives. If what Burke argues in *A Grammar of Motives* and *A Rhetoric of Motives* is accurate, then human beings are motivated (in the passive sense) as much as they have motives (in the active sense).

During my archival research, I repeatedly wondered why Burke does not directly define human motivation despite the fact that *motives* are the salient theme in his motives trilogy. For a time, I thought that the books might have been better titled *A Grammar of Symbolic Action* and *A Rhetoric of Symbolic Action* (though *A Symbolic of Symbolic Action* is admittedly clunky). Had he chosen these titles, many of the concerns with his action/motion distinctions, and the biological assumptions that underwrite them, would be more or less resolved.

Today, I am less convinced by my imagined revision. Although this revision captures what is arguably Burke's fundamental preoccupation (symbolic action), and does so in a manner that deliberately departs from the psychoanalytic assumptions of Freud, I'm not sure the solution is to be more theoretical—to focus, that is, on the "universal" features of the dialectic principle. Instead, I think critics should become more historical in their focus and develop an archival genealogy of human motives. This approach would place Burke's definition of human motives within a broader episteme that would allow us to evaluate, for example, *where* such terms emerged in human history, *what* disciplinary practices are associated with them, *how* such disciplinary practices were implemented, and *why* the social effects they produced qualified as desirable.

Mythic historiography may provide a linchpin for this line of inquiry. Freud and his contemporaries were not shy about connecting theories of human consciousness to myth, as Mikkel Borch-Jacobsen argues in *The Freudian Subject*. The center view of literary criticism and poetry in mid-twentieth-century America was concerned with myth as well.[7] And this is to say nothing of foundational works in cultural anthropology, structural anthropology, evolutionary biology, comparative religion, theology, philosophy, comparative philology, political science, cybernetics, and semiotics.[8]

So I am proposing that we view human motives as a technology for disciplining human consciousness. Like any technology, this would form and naturalize an interface that organizes human perception and action. It would also establish rhythms of expectancy that allow individuals and groups to identify with broader institutional imperatives through origin and eschatological stories. Burke's drafting notes and chapter fragments on scientific rhetoric and the rhetoric of bureaucracy in particular indicate that this is where he was headed before consigning the "War of Words" manuscript to the filing cabinet. Burke's place in the history of ideas indicates that he was hardly alone in trying to promote an alternative future by appealing to the poetic universal in humanity.

In an earlier draft of this book, there was a chapter dedicated to this topic, but that must await publication in a separate volume. For the time being, it is enough to say that in digging in the weeds with Burke, I have found a sufficient array of ideas to suggest that the direction I am proposing warrants more digging. In time, I may be cured of such a conviction and seek new terrain. Maybe this work will lead to new ideas. Maybe it won't. Either way, I am back where I started before this book began: with a question and some tools. May all our work yield such returns.

Notes

Part I: An Archive of Motives

Introduction

1. This is plausible fiction. What I've tried to do in this opening paragraph is capture the spirit of Burke's letters by setting a scene in which Burke's struggle against the briars and weeds echoes his composition of *A Rhetoric of Motives*. To create this scene, I cite and adapt lines from William Carlos Williams's poem "On the Road to the Contagious Hospital" and lines from Kenneth Burke's poem "The Wrens Are Back," which appears in *The War of Words*. As for exactly where Burke happened to be writing while on his Andover, New Jersey, farm, there are a couple of possibilities. During a visit to the farm in 2013, Julie Whitaker mentioned offhandedly that Burke wrote at the kitchen table. He also wrote upstairs in his personal study, which was not much larger than a coat closet (he called it his "cell"—see below); for more on Burke's personal study, particularly as it relates to his famous phrase *ad bellum purificandum*, see Zappen, Halloran, and Wible. Evidently, he also wrote in his living room. As Burke explained in a letter to Matthew Josephson dated 9 June 1948 (MJP), "Lo! whereas I had abandoned my study upstairs, and had written the entire Grammar in the living room, disliking the thought of being alone: I now found it pleasant to think of going back to the cell. Also, I of a sudden realized, I was only now at the point where I had originally begun my project." Knowing where Burke wrote is not particularly important, except that it draws attention to factors that may have influenced his drafting process as it evolved. Burke described his struggle with the briars and weeds in the same letter to Josephson: "For years a mystic sorrow has been upon me. Daily I suffered the defeat of knowing that the Jungle was coming ever closer." He continued to struggle with the weeds even after *A Rhetoric of Motives* was complete. In a letter dated 6 June 1952 to Malcolm Cowley (MCP), he wrote, "Meanwhile, know that I am trying to get things all cleared away, as preparation for the six-week stint at Indiana. And the muddle is tremenj. And my heart, he, she, or it doan work right, though the crude mechanisms of recording assure me otherwise (probably because I'm several, and the one on parade in the doctor's office aint the one I write by, or the one I go to bed with, or the one that is at-one-with the hesitancies of critical reading, or the one that loves to race behind the putt-putt a-slaying of the weeds, etc.)." Burke may have gotten the idea to purchase "Putt-Putt" from Cowley. In a letter dated 13 March 1946 (MCP), Cowley wrote, "Meanwhile the sun shines, the frost gets out of the ground, and I have a hotbed now where I'm trying to start plants for the garden. And I have ordered (did I tell you?) an expensive garden tractor, supposed to do everything, so that instead of working to swing a hoe, you work to tighten

a bolt or start a balky motor." Ian Hill explains in "'Human Barnyard'" that Cowley doubted whether Burke would ever buy such a machine, though Cowley notes, "it would greatly simplify your lawn problem, which, I suppose, you don't want simplified." It appears that Cowley was wrong on both counts.

2. Stanley Hyman was a former student of Burke's and an eventual colleague at Bennington College.

3. In a letter to Matthew Josephson dated 9 June 1948 (MJP), Burke wrote, "When I originally began this project, I had a batch of notes on what I called 'Devices' (various tricks that people play upon one another, in the course of Human Relations). It was my intention to write up those notes. But I found that they needed an introduction of what I thought would be three or four thousand words. As I wrote that, I found that it in turn needed an introduction. So, in fantastic impatience, I began by racing backwards, each step needing a step before that. I began to puff up like a toad, my eyes got red, my mouth was full of cotton—and medical examination disclosed a fancy case of high blood pressure. I made a certain amt. of peace with my complaint (as one learns how to keep an old car running). But I was always a step behind, until, in that state, I had written what I call a Grammar, and had written circa 125,000 words of what I call a Rhetoric. As I reached the end of that section of the Rhetoric, where the subject was a kind of suspended animation that applies to one aspect of Rhetoric (an attitude that, in the book, I call 'Pure Persuasion') my ever-cardiac heart became so sluggish that, for a few days, I thought I'd melt away. Then I finished, and things came back to their normal degree of discomfiture." In "Foreword (to end on)," published in *The War of Words*, Burke similarly writes, "Though most of this material . . . was finished some decades back and attained the hopeful stage of a fair copy, I laid the MS aside while I worked on <u>Grammar of Motives</u> and <u>Rhetoric of Motives</u>, that I then judged to be needed as preparatory grounding. This notion was all wrong. The books should have been published exactly in the order in which they were written, with the Devices as preparation for what followed" (*WW* 265). Burke also writes about media devices in *A Grammar of Motives*: "the concept of incipient acts is ambiguous. As an attitude can be the substitute for an act, it can likewise be the first step towards an act. Thus, if we arouse in someone an attitude of sympathy towards something, we may be starting him on the road towards overtly sympathetic action with regard to it—hence the rhetoric of advertisers and propagandists who would induce action in behalf of their commodities or their causes by the formation of appropriate attitudes" (236).

4. Burke did not just associate spiritualization with postwar geopolitics. In an earlier set of notes catalogued in the folder "Moral Equivalents of War" in KBP, Burke-3, he has a typescript on how modern science relies on spiritualization. The title of the short document is "Critique of Science," and it reads in part, "Science, I grant, is 'full of spirituality.' And, when considered in the widest sense, it possesses all the nobility that one cd. ask of any human activity . . . but, at the same time, one must be on guard against the black magic and paganism of science, the symbolic subterfuges whereby people seek to get, through material purchase or operational manipulation, results that even a savage knew were in the realm of ritual. It is the damned 'godifying' line that must be criticized, to the very last iota, before people are sophisticated enough to be equal to science. Otherwise, men must be the victims of one another's greatest invention." He then goes on to critique Deweyan pragmatism.

5. In a letter to Cowley dated 27 September 1946 (KBP, Burke-1), Burke wrote, "The Rhetoric material, as I had foreseen in principle, is undergoing quite some change. (Mainly, it becomes less thumbs-down in its emphasis, bringing out more the happy side of Rhetoric and the general contemplation of the subject—a change in emphasis which will, I think, serve eventually to make the thumbs-down section, on the Logomachy, more effective. Also, it becomes more systematic." In an undated draft titled "problems of rhetoric (from letter to DM)," Burke writes, "problem is essentially: how to write a modern rhetoric which is on the subject, without having it sound like Seldes' In Fact. here, the area, above all, that urges you to become a Debunker Hillbilly." In a note titled "to McKeon," Burke elaborates: "once one gets into the rhetoric-vs. science business, there is much invitation to become

downcast. indeed, my own struggle through rhetoric is obviously going to be the struggle to keep myself from falling into some variant of the scientifico-debunko-semanticist attitude, I find that I can write of rhetoric happily enough when I am applying rhetorical coordinates to poetry; but as soon as I turn to consider the concealed rhetoric in our journalistic version of 'reality,' I can prevent myself from becoming homicidal only by becoming homicidal, and can prevent myself from becoming suicidal only by becoming suicidal." George Seldes was a journalist who wrote the famous newsletter *In Fact*.

6. Burke discusses modern rhetorical devices in "Rhetoric—Old and New"; see especially 208-9, where he writes about "Deflection" and "Spiritualization." Although Burke's essay "The American Way" appeared prior to the publication of *A Rhetoric of Motives*, Burke planned to include it as an appendix to the two-volume work. In a letter to Watson dated 15 February 1948 (JWP), Burke wrote, "American Way cd. either go into the Bureaucracy section or be printed as part of the appendix. wd. also like to do an essay on New Yorker cartoons, for inclusion in appendix, but may not have time. If book were to be published in Dec., material would have to be in hands of publisher probably not later than sometime in June." A couple of weeks later, as Burke finished a draft of what would become the published *Rhetoric of Motives*, he decided to place "Ideology and Myth" in the appendices as well. He told Watson in a letter dated 24 February 1948 (JWP), "Incidentally, while trying to write the pages that were meant to serve as transition into the original Ideology and Myth lecture, lo! I came instead upon an ending—whereupon, bing, down went the curtain, and the lecture was relegated to the Appendix. I'll probably add an addendum to it there; but there was great rejoicing when I discovered definitely that I would not have to attempt fitting it into the book proper. But the present ending is a bit vatic, though I can take some of that out when revising, and then might tone it down some more when looking it over finally for the printer." Finally, in what appears to be an unsent letter to Watson, Burke mentioned a "Thesaurus of Deaths" to be included in *The War of Words*: "There are many notes, for instance, that still need typing. (And I live in fear lest a fire destroy them before I have distributed duplicates.) There are, besides, many problems of classification still unresolved. And there is a whole other area (what I call 'channels of affinity') which I have notes on, but which I have not yet put into shape. (The enclosed item, on the 'Thesaurus of Deaths,' is the sort of thing that belongs in this bin.)" Eventually, Burke would publish an essay titled "Thanatopsis for Critics: A Brief Thesaurus for Deaths and Dyings." Burke lectured from *The War of Words* while in residence at the University of Chicago. He wrote to Watson on 7 April 1950 (JWP), "Meanwhile, think I'll try, on the side, to get out some of the Devices. Shall try to present them as short independent articles. Reason for haste: at Chicago, gave some talks before the sociologists on the theory of the devices, plus some illustrations; and since it's obviously a line of thought they should have been following all along, and since they immediately began to discover that one or another of them had already been following it, I decided I had better publish mine, before I found myself obliged to do some fantastic apologetic squirming, etc." The Burke Literary Trust also holds lecture notes under the title "Towards a Science of Human Comedy," in which Burke discusses such devices as "deflection," "undoing by overdoing," "tithing by tonality," and "shrewd simplicity." I have not been able to determine where he delivered the lecture. Burke also presented aspects of his material on myth and rhetorical counteraction during his lecture at the Harvard Summer School Defense of Poetry conference held in August 1950. In this lecture, he drew from J. W. Mackail's work on Virgil, which outlined the ingredients that distinguished the *Aeneid* as a representative example of epic poetry. As in his 1947 Bennington lecture "Ideology and Myth," Burke drew specifically from Mackail's research on the *Aeneid*, which outlined how the myth may be adapted to the present. With some revision, Burke believed that a new national myth could help respond to the dangers of thermonuclear warfare. The goal of inventing such a myth, Burke explained, would be to imagine a future that circumvented the "almost paranoiac impersonality of modern instruments of destruction" ("Harvard Summer School Conference" transcript 125). Accordingly,

the poet's job would be to imagine "a wholly humanizing art of epic scope" (128). The discussion following Burke's lecture began amicably enough, but it soon turned sour when the conference chair, W. Y. Elliott, took the floor. Elliott took issue with Burke's argument that the threat facing the poet, if not humanity in general, was that "a war would be the end of all civilization and that a war of pacification was not the war to be fought" (130). Elliott asked attendees to remember the transhistorical values that distinguished the epic poem: "the ultimate affirmation of freedom" and a "willingness to stand [up for] the last supreme, the ultimate measure, the last measure of devotion" to the nation (130). Affirming human civilization and freedom in this manner would transcend considerations of government and capitalism, which to Elliott's mind would survive future wars. Elliott asked Burke to clarify his position and Burke obliged. Burke acknowledged Elliott's concerns but insisted on the need to address the threat of nuclear catastrophe. Echoing Stephen Spender, another distinguished attendee, Burke reiterated the claim that "new super-weapons have brought a new condition into the world that complicated the whole problem of heroism" (130). In Burke's view, willful ignorance on this point would trigger the scapegoat mechanism and thereby foster rather than redress catastrophic violence. Before Burke could complete his thoughts, however, Elliott cut him off. The conference transcript indicates that Elliott was unwilling to entertain the possibility that human freedom should be qualified by the threat of catastrophic war. Speaking for the group, Elliott ended the debate and asked to return to the subject of the conference: "ars poetica" (132). Though Levin spoke on Burke's behalf in claiming that the group had not finished discussing "these momentous issues" and should not thereby "exclude the relevance that has been so impressively established," Elliott directed the attention of the group toward questions from the crowd. Although Burke's provocations continued to shape the ensuing discussion, Burke did not speak again. In fact, he left the conference early and did not return as scheduled.

7. Here is a small list of recent scholarship that has extended Burke's insights into new terrain: Anderson and Enoch, *Burke in the Archives*; Clark, *Civic Jazz*; Crable, *Ralph Ellison and Kenneth Burke*; Davis, *Inessential Solidarity*; Gross, *Being-Moved*; Olson, *Constitutive Visions*; Ratcliffe, *Rhetorical Listening*; Rickert, *Ambient Rhetoric*.

8. Donald Stauffer was a professor in the English Department at Princeton University.

9. Scholars of *A Rhetoric of Motives* have tended to argue that the project is incomplete. Ross Wolin's *Rhetorical Imagination* claims that the book is "more suggestive than systematic" (172). Bryan Crable has argued that the aforementioned footnote "signals the presence of an absence, material removed during Burke's process of revision" ("Distance" 215). Although these and other scholars draw different conclusions about what the incompleteness of *A Rhetoric of Motives* means for modern rhetorical studies, all seem to agree that its incomplete status compromises the coherence of the published edition. Consequently, there is at present no coherent explanation of how the constituent parts of *A Rhetoric of Motives* constitute a systematic approach to modern rhetorical studies.

10. My archival account of *A Rhetoric of Motives* borrows primarily from the research methods of Jack Selzer. Whether we find Burke in Greenwich Village or delivering a paper at the First American Writers' Congress, Selzer stresses the need to situate Burke among his contemporaries. Doing so grounds interpretations of Burke's writings in the historical and material complexity of the archival record and thereby tends to generate more nuanced interpretations. My reconstruction of the compositional evolution of *A Rhetoric of Motives* adds to Selzer's approach the methods of textual scholarship. In particular, I draw from the work of John Bryant, who demonstrates the value of tracking the differences between different versions of the same work. Tracking such differences discloses "a larger and broader community of writers" that includes, but is not limited to, the friends and collaborators from whom Burke consistently sought feedback (7). Tracking Burke's epistolary conversations with collaborators is a well-established method in rhetorical studies. Elizabeth Weiser makes an eloquent case for their inclusion when she writes, "Exploring the implications of theories as conversationally constructed entities allows

rhetoricians to shed new light on these theories, reconstructing threads in their argument that have been less noticeable as the scenes shift over time" (Burke xvi). But rhetorical historians have placed less emphasis on how Burke's collaborations affect his writing process prior to publication. By focusing on the prepublication drafting process of *A Rhetoric of Motives*, we can admit to Burke's community of collaborators news reporters whose work was just as important to Burke's revision process. As Bryant argues, "A text may vary radically from one version to the next, yielding significant interpretive differences" (5).

11. The list of scholars who recognize the centrality of the concept of identification to Burke's philosophy of modern rhetoric is long and distinguished. See, for example, Anderson, *Identity's Strategy*; Biesecker, *Addressing Postmodernity*; Clark, *Civic Jazz*; Crusius, *Kenneth Burke*; Davis, *Inessential Solidarity*; Day, "Persuasion"; Heath, *Realism and Relativism*; Nichols, *Rhetoric and Criticism*; Ratcliffe, *Rhetorical Listening*; Rueckert, "Field Guide"; Wess, *Kenneth Burke*; Wolin, *Rhetorical Imagination*; Wright, "Burkeian and Freudian Theories." Both Laurence Coupe and C. A. Carter emphasize the fundamental role of myth in Burke's philosophy of human motives. While both cite *A Rhetoric of Motives* in their arguments, neither explicates the infrastructural role it plays in Burke's philosophy of modern rhetoric.

12. In an early draft titled "conclusion—," Burke writes, "our rhetorical job—to keep our nation out of war." Burke goes on to explain how that rhetorical job focuses on the dangers of Western nationalism: "limitations of nationalism—need to see, if possible, that East doesn't pick it up, and go through the crudities of the Western nationalist orgies—help them to pass over these stages, like going from oxcarts to airplanes in the Andes . . . danger: we are teaching them our worst ways—indeed, we are forcing them to learn these, as the only way of gaining independence—ironic likelihood: that just when we are past such excesses, the 'backward peoples' will have been forc<u>ibly</u> taught our raw ways, and be ready to imitate them thus starting the worthless turmoil all over again. . . . maybe we have already gone too far—our complicity: to boast of <u>our</u> nationalism, we had to extoll nationalism per se. most disastrously of all, we <u>forced</u> nationalism upon the Russians, as the only way whereby their international doctrine could survive even within their own borders—even so: it is good to remember that Russian nationalism, at its most conceivably worst, lacks the arrogant theories of race that plague white capitalism. —hence, Russia may help to mitigate this, to act as a bridge with other races—such will be needed, if our future generations are to survive, not as members of a 'privileged class,' but simply to survive <u>at all</u>." From what I can tell, Burke used this "conclusion—" document to state major claims that would organize the book. For instance, the epigraph that opens this introduction is also titled "conclusion," as are a number of other documents stored alongside it.

13. Scholars such as Bryan Crable ("Distance") and Jim Zappen ("Kenneth Burke") have argued that Burke's major contribution in *A Rhetoric of Motives* lies adjacent to the concept of *identification*; Crable focuses on *pure persuasion* and Zappen focuses on *dialectical-rhetorical transcendence*. Both scholars make compelling cases in support of their insightful conclusions; I simply do not agree with those conclusions. As I show throughout this book, Burke was unequivocal about the centrality of identification to *A Rhetoric of Motives*. I believe that the limits in Crable's and Zappen's arguments lie predominantly in their tendency to overstress the value of "Order" to the published version of *A Rhetoric of Motives*. This interpretive tendency is not new. In fact, published reviews, essays, and book chapters from Donald Stauffer to Barb Biesecker argue the same point.

14. As I argued in my essay "Rhetorical Counteraction," "When referring to Burke's theory of identification in this essay, I use the term nonconscious. As far as I can tell, this is not a term that Burke employs in his discussion of identification either in *A Rhetoric of Motives* or *The War of Words*. I have chosen the term nonconscious instead of subconscious because the former is more clearly differentiated from the search for deep motivations that Burke clearly opposes. In addition, contemporary research on nonconscious processes adopt a system-based approach to its analysis, which is largely consistent with Burke's study of symbolic

action" (397–98). For more on this, see Hayles 398.

Prolegomena

1. I focus on the years 1945–50 because Burke composed *A Rhetoric of Motives* during that time span. Burke wrote notes toward *A Rhetoric of Motives* prior to 1945 and continued to work on it after the book's publication in 1950. In choosing not to include the *before* and *after* in my account, I am not saying that they are unimportant to the study of *A Rhetoric of Motives*. I am simply saying that they are not relevant to my specific purpose in writing this book.

2. Landmark works on this topic include Bryant, *Fluid Text*; Bushell, *Text as Process*; Parker, *Flawed Texts*; Cohen, *Devils and Angels*; Greetham, *Theories of the Text*; Shillingsburg, *From Gutenberg to Google* and *Resisting Texts*; Sutherland, *Jane Austen's Textual Lives*; Kelemen, *Textual Editing*; Bruns, *Inventions*; Deppman, Ferrer, and Groden, "Introduction"; and McGann, *Textual Condition*.

3. For more on this, see esp. Bryant 30–43; Bushell 9–37.

4. For more on this, see esp. Bryant 64–87; Bushell 57–74.

5. For more on this, see esp. Bryant 88–111; Bushell 38–56.

6. It is important to recognize that the status of *The War of Words* has changed since the publication of *A Rhetoric of Motives* in 1950. Whereas Burke's footnote on p. 294 refers to it as a "section" and a "volume," it is now a scholarly edition that has been published separately from its companion volume. As with any published version of a rhetorical work, this status could change in the future. The status of *The War of Words* is complicated by the fact that archived manuscript versions and a published scholarly edition remain extant. To denote which version I am referring to in this book, I characterize extant archived manuscripts as chapters that make up a second volume of the larger work *A Rhetoric of Motives*, and I refer to the published scholarly edition as *The War of Words* to underscore its status as a collated, edited, and published version of the archived manuscripts. I draw primarily from the scholarly edition of *The War of Words* in subsequent discussion. My references to the drafted, archived manuscripts held in the Berg Collection at the New York Public Library should be obvious.

7. The main parts of the manuscript are held in several locations—namely, the New York Public Library, the Eberly Family Special Collections Library at Pennsylvania State University, and the Kenneth Burke Literary Trust in Andover, New Jersey. The latter two sites are connected by the collaboration between members of the Burke family at Penn State, who have acquired materials for the Kenneth Burke Papers over the years. Burke-3 (Burke's correspondence and MSS), acquired in 2008, included drafting notes for both *A Rhetoric of Motives* and *The War of Words*, indexes of chapters, early drafts of both works, and fair copies of what came to be the published version of *A Rhetoric of Motives*. The major chapters that make up *The War of Words* are held at the Burke Literary Trust. Earlier versions of those chapters are held in the Berg Collection at the New York Public Library.

8. The scholarly edition of *The War of Words*, published in 2018, reproduces the typeset versions of "Of the Devices" and "Scientific Rhetoric" held by the Burke Literary Trust, since they are the most fully formed manuscripts that Burke produced on each topic. The scholarly edition uses more elaborate versions of "The Rhetorical Situation" and "The Rhetoric of Bureaucracy" from the Kenneth Burke Papers at Penn State University.

9. For more on this, see Genette.

10. Even if, at some point in the future, the two published volumes were fitted into the same binding, the published version of *A Rhetoric of Motives* would still exist (along with its subsequent printings) and would retain its status as such—as would the 2018 scholarly edition of *The War of Words*. I have argued that tracking the various iterations of a rhetorical work over time facilitates a more precise orientation toward textual criticism.

11. For example, there's an entire book to be written about how Burke analyzed the unfolding events reported in the news media. I incorporate some of the highlights, but there remains a significant opportunity to understand Burke's engagement with the *New York Times*, in particular.

Chapter 1

I take this title from Burke's novel, *Towards a Better Life* (214). Burke drew a direct correspondence between his early drafts of *A Rhetoric of Motives* and *Towards a Better Life* in a letter to Malcolm Cowley dated 3 April 1946 (Jay 274-75): "First draft of the Rhetoric goes bumping along. Instead of writing it from start to finish, I seem to be writing it from the middle out. Each day I drive in more wedges that push the two ends farther apart. And there's just the possibility that I may, this time, be lambasted for being too easy to read. The book is as anecdotal as T.B.L., except that this time the anecdotes are strung along an idea instead of a story. The clothesline method. Except that there is a shortage of clothespins, so that you have to hang several items at each spot along the line. The anecdotes treat everything as of equal importance: what two diplomats solemnly announce at an International conference is valued no higher than something that Butchie and Michael say at the sand pile. I gave as the formula, 'benevolently caustic,' but out of some correspondence with Knickerbocker I have found a more tonal way of expressing the same design 'ironically irenic.'" When Burke returned to his "Devices" chapter in 1948, he once again mentioned the correspondence between *A Rhetoric of Motives* and *Towards a Better Life*. In a letter to James Sibley Watson dated 7 May 1948 (JWP), he wrote, "The reading should be much easier in one sense at least. The reader can take up one thing at a time, confining his speculations, if he wants, to the limits of the given example. On the side, I keep digging into Aquinas and going over my books of proverbs. (Ideally, my method should be a mixture of the two styles.) Or some of the incidental 'case histories' in T.B.L. but with a wholly changed tonality."

1. Early and late drafts of what became the published version of *A Rhetoric of Motives* are held in the Kenneth Burke Papers (Burke-3, Q4 B9-10); indexes for "Traditional" and "Order" (Q4 B9 F9); "Traditional Principles," also titled "Landmarks of Rhetoric" (B9 F23-26); "Order," also titled "Dialectic, Ideology, and Myth" (Q4 B9 F27-29); fair copy of "A Rhetoric of Motives" MS (Q4 B10 F2-10).

2. Guerard 8. Albert Guerard was a noted novelist, short-story writer, and literary critic. He taught at Harvard and Stanford.

3. For more on Hyman, see George and Selzer 46.

4. McKeon was a professor of philosophy at the University of Chicago. See ibid. 226.

5. An early edition of *A Rhetoric of Motives* interprets the published version in exactly this manner. The dust jacket reads, "Though not specifically a 'How To —' book, *A Rhetoric of Motives* does incidentally deal with many devices that have been used for producing effects by words, not only upon others, but also upon oneself. For, according to the author, many aspects of psychology (such as psychoanalysis) involve rhetorical factors, with one part of the mind as the 'speaker' and the other part as the 'spoken to.'"

6. In an early drafting document titled "conclusion (or introduction)," Burke writes explicitly about the relevance of rhetoric in a nuclear age: "Rhetoric can make its contribution too; and its contribution is just as momentous as the contributions of physics, chemistry, and biology, and any other science that contributes to the resourcefulness of war. For if the men in those departments have done their part to make war little short of universal suicide, it is those in our department who will make you want to get into such a war. It is the rhetoricians, the editors, the commentators, the politicians, the priests, who will invent the distortions and the slogans that alone are capable of goading you into the holocaust, of making you actually demand it, or at least making you <u>think</u> you had demanded it. And they have started their work already" (2).

7. It is worth noting that Burke associates the dangers of complicity with efforts to challenge the "doctrine of 'white supremacy'—as vs. 'sociologists.'" He drafted a more elaborate analysis of white supremacy in the published version of *The War of Words* (151).

Chapter 2

1. Burke published an essay in 1973 titled "The Rhetorical Situation," but there is no evidence to suggest that this essay is a continuation of the section he proposed in the 1946 prospectus.

2. By "extra-literary factors," Burke means factors outside the text that impinge upon its meaning. These factors include sociopolitical, material, economic, and contextual matters. They also include any aspect of the text that is not literary in self-reference, such as appeals to specific audiences.

3. Matthew Josephson was a poet, literary and economic critic, and biographer. For more on the relationship between Burke, Cowley, and Josephson, see Selzer 108.

4. Burke's discussion of implicational criticism claims Marxist rhetoric ("red rhetoric") as a representative example. Eventually, Burke's engagement with Marx's red rhetoric produced a sustained consideration of mystification, among other concepts.

5. "The Moral Equivalent of War" is the title of William James's 1910 essay, based on a 1906 speech, which imagines nationalist methods of counteracting warfare.

6. William S. Knickerbocker was the editor of the *Sewanee Review* from 1926 to 1942.

7. T.B.L. refers to Kenneth Burke's novel, *Towards a Better Life* (1932).

8. Will Rogers was, among other things, a famous actor known for his roping skill and over-the-top performances as a cowboy.

Chapter 3

1. For more on Burke's tense history with Sidney Hook, see George and Selzer 170.

2. Gorham Munson was a friend and collaborator who helped Burke secure a publisher for the motives trilogy. For more on Burke's relationship to Munson, see *WW* 11.

3. Burke also seems to have been planning for his long history of rhetoric, which would evidently include medieval philosophers. In a letter to Richard McKeon dated 12 May 1946 (RMP), he wrote, "I have not been successful in getting copies of the two volumes on medieval philosophers which you once put out. And I wonder whether you have any available. And whether you would be willing to trade me a set for a genuine first edition of my Grammar of Motives." Burke's sections on McKeon and medieval philosophers appear on pp. 101, 169–73, and 206 of the published version of *A Rhetoric of Motives*.

4. The original index, drafts, correspondence, and editorial prospectus for this special issue of *Esprit* are all held in KBLT, C12. A number of writers at the time were tasked with determining the character of American culture. See, for example, Gorer, *American People* and Riesman, *Lonely Crowd*.

5. In a letter to Watson dated 12 March 1947 (JWP), Burke painted a grimmer picture: "And I don't see any hope. For it seems obvious to me that Communism is gaining throughout the world, not because of pressure from Russia, but simply because most of the world can't support the kind of govt. we can support in the U.S. Hence, the 'threats to the American Way of life' are going to continue. If we stop 'loans' to a given area on Tuesday, the 'threats' will be resumed on Wednesday. Hence, the more we pour into them (with a large part of it, at that, going for economically unproductive assistance, war materials to bolster up administrations that, unaided, would fall by their own weight), well, the more of such backing we give, the meaner we'll be, when the inevitable fact [is] that most of the world today simply cannot support capitalism. And in proportion as this fact makes itself manifest, there'll be increasing zest for letting loose with the atomic bomb."

6. If this assertion seems confusing, remember that Burke's definition of poetry did not require him to make reference to Aragon's temporal context. He could have simply read the poetry in and of itself without consideration of audience. Yet Burke characterizes Aragon's poetry as a form of resistance in order to demonstrate that the poetic can have rhetorical elements. To understand these elements, we need to learn how to read the content of the form. This point comes into clear relief in the final sentence of the quoted passage, in which Burke implores his (French) audience to scrutinize Aragon's poetry carefully. Just as Aragon scrutinized love, war, and work, so too must Burke's audience. That work begins by scrutinizing the exemplar himself.

7. In *Attitudes Toward History*, Burke uses the term "curve of history" to "chart the over-all problems of merger and division (with corresponding confusion and profusion of orthodoxy, heresy, sect, and schism) that marked our particular Western culture" (second page of unpaginated introduction).

Chapter 4

1. In an early set of notes, Burke argues for "a minimum grounding for unity": "Rhetorically, what is needed is a minimum grounding. For as thorough rhetoricians, we shall also use our shrewdness against ourselves, allowing ourselves nothing beyond positivist, pragmatist, empiricist, behaviorist, operationalist grounding, except insofar as the 'hard facts' themselves point to more edifying grounds. In brief, edification must here be made difficult, quite as by idealizations it is made easy." He goes on to explain that such grounds ought to be based on our existence as symbol-using animals: "But a man, to be himself, must first of all be human. That is, he must follow to completion the logic of his nature as a symbol-using animal. And this nature is, first of all, generic; for however individually he may use language, the linguistic resources themselves are those of his kind. Language is in essence as universal as the global traffic developed by its help, and as the ultimate universal classification towards which its own genius impels those who would freely follow the logic of linguistic resources to its ultimate" ("Conclusion—on minimum grounding," 3).

2. In a letter to Richard McKeon dated 2 December 1946 (RMP), Burke mentions this student's question again, writing: "No, damn it; some of my students are really excellent. They have taught me a great deal. And perhaps they taught me most at those times when they wouldn't budge, or just sweetly let me tie myself into knots and find my own way out. One very blunt question, in a flash, like a catalytic agent, organized a whole third of my book for me."

3. The list of lectures is available electronically via Bennington College's archives under the title "The Myth-Lecture Series Listing of Speakers and Topics." See https://crossettlibrary.dspacedirect.org/handle/11209/8497. We know that Burke attended Campbell's lecture because he took notes on it and sent them to Watson (Burke to Watson, 27 April 1947, JWP). Burke's notes are also held in KBP, Burke-3 (P17 B5 F4). It appears that he also attended, or at the very least read, Salvadori's lecture ("The Myth of the State") and Drucker's, because his archives contain typescript copies of their lectures. See KBP, Burke-3 (P17 B5 F3–4). Burke's copy of Drucker's lecture is untitled. The titled copy of Drucker's lecture can be found in Bennington's archives at https://crossettlibrary.dspacedirect.org/bitstream/handle/11209/5404/Drucker%20Lecture%203.25.47%20%20Myth%20of%20the%20State.pdf.

4. When discussing the transmigration of souls, Burke considers "the place that animals have" in such an arrangement. He writes, "there is the 'natural sociality' of children (and seers), whose sense of a 'community' is not bounded by purely human limits, but includes other forms of life and even 'inanimate' nature. next: there is the fact that, as with Aesop's Fables, the names for animals are a kind of primitive vocabulary for 'systematizing' ethical types. the different animals are taken to represent different kinds of people. they are thus a mode of abstract classification, expressed in concrete terms. . . . similarly, different animals cd. be taken to symbolize the different stages or 'selves' of an individual's development. (as with Nietzsche and the camel-lion child series). the real experience of character change within the self wd. thus be 'mythically' expressed in terms of 'metempsychosis,' a transmigration of souls through a succession of 'animal natures.' . . . Thus, 'transmigration of souls' would be a 'dramatic' way of expressing one's real experience of moral development. and the 'form' behind it (the experience of development or the transformation per se) wd. be 'true.' but it wd. be a 'mythical' truth (a truth 'truer' than the particular concrete images in which it was expressed)." "myth—."

5. Burke's attraction to Reich is not surprising given his definitions of identity and identification in *Attitudes Toward History*—"the so-called 'I' is merely a unique combination of partially conflicting 'corporate we's'" (264). What is perhaps less obvious is how Reich's research aligned with the argument Burke would make in *A Symbolic of Motives*. In the aforementioned letter to Watson dated 17 March 1947 (JWP), Burke noted that Reich's research interested him because of its commentary on the "psychosomatic business." Burke would later characterize *A Symbolic of Motives* as the study of the internalized war of words. So even though Reich does not figure prominently in the published versions of *A Rhetoric of Motives* or *The War*

of Words, his book on the orgasm advanced Burke's thinking about the relationship between rhetoric and poetics.

6. For more on these terms, see Burke, "principles (categories)."

Chapter 6

1. On 18 February 1948, Burke wrote to Richard McKeon (RMP), "The book itself finally fell into two sections, the first called Rhetoric and Dialectic, and the second The World of Publicity. (Roughly, an Upward Way and a Downward Way?) If, after I get home, I find that Aristotle's Topics would have destroyed the entire work, I'll add a footnote to that effect. If all goes as per schedule, I should have finished the Upward Way in another ten days or so, and should be sitting pretty, on top of the world. It remains to be seen whether the parachute will work properly, on the way down. (The other day I saw a news reel of a dog descending in a parachute. Not knowing what else to do, but obviously feeling a bit embarrassed as he floated slowly down, he wagged his tail. It was very winsome, and I decided to remember it.)"

Chapter 7

1. On the process of Robert Oppenheimer's appointment as director of the Institute for Advanced Study, Kai Bird writes, "Late in 1946, Lewis Straus, one of Truman's appointees to the new Atomic Energy Commission, flew out to San Francisco and was met at the airport by Ernest Lawrence and Oppenheimer. Before discussing AEC business, Strauss took Oppenheimer aside and said he had something else to talk to him about. Strauss had met Oppenheimer only once before, late in the war. Pacing about on the concrete tarmac, Strauss explained that he was a trustee of the Institute for Advanced Study in Princeton, New Jersey. At the moment, he chaired the trustees' search committee for a new director of the Institute. Oppenheimer's name was at the top of a list of five candidates, and now the trustees, Strauss said, had authorized him to offer Oppenheimer the post.... Oppenheimer was inclined to accept this new challenge. It played to his administrative talents, it promised to leave him ample time to pursue his extracurricular government responsibilities, and its location was perfect" (Bird 359–60). See also Monk 527.

Chapter 8

1. In a document titled "Notes on the Director's Fund" dated 16 December 1947 (SWLL), Beatrice Stern wrote, "There are many fields, in the Director's opinion, in which a beginning could be made. He pointed to two main classifications of effort: (1) the application of scientific methods to fields in which there is really pioneering, and (2) the encouraging of work by men to whom experience in the creative arts has brought deep insight. The Director outlined no specific program for such efforts. His suggestion was that there would be opportunity for exploring new fields outside and beyond specific areas of the schools, which in some cases have narrow interests. For this purpose, the Director asked that there be members who are not members of the Schools. To accomplish his plan, he asked the Trustees to establish a General Fund of $120,000 on a five-year basis."

2. IAS policy prevented Fergusson from recommending Burke for a short-term appointment, so he enlisted the help of permanent faculty member W. W. Stewart, a noted historian of economics, who submitted the formal recommendation to Oppenheimer on 30 March 1948. See Stewart to Oppenheimer, 30 March 1948, SWLL.

3. See Dyson, *Turing's Cathedral* 7–10 for a brief synopsis.

4. The IAS offered faculty and membership positions to a number of world-famous mathematicians and scientists, including Albert Einstein, Marston Morse, Robert Oppenheimer, Kurt Gödel, John von Neumann, Oswald Veblen, Abraham Pais, Paul Dirac, Freeman Dyson, Clifford Geertz, George Kennan, and numerous others. For a history of the IAS, particularly as it relates to the Electronic Computer Project, see ibid.

5. Max Radin was a philologist and legal scholar and a fellow member of the IAS.

6. Gregory Bateson was an English anthropologist who was famous for such works as *Steps to an Ecology of Mind*. George Boas was a philosopher at Johns Hopkins University. Frank Lloyd Wright was arguably

the most influential American architect of the twentieth century. Marcel Duchamp was a French painter and sculptor famous for such works as *Nude Descending a Staircase (No. 2)* (1912) and *Fountain* (1917). Andrew C. Ritchie was a Scottish-born art historian and director of painting and sculpture at the Museum of Modern Art. The complete transcript of the event can be found at http://ubu-mirror.ch/historical/wrtma/transcript.htm.

Chapter 9

1. Richard McKeon had been inviting Burke to the University of Chicago routinely since at least 1946.

Part II: A Theory of Motives

Chapter 1

1. Archetype would have been a good candidate. Archetype was the organizing concept in Carl Jung's theory of the collective unconscious, which was highly influential at the time of Burke's writing (*Symbols of Transformation* would be updated and reissued in 1952). Burke was familiar with Jung's work and had been discussing its merits since 1925. In a letter to Malcolm Cowley dated 20 January 1925, Burke wrote, "The psychology of the type of Jung deals with art's failure to be universal, in the sense that a pure introvert could not find sympathetic expression in the work created by a pure extrovert. . . . Jung, for instance, says that there are certain basic divisions of mankind which are continually re-individuated. If I, that is, have the type of mind of a Plato rather than an Aristotle, I shall find in Plato a fuller response to my requirements" (Jay 170). In Burke's drafting notes, there is a typescript note titled "archetype" (KBP, Burke-3) that reads, "Grammatically, I take 'archetype' to be another perfect instance of the ambiguity whereby we can express a 'logical priority' in terms of a 'temporal priority.' That is, in seeking to enunciate a principle for our national conduct now (in seeking to enunciate a 'first'), we can state it in temporal terms, as against logical terms, by locating it in the past. And the Platonic myth, as thus similarly viewed grammatically works in this same area of ambiguity. (The argumentative parts of the dialogue establish a 'logical' principle; and the 'myth,' or imaginative anecdote, then translates this same principle into a 'vision' of a representative incident that happened in the 'mythic' past."

2. Bruce Lincoln argues that the scholars driving postwar research on myth were Mircea Eliade, Claude Lévi-Strauss, and Georges Dumézil. Though each scholar approached myth from a different angle, they all defined myth as a narrative taxonomy and narrative ideology (Lincoln 147). For some representative texts on myth written around the same time as Burke's drafting and publication of *A Rhetoric of Motives*, see Beauvoir, *Second Sex*; Campbell, *Hero*; Camus, *Sisyphus*; Chase, *Quest*; Cassirer, *Language* and *Myth of the State*; Eliade, *Cosmos*; Fromm, *Forgotten*; Horkheimer and Adorno, *Dialectic*; Jung, *Symbols*; Langer, *Philosophy*; and Slochower, *Mythopoesis*. For more on the relationships among modernist painting, mythmaking, and the creation of the modern primitive in anthropology, see Leja 49–120. For more on how myth figures in modern poetry, see Feder. For more on how myth figures in a number of disciplinary fields, see Doty. For more on how mythic images shaped American culture, see Cmiel and Peters 152–76.

3. A handful of scholars have addressed the function of myth in *A Rhetoric of Motives*. Carter and Coupe emphasize the centrality of myth to Burke's work but give very little attention to *A Rhetoric of Motives*. Crable and Zappen emphasize the function of myth to *A Rhetoric of Motives* but focus on the third section, "Order," to the near exclusion of the others, thus obscuring myth's infrastructural relationship to identification and especially to poetry. Michael McGee recognizes the organizing function of myth in Burke's argument but is more interested in moving beyond its apparent limits. The most notable book on Kenneth Burke and myth is Coupe, *Burke on Myth*. Mythic terms show up variously in Wess, *Kenneth Burke*; see also Lentricchia.

4. Burke sometimes treats myth as an object of inquiry. See, for example, "Revolutionary Symbolism"; "Myth, Poetry, and Philosophy," in *Language as Symbolic Action* (380–409); "Ideology and Myth"; and "Doing and Saying."

5. Although Coupe does not discuss *A Rhetoric of Motives* at length, he nails the function of myth: "Mythology for Burke is at once historical and universal, temporal and transcendent" (*Burke on Myth* 4).

6. Susan Wells explains Burke's stance well: "Rhetoric and poetics are not sorting devices for bodies of texts, or fancy words for 'fiction' and 'nonfiction.' They are terms for perspectives on texts, bundles of questions that might be asked" (66).

7. For more on this, see Borch-Jacobsen 116–17, 237–39.

8. Burke explains in an unpublished note that myth is "a way of naming essence in a vocabulary prior to the development of a philosophical, or metaphysical (theological) vocabulary of essence, principles, and the like." Burke, "when on myth."

9. Placing Burke in conversation with Joseph Campbell is helpful when discussing mythic images. Campbell says that "universals are never experienced in a pure state, abstracted from their locally conditioned ethnic applications. It is, in fact, in their infinitely various metamorphoses that their fascination resides. And so, while it has been my leading thought in the present work to let sound the one accord through all its ranges of historic transformation, not allowing local features to obscure the everlasting themes, it has also been intended and arranged that the wonder of the revealed accord should not diminish our appreciation of the infinite variety of its transformations." *Hero* 11–12.

10. As George and Selzer demonstrate, Burke sought a poetic society that "fosters participation as in a great drama, a state that might fuse diverse cultures the way a lyric fuses images, a state in which the most important business is the creative act, a state that would be as politically engaged as it would be attentive to the values of aesthetes" (110). George has since built on this discussion in her outstanding book *Burke's "Permanence and Change"* (86–126). See also Clark, *Civic Jazz* 22–38.

11. Influential scholars such as Claude Lévi-Strauss also viewed myth in transformational terms. François Dosse writes, "Levi-Strauss saw mythic structure as the product of a veritable syntax of transformations" (250).

12. A number of important works have explained how twentieth-century critics were preoccupied with redefining the status of "man." For example, Mark Greif argues, "The world had entered a new crisis by 1933, the implications of which would echo for nearly three decades to follow: not just the crisis of the liberal state, or capitalist economy generally, and not only the imminent paroxysm of the political world system in world war. The threat was now to 'man.' 'Man' was in 'crisis.' This jeopardy transformed the tone and content of the intellectual, political and literary enterprise from the late thirties forward, in ways that—because they are so intertwined with panic, piety, and the permanent philosophical questions of human nature—have still not been given an adequate accounting" (3). For representative books published around the same time as *A Rhetoric of Motives*, see Cassirer, *Essay*; Weaver, *Ideas*; Mumford, *Condition*; and Cousins, *Modern*. The latter two establish the threat of death—in Cousins's case, the threat of "irrational death"—as the foundation for redefining "man's" status in history (7). A focus on death and, by implication, transformation tethers this research to the study of myth according to Burke's arguments in both *A Grammar of Motives* and *A Rhetoric of Motives*. Griffin explains that the appeal of myth is strong because it provides a "sacred canopy" that "transcends . . . chaos, the intimation of nothingness" (75). In making this argument, Griffin echoes Lévi-Strauss in *Naked Man* (535–624); Berger in *Sacred Canopy* (3–28); Eliade in *Cosmos* (139–62); and Kermode in *Sense* (93–124). For more on how the crisis of man played out in art and literature, see Leja 203–74.

13. For more on this, see Pan 45–78; see also Niebuhr.

14. Burke defines *representative anecdote* as a "form" that critics use to build a vocabulary that represents and thereby describes reality (or at least presumes to do so). Burke argues that it must "be supple and complex" and have "scope" while also possessing "simplicity" as a reduction of the subject under consideration (*GM* 59–60).

15. Burke writes extensively about the dialectic, especially in *A Grammar of Motives* (see 29–58, 323–98, 402–43). A number of scholars have written sophisticated analyses of how the dialectic functions in Burke's

writings, among them Anderson; Biesecker 59–73; Brock, "Evolution"; Clark, *Rhetorical Landscapes* 78–79, 89–92; Crable, "Burke's Perspective" and "Burkean Perspectives"; Crusius, *Kenneth Burke* 192–96; Heath 157–94; Weiser, *Burke* 124–48; Wess, "Burke's 'Dialectic'"; Wolin 162–66; and Zappen, "Kenneth Burke."

16. In "Rhetorical Listening," I argue, "According to Burke, constitutions establish a set of ideal principles that seek to alter an existing scene both in the present and into the future. They do so by declaring what a situation is substantially in order to alter that situation for the purposes of gaining a motivational advantage. In this way, constitutions establish the motivational coordinate points for individuals to identify with one another (or con-substantiate)" (189). For more on this, see Anderson 42; Clark, *Civic Jazz* 4.

17. Burke's definition of poetry is not unique, though critics have called it "rare" (Abrams 26). In *The Mirror and the Lamp* (1953), M. H. Abrams writes, "To pose and answer aesthetic questions in terms of the relation of art to the artist, rather than to external nature, or the audience, *or to the internal requirements of the work itself*, was the characteristic tendency of modern criticism up to a few decades ago, and it continues to be the propensity of a great many—perhaps the majority—of critics today" (3, emphasis added). Burke's definition of poetry accords with research on myth outside literary studies. For example, according to François Dosse, Claude Lévi-Strauss defines myth as a subjectless, atemporal form: "There was no place for a 'cogito'—'Myths are anonymous'—and Lévi-Strauss pursued his enterprise of decentering a subject dominated by the mythological universe that speaks to him but unbeknownst to him" (253).

18. Jim Zappen notes the presence of poetic myth in Burke's philosophy of modern rhetoric ("Kenneth Burke" 280, 290–91). Zappen's argument implies that Burke discusses poetic myth prior to the third part, "Order." But his focus is limited to the argument Burke advances in "Order."

19. The best way to conceptualize what Burke means by "secondary order of reality" is via Niklas Luhmann's theory of second-order systems. For more on this, see J. Jung. The roots of second-order systems theory were being developed as Burke was drafting *A Rhetoric of Motives*. In a lecture series titled *What Is Life?* (1944), Erwin Schrödinger posited the existence of second-order systems that create operational closure in order to increase in complexity. For more on this, see Schneider and Sagan.

20. For more on this, see Doyle.

21. Burke might argue that Eliade's capacity to identify archetypes is a function of the capacity to transcend differential gridlock via the dialectical principle; Burke would note that Eliade is drawing a curve of history to encourage a particular type of action that is more or less suited to his local and universal rhetorical situation (*RM* 146–49).

22. Burke's description of the transition from the upward to the downward way closely follows Joseph Campbell's description of the hero's journey: "The so-called rites of passage, which occupy such a prominent place in the life of a primitive society (ceremonials of birth, naming, puberty, marriage, burial, etc.), are distinguished by formal, and usually very severe, exercises of severance, whereby the mind is radically cut away from the attitudes, attachments, and life patterns of the stage being left behind. Then follows an interval of more or less extended retirement, during which are enacted rituals designed to introduce the life adventurer to the forms and proper feelings of his new estate, so that when, at last, the time has ripened for the return to the normal world, the initiate will be as good as reborn." *Hero* 10.

23. Burke had reviewed Cassirer's *Myth of the State* for the *Nation* in 1946 (see "Homo Faber").

24. Robin Coste Lewis's *Voyage of the Sable Venus* transforms mythic figures as an act of civic engagement.

Chapter 2

1. Scholars tend to assume that Burke's discussion of identification in *Attitudes Toward History*, for example, is equivalent to his discussion of identification in *A Rhetoric of Motives*. In unpublished notes titled "Range of Rhetoric—," Burke explains why such assumptions are faulty: "The beginnings of our systematic concern with 'identification' are in <u>Attitudes Toward History</u>,

notably Vol. II, pages 138–53. In The Philosophy of Literary Form, 'Twelve Propositions on the Relation Between Economics and Psychology,' the implications of the term are developed further. This book also contains a review of John Dewey's Liberalism and Social Action (review entitled 'Liberalism's Family Tree'), where the concept of identification is applied thus. . . . However, in these references, we were using 'identity' and 'identification' in terms of their similarities rather than in terms of their distinction. We had not yet adopted the present scheme which treats 'identity' as [the] generic name for a thing in its uniqueness, and 'identification' as the name for the thing in its substantial union with other things." By emphasizing that Burke's definition of identification evolved as his thinking evolved, I am in agreement with Jodie Nicotra, who similarly calls for the need to "see how a single concept such as mysticism can operate differently at different times over the course of one thinker's work" (173). For more on how concepts form different attachments, see Bal.

2. In August 1950, Burke presented a paper at Harvard Summer School's Defense of Poetry conference. Harry Levin's introduction of Burke on the third night of the conference is similar to Crusius's assessment of *A Rhetoric of Motives*. Levin described Burke as a "new subtle doctor" whose grammar, logic, and rhetoric offered "perhaps the best approach to poetry." However, Levin's introduction took a curious turn when he compared Burke to a "nuclear physicist in science." Levin went so far as to claim that Burke was a "nuclear critic" who "makes those of us who live by our words, manipulators of the phrase, rather self-conscious in his presence." The conference papers, and Levin's introduction, can be found in KBP, Burke-3 (P33 B8 F22–23). It is possible that Levin's analogy, like Crusius's assessment of Burke, was designed to underscore Burke's singular influence on the American literary scene. Or maybe it was designed as an intertextual nod to Burke's characterization of perspective by incongruity as a form of verbal atom cracking (see, for example, *Permanence* lv; *Attitudes* 308). Either way, Burke probably found Levin's characterization irritating. Passages on the threat of war abound in both *A Grammar of Motives* and *A Rhetoric of Motives*, evincing a writer consciously opposed to "those for whom war is a vocation, to whom the thought of the universal holocaust is soothing, who are torn by internal strife unless, in their profession as killers, they can commune with carnage" (*RM* 332). Burke was acutely aware of how being identified with nuclear physicists, irrespective of their national stature, enlisted him as a participant in the national project of carrying out economic exploitation and international war. Levin's enlistment was one from which Burke sought to dissociate himself, and the paper he delivered at the Defense of Poetry conference left no doubt about his stance on the matter. Crusius's assessment, obviously, does not go as far as Levin's. Still, it identifies Burke's argument with a metaphor he would have opposed.

3. Again, see Wolin, who writes that *A Rhetoric of Motives* "is still more suggestive than systematic" (172). Singling out Wolin as a representative of this argument is not fair. There are a number of scholars who simply lift concepts out of *A Rhetoric of Motives* without contextualizing them within Burke's broader philosophy of modern rhetoric. Ironically, Wolin makes this point explicitly in his chapter on *A Rhetoric of Motives*: "Several subsections that follow 'Identification' and 'Identification and Consubstantiality' have been largely ignored in analyses of Burke's work and even in discussions of identification. That is unfortunate, for in these sections Burke further indicates how identification is to be used" (181). To be clear, I don't think critics should be prevented from using concepts in Burke's writings to solve problems in their research. I do, however, think it is important to contextualize the role each concept plays within Burke's broader philosophy of modern rhetoric.

4. Diane Davis's engagement with identification in *Inessential Solidarity* is a good example of the problem I am defining. When presenting Burke's approach to identification, Davis writes, "Burke's quiet rivalry with Freud drops anchor here, in Burke's insistence that identification is a symbolic act—whether conscious or unconscious—that therefore remains available for sober critique and reasoned judgment" (*Inessential* 20–21). Davis is correct: Burke believed that

identification was a symbolic act available for sober critique and reasoned judgment. As Burke explains in *A Rhetoric of Motives*, "In our projected *Symbolic of Motives*, we hope to show, by analysis of Freud's work, how many logical and dialectical principles are, by his own account, involved in the operations of the dream. These elements are 'prior' to dream life insofar as they are the basis of all 'rational' thinking as well. But while psychologistic accounts of human motives seem, in their important stress upon symbolism, closer to the origins of *homo dialecticus* than institutionalist explanations are, we must discount Freud's own vocabulary somewhat; otherwise we cannot appreciate his great prowess as a dialectician, or note how well his analysis of the child's early experiences within the family reveal the operations of the hierarchic motive" (283–84). Davis is incorrect to assert that identification was interested in the unconscious. In the introduction to the book, Burke goes out of his way to emphasize that identification is more than the study of conscious and unconscious motives: "There is an intermediate area of expression that is not wholly deliberate, yet not wholly unconscious. It lies midway between aimless utterance and speech directly purposive. . . . And we would treat of it here" (xiii–xiv). By defining Burke's definition of identification this way, Davis undercuts the variety of ways in which Burke defines the concept and thus the variety of methods associated with its functions. As I wrote earlier in the book, this difference in interpretation does not diminish Davis's accomplishment as a scholar of Burke's work. Her insights are sharp and the directions she proposes are unquestionably worth pursuing. We simply disagree on how to define Burke's concept of identification in *A Rhetoric of Motives*.

5. This claim simply reiterates what we learned when tracking Burke's drafting process in Part I. However, it is important to note that Burke was not the only scholar studying identification in the early postwar period. For example, in his drafting notes on identification, titled "Range of Rhetoric—," he writes, "For other applications, see M. Sheriff and H. Cantril, The Psychology of Ego-Involvements, where 'ego-involved' judgments and behaviors are said to result from 'identification of one's self with a certain constellation of values.'" Sheriff and Cantril's book was published by Wiley in 1947.

6. For recent research that has engaged, applied, or reconsidered Burke's "theory of identification," see Belk; Davis, "Identification"; Enoch, "Claiming"; Hawhee, "Language"; Olson 1–24; Walsh; Weiser, "National."

7. The background image of an upside-down tree in figure 3 is a reference to the myth of Yggdrasil. For more on this, see Gaiman 37–42. I have selected this image because Burke refers to "roots" in his definition of rhetoric on p. 43 of *A Rhetoric of Motives*. I have also selected it because the myth's hero, Odin, commits suicide, which, as we have established, opens Burke's discussion of identification. Gaiman writes, "The world-tree can be climbed. It is from this tree that Odin hanged himself in sacrifice, making the world-tree a gallows and himself the gallows-god" (40). I deliberately selected a tree that branches out further than the diagram to signify that there is more to Burke's philosophy of modern rhetoric than what he addresses in his notes, letters, and published versions of the two-volume work. Again, I have diagrammed only what Burke discusses in the published version of the work. The solid lines in the diagram are (1) the line that separates pre-linguistic unity from the rest, and (2) the lines that form the boxes that encase each concept. I use a solid line for the former to represent Burke's argument that there is no return to pre-linguistic unity; that line runs through the word "division" in order to signify how Burke conceptualizes the principle of division that inaugurates our existence as symbol-using beings. To be clear, he doesn't use the phrase "principle of division"; I am inferring his meaning based on his argument about, for example, the principle of identification. In any case, the division in this diagram is the "universal" kind that frames the local divisions between individuals in context. I use solid lines to encase each concept to signify that these concepts are operational (i.e., they have specific functions, including self-reference) in Burke's philosophy of modern rhetoric. For more on this, see Luhmann xxii–xxiv. I am aware that Luhmann and Burke hold different views of how symbol systems work; Luhmann's systems

theory is nevertheless helpful for explaining how Burke's philosophy of modern rhetoric works. For example, Luhmann's theory helps explain how symbol systems "interface between conscious systems and social systems and permit their structural coupling by encoding the difference between information and utterance in ways that stabilize the coordination between the two and in so doing increase their internal complexity" (xxxii). The oval connecting pre-linguistic unity and the dialectic principle is broken to signify that we can posit pre-linguistic unity only through the failure of representation via a mythic image. The dotted lines that connect the boxed concepts to one another signify (a) that each concept is connected, and (b) that the paths between them can signify more than their internal relationships. In other words, I am suggesting that Burke's philosophy of modern rhetoric does not comprehensively explain how each concept relates to each other concept. The shaded boxes to the right of the primary diagram are two of the primary examples that Burke draws on to make his argument. I could have included more such examples, but it would have made the diagram visually muddled.

8. Dana Anderson's insightful reading of the relationship between transformation and constitutions emphasizes both poetic and rhetorical dimensions (33–57). Jeffrey Walker discusses the intimate relationship between rhetoric and poetics (17–41). Ann George discusses the fundamental role that poetry plays in Burke's conception of the good life (86–124).

9. See *RM* 23, 31, 139, 168, 266; *WW* 126. Barbara Biesecker argues, "To be sure, when Burke addresses identification his preoccupation with questions of origin gives way to a preoccupation with questions of process, his concern with structure gives way to a preoccupation with history" (48). I agree that Burke is interested in history and process, but this argument obscures the mythic dimensions of identification that allow it to explain movements across history via an origin-based social philosophy.

10. For more on this, see Doyle 126–33; Campbell, *Mythic* 87. Campbell's discussion of the Tower of Babel is particularly interesting because it stresses that the Judaic version of the story is unusual in its implication when compared to other cultural traditions. "The word 'ziggurat,'" says Campbell, "by which such towering Mesopotamian structures are designated, is from the Babylonian verb *zagaru*, meaning 'to be tall, to be lofty,' and—contrary to the view of the authors of the Biblical tale of Babel (Genesis 11:1–9)—such towers were not meant to storm the heavens but to elevate the mind and heart to supernatural contemplation and to provide, as well, a scale of descent for the gods to come down to hearth. . . . This old Sumerian idea of the graded stages of a universal manifestation of divinity, symbolized in the towering ziggurats and understood to correspond to grades in the powers of human consciousness, survived through many transformations of myths and monuments, not only throughout antiquity, but also (in the Orient) even to modern times" (87). The affinity between Campbell's description and Burke's language is unmistakable. Note, for example, the emphasis on different forms of consciousness, the upward and downward path, the graded series, etc. Campbell's description also calls to mind research on the relationship between Burke and mysticism. For more on this, see Hawhee, *Moving* 30–54; Nicotra. As discussed in Part I, Burke took part in a lecture series on myth with Campbell at Bennington College in 1947 and attended Campbell's lecture. Burke's notes on the lecture indicate that Campbell discussed mysticism at length; in response, Burke wrote the following: "The speaker also made an important distinction as regards the common essence of self and cosmos. It matters greatly, he said, whether the dreamer's dream symbolizes the cosmos or the self. (This would be the difference between psychoanalysis and myth.) When one seeks the common essence uniting himself and the universe, he may mistake his own private self for the universal self (may see the universe merely in terms of himself writ large). Whether the distinction can be kept clear, I do not know. But certainly here is the point at which mysticism and neurosis merge. The mystic may perhaps be one who can commune with a universal self, I don't know; but assuredly the would-be mystic becomes the neurotic when, in his transcending of the particular conditions, he <u>thinks</u> he is communing with a higher power, but is actually but confronting a disguised replica of his

own identity" ("Notes on Joseph Campbell's lecture"). So, while there may be an affinity in terminology between Campbell and Burke, Burke is clearly suspicious of the cosmic unity Campbell promises.

11. "Such would be the Edenic paradigm, applicable if we were capable of total acts that would produce total transformation. In reality, we are capable of but partial acts, acts that but partially represent us and that produce but partial transformations. Indeed, if all the ratios were adjusted to one another with perfect Edenic symmetry, they would be immutable in one unending 'moment'" (*GM* 19).

12. Scholars such as Bryan Crable have argued that *pure persuasion* is the organizing concept in *A Rhetoric of Motives* because it represents the furthest that one can go in the study of rhetoric (Crable, "Distance"). Crable goes so far as to call pure persuasion a mythic image. For the reasons I outline in "Rhetorical Counteraction," I do not agree with Crable's final assessment, though I do think he offers a provocative case for paying greater attention to pure persuasion's role in Burke's philosophy of modern rhetoric. For more on this topic, see Wess, *Kenneth Burke* 211–16.

13. See Zappen, "Kenneth Burke"; Crusius, *Kenneth Burke*.

14. In figure 3, I place "ultimate identification" under the heading "principle of identification" because ultimate identification collapses the temporal and the universal via transcendence, which Burke's definition of rhetoric does not allow. Burke suggests that ultimate identification exceeds rhetoric when he writes, "And finally let us observe, all about us, forever goading us, though it be in fragments, the motive that attains its ultimate identification in the thought, not of the universal holocaust, but of the universal order—as with the rhetorical and dialectical symmetry of the Aristotelian metaphysics, whereby all classes of beings are hierarchically arranged in a chain or ladder or pyramid of mounting worth, each kind striving towards the *perfection* of its kind, and so towards the kind next above it, while the strivings of the entire series head in God as the beloved cynosure and sinecure, the end of all desire" (*RM* 333). As I argue in the body of this chapter, the hierarchical order referenced in this passage is not peculiar to rhetoric but is symptomatic of all language use. In addition, the references to war that act as a counterpoint to Burke's example in this passage include nonrhetorical forms such as poetry.

15. Burke uses the term *Homo dialecticus* at various points in *A Rhetoric of Motives*. I have been unable to locate a reference to *Homo rhetoricus* in Burke's work, which I think is suggestive of the role rhetoric plays within Burke's trilogy on motives (it is subsidiary to broader language functions). Heath's *Realism and Relativism* notes the role *Homo dialecticus* plays in Burke's work, but it does so in reference to *A Grammar of Motives*, not *A Rhetoric of Motives* (157–94). Both Biesecker and Davis refer to *Homo dialecticus* in the context of *A Rhetoric of Motives* (Biesecker 49; Davis, *Inessential* 23); Burke refers to *Homo dialecticus* in *GM* on p. 235.

16. See Zappen, "On Persuasion."

17. See *RM* 130. A number of scholars have engaged Burke's argument about biological division—most notably (and persuasively) Condit; Hawhee, *Moving* 1–11; and Davis, *Inessential* 18–36.

18. For more on this, see Jensen and Ratcliffe 89n2.

19. I read Gregory Clark's *Rhetorical Landscapes* as an exemplary demonstration of this point.

20. A handful of scholars have stressed the importance of reading Burke's argument in the published *Rhetoric of Motives* as a Cold War work. See, for example, Enoch, "Becoming"; Jameson 520; O'Gorman, *Spirits* xviii; Wess, *Kenneth Burke* 199–200; Wolin 171.

Chapter 3

1. As I argued in Part I, *A Rhetoric of Motives* is dedicated to counteracting nationalistic aggressions that culminate in war, particularly nuclear war. In an early draft of the introduction to the book titled "conclusion (or introduction)," Burke makes his purpose clear: "We are not in the least discomfited. Indeed, we are quite confident. Rhetoric can make its contribution too; and its contribution is just as momentous as the contributions of physics, chemistry, and biology, and any other science that contributes to the resourcefulness of war. For if the men in those other departments have

done their part to make war little short of universal suicide, it is those in our department who will make you want to get into such a war. It is the rhetoricians, the editors, the commentators, the politicians, the priests, who will invent the distortions and the slogans that alone are capable of goading you into the holocaust, of making you actually demand it, or at least making you think you had demanded it. And they have started their work already. There is still a long way to go, perhaps, but they are well subsidized, and they don't have much else to do" (2). Burke's argument is noteworthy for a couple of reasons. First, it characterizes rhetoricians as a catalyst of nuclear holocaust in order to justify an investment in rhetorical education. In the next paragraph, for example, Burke writes that rhetoricians "can do as much damage as any—for science piles up the resources of war, but only rhetoric can make people crazy enough to use them." So, in tracking modern rhetorical devices, Burke is counteracting rhetoricians as much as he is scientists. Second, Burke addresses the audience directly. Notice, for instance, his claim that rhetoricians are guilty of "goading you into the holocaust, of making you actually demand it, or at least making you think you had demanded it." Clearly, Burke is not writing to fellow scholars but to public audiences who are susceptible to such appeals.

2. I take the term *rhetorical counteraction* from the opening pages of *A Rhetoric of Motives*, where Burke announces his purpose for the book: "We do not flatter ourselves that any one book can contribute much to counteract the torrents of ill will into which so many of our contemporaries have so avidly and sanctimoniously plunged. But the more strident our journalists, politicians, and alas! even many of our churchmen become, the more convinced we are that books should be written for tolerance and contemplation" (xv). For more on this, see Jensen, "Rhetorical Counteraction."

3. The formal tendencies of public media discouraged rhetorical counteraction. In a 29 June 1948 letter to Watson (JWP), Burke described "the chapter on news" as "stylistically... perhaps the most difficult problem in the book. For one must look closely at things that don't deserve a glance. So it is a search for subterfuges." Unlike other periods in history in which public argument could be characterized as a "sustained attack," in the late 1940s it was "done in quick raids, as with Indian warfare, guerilla tactics, commando operations. It is neither good argument nor bad; it is not argument at all. For argument it substitutes identification and dramatization" (WW 134).

4. Among Burke's drafting notes is a February 1946 article by Julian Huxley titled "Is War Instinctive—and Inevitable?" Huxley writes: "To sum up very briefly, the biologist denies emphatically that there are human war instincts, either for the waging of war in a particular way, or to make war in general. But there does exist a human drive or impulse of pugnacity, which can be used as the foundation of a war sentiment; and this will continue to express itself in war as long as external conditions encourage or permit this expression of human nature. It is up to us to alter the conditions so as to prevent human pugnacity from expressing itself in war, and to encourage its use in other sentiments leading to activities and outlets of use or value."

5. See, for example, Beasley and Selzer 45; Crable, "Distance" 215; Murray 40; Enoch, "Becoming" 285.

6. As Burke explains early in *The War of Words*, "The aspect of the Scramble will change with changing conditions. These conditions themselves can be better or worse. But the human relations expressed through the Scramble will, *mutatis mutandis*, prevail under all historical conditions. 'Human nature changes,' in the sense that the means of livelihood, the quest for advantage, and the idea of order change. But 'human nature cannot change,' in the sense that we can abstract from various situations an essence common to the lot, transcending all details" (45–46).

7. See Jensen and Selzer. See also Meyers 153–70.

8. McKeon encouraged Burke to incorporate Aristotle's *Topics* into *A Rhetoric of Motives*. Their correspondence on this subject can be found in RMP.

9. Within the context of Burke's argument, Aristotle's appeal to good form is meaningful in at least two ways. First, form can mean *comportment*—as in, "When it comes to public argument, it would be better to comport oneself in a manner that is reasoned and deliberative rather than

obstructive and self-interested." According to Aristotle, one may exhibit good form by "reason[ing] from generally accepted opinions [and] principles" (*WW* 131). Second, form can signify the *discernible shape or structure that arguments take* in order to achieve a particular outcome. According to Aristotle, the antidote to freewheeling form is to emphasize a "realm of principle" that "remind[s] us of the turns, point-work, arabesques, and attitudes of formal dancing" (131). This emphasis does not discount informal dance as a practice so much as it demonstrates how a study of argumentative patterns can yield more complex approaches to argumentation.

10. "Persuasion involves choice, will; it is directed to a man only insofar as he is *free*. This is good to remember, in these days of dictatorship and near-dictatorship" (*RM* 50).

11. For more on this, see Adams; Crusius, "Question."

12. According to Burke, classical devices reveal different orders of motives. For example, in the *Topics*, Aristotle "calls particular attention to the use of a shift between public and privation orders of motivation." "In public," Burke explains, "one praises the just and the beautiful; but in private one prefers the test of expediency." Recognizing this distinction helps speakers (a) identify resources that are best suited to their purpose, and (b) conceptualize devices in terms that exceed stylistic embellishment. For example, knowing that certain devices are better suited to private situations, the speaker can frame devices as resources for invention and anticipate that their "profusion and vitality" will increase as material conditions place greater urgency upon those who use them (*RM* 57).

13. In her exceptional book *Forms*, Caroline Levine argues that we need to think about forms in terms of their *affordances*, as doing so will close the loop between ideas and material objects: "Affordances point us both to what all forms are capable of—to the range of uses each could be put to, even if no one has yet taken advantage of those possibilities—and also to their limits, the restrictions intrinsic to particular materials and organizing principles. Ballot boxes, biological clocks, and lyric poems all take organizing forms. Each of these forms can be repeated elsewhere, and each carries with it a certain limited range of affordances as it travels. But a form does its work only in contexts where other political and aesthetic forms also are operating. A variety of forms are in motion around us, constraining materials in a range of ways and imposing their order in situated contexts where they constantly overlap other forms. Form emerges from this perspective as transhistorical, portable, and abstract, on the one hand, and material, situated, and political, on the other" (10–11).

14. In *Postwar*, Tony Judt outlines the consequences of the Berlin Blockade of 1948: "The Berlin crisis had three significant outcomes. In the first place, it led directly to the creation of two German states, an outcome none of the Allies had sought four years earlier. . . . Secondly, the Berlin crisis committed the United States for the first time to a significant military presence in Europe for the indefinite future. . . . But thirdly, and this followed from the first two, the Berlin crisis led directly to the reappraisal of Western military calculations. If the West was going to protect its German clients from Soviet aggression then it would need to give itself the means to do so" (147).

15. Burke spends a majority of his "say anything" section (119–31) critiquing the US government and US news media's portrayals of the USSR. As we noted in Part I, Burke doesn't come right out and identify each country in *The War of Words*; he alludes to them via the names "Perfectists" (the United States) and "Loathesomites" (USSR). Still, his "allusions are about as ambiguous as a right to the jaw" (Burke to Hyman, 20 July 1948, SHP). It's worth noting that Burke, in his letter to Hyman, characterizes these proxy names as "mythic" in quality.

16. For more on this, see O'Gorman, "Longinus's"; Hawhee, "Looking."

17. See Beatty.

18. See Adams.

19. See Powers for one particularly poignant example.

20. See Seigel.

21. For a detailed account of Robert Oppenheimer's experience of being a suspected communist sympathizer, for example, see Monk 620. See also George 173–77 for a discussion of Burke's failed appointment at the University of Washington.

22. For more on this, see Clark, *Civic Jazz* 60–61; George 86–124.

Chapter 4

1. When critics approach *A Rhetoric of Motives* in piecemeal fashion or assert that the concepts it introduces are loosely connected, they imply that no underlying methodology organizes Burke's selection and analysis of textual examples.

2. Kris Ratcliffe and I first introduced this term in "Mythic Historiography."

3. As Burke uses mythic historiography in his philosophy of modern rhetoric, he naturalizes unstated assumptions that demand qualification—particularly assumptions related to the "universality" of white, masculine logic. Being mindful of the liabilities in Burke's selection process, contemporary rhetorical critics may use mythic historiography to achieve their own purposes, even or *especially* if those purposes involve challenging the parameters of the rhetorical tradition that Burke established.

4. Dosse argues that many structuralist critics consciously "excluded the subject" in their research. For example, Lévi-Strauss "pursued his enterprise of decentering a subject dominated by the mythological universe that speaks to him but unbeknownst to him." In this sense, myth is "anonymous." I believe that Burke, by focusing on the functions of the dialectic principle, adopted a similar stance. In making this argument, I am not in agreement that myths are anonymous or that by excluding the subject, structuralist critics become more scientific in their pursuits (Dosse 253). Burke was appropriately skeptical of scientific distancing. Nevertheless, he does collateral damage to excluded subjects by advancing a "universal" approach, regardless of how much he may have qualified his claims. Bryan Crable has explained how Ralph Ellison called Burke to task on this point; see "Antagonistic Cooperation" in *Ralph Ellison* 46–78. Kris Ratcliffe and I make a similar point in "Mythic Historiography."

5. Burke addresses this possibility directly in *The War of Words*, when he discusses the trial of suspected Communist spy Alger Hiss. "A 'spy scare' or a 'witch hunt' engineered by some Congressional committee could serve its purposes even though no single charge could be legally proved. For if one person after another is publicly questioned on suspicion of being secretly a member of Faction X, though each of them indignantly denies the charge, you have material for a succession of headlines that keep the name of Faction X vibrant with dyslogistic tonalities" (WW 191). To the extent that its audience did not or could not pause to assess its implications, they were subject to the formal rhythms such tactics engendered. Burke was concerned that familiarity with association was taking the place of justification from reasoned deliberation. The public trial was organized by the House Un-American Activities Committee, which proposed the Mundt-Nixon bill in 1948, which would have made "membership in communist political organizations" illegal and would have punished members of the Communist Party who failed to register with the US attorney-general "liable to denaturalization, a loss of passport privileges, and denial of government positions" (Steinberg 104). This bill laid the groundwork for the investigation of other Communist sympathizers, such as Burke and Robert Oppenheimer, who were deemed national security threats. As the red scare episode in US history demonstrates so forcefully, those who exploited familiarity with certain associations furnished "a 'worldview' for people who had previously seen the world but piecemeal" (Burke, *Philosophy* 218). In doing so, they stoked an ardent form of nationalism committed to capitalist expansion.

6. A good example of pure persuasion is cursing at another driver who has cut you off (assuming the driver can neither hear nor see you yelling). You are yelling not to convince him to drive more carefully but to vent frustration and to underscore your virtues as the better driver. Though physical confrontations on the road do occur, most drivers avoid direct physical confrontations with others.

7. In *Ritual Theory*, Catherine Bell argues for a definition of ritualization that is highly rhetorical: "It is a way of acting that sees itself as *responding* to a place, event, force, problem, or tradition. It tends to see itself as the natural or appropriate thing to do in the circumstances. Ritualization does not see how it actively creates place, force, event, and tradition, how it redefines or generates

the circumstances to which it is responding. It does not see how its own actions reorder and reinterpret the circumstances so as to afford the sense of a fit among the main spheres of experience—body, community, and cosmos. Ritualization sees its end, the rectification of a problematic. It does not see what it does in the process of realizing this end, its transformation of the problematic itself. And yet what ritualization does is actually quite simple: it temporally structures a space-time environment through a series of physical movements . . . thereby producing an arena which, by its molding of the actors, both validates and extends the schemes they are externalizing. Indeed, in seeing itself as responding to an environment, ritualization interprets its own schemas as impressed upon actors from a more authoritative source, usually from well beyond the immediate human community itself" (109–10).

Epilegomena

1. Many thanks to David Blakesley for the invitation.

2. Derrida makes this point in *Archive Fever*. See especially 19.

3. A number of scholars have identified the non-Western roots of the rhetorical tradition. See, for example, Kennedy, *Comparative Rhetoric*; Lloyd, *Routledge Handbook*; Mao, *Comparative Rhetoric*.

4. Research on rhetoric's relationship to animals is growing by the year. To get started, see Hawhee, *Rhetoric*; Rowland; Worsham, "Toward."

5. See, for example, Bernal. Bernal has been criticized for relying too much on myth and not enough on historical evidence. Although such critiques are reasonable in light of the archaeological and linguistic evidence, I think critics who make these arguments miss the point.

6. For a parallel case, see Lewis: "'Art' included paintings, sculpture, installations, photography, lithographs, engravings, any work on paper, et cetera—all those traditional mediums now recognized by the Western art-historical canon. However, because black female figures were also used in ways I could never have anticipated, I was forced to expand that definition to include other material and visual objects, such as combs, spoons, buckles, pans, knives, table legs" (35). For more on the challenges associated with this work, see Hawhee and Olson.

7. For more on this, see Brunner; von Hallberg.

8. See note 3 in "Mythic Palingenesis," above.

Works Cited

Information about archival manuscripts appears here. Detailed information about Kenneth Burke's correspondence, including dates and archival location, can be found in the text and endnotes.

Archives

Bennington College Archive, Bennington, Vermont

Manuscripts

Drucker, Peter F. "The Myth of the State." 25 March 1947. https://crossettlibrary.dspacedirect.org/bitstream/handle/11209/5404/Drucker%20Lecture%203.25.47%20-%20Myth%20of%20the%20State.pdf. Accessed 4 September 2020.

"Bennington College Lecture Series, 1947: The Myth." https://crossettlibrary.dspacedirect.org/bitstream/handle/11209/8497/Bennington%20College%20Lecture%20Series%2c%201947.%20The%20Myth-List.pdf. Accessed 4 September 2020.

Kenneth Burke Literary Trust, Andover, New Jersey (KBLT)

Manuscript Images and Drafts

"Kenneth Burke Scything 1947" (photo)
"Scientific Rhetoric"
"Towards a Science of Human Comedy"

Kenneth Burke Papers, Eberly Family Special Collections, Pennsylvania State University, University Park, Pennsylvania (KBP)

Burke-1: Correspondence
Malcolm Cowley, Francis Fergusson, James Sibley Watson

Burke-3: Correspondence
L. E. Christie, Malcolm Cowley, Donald Stauffer, James Sibley Watson

Burke-3: Manuscripts
"archetype" (P17 B5 F3)
"conclusion" (P23 B7 F4)
"Conclusion" (P23 B7 F4)
"conclusion—" (P23 B7 F4)
"Conclusion—on minimum grounding for unity" (P23 B7 F2), 1–3
"conclusion (or introduction)" (P23 B7 F2), 1–2
"Critique of Science" (P23 B7 F2)
"The Desert Fathers. tr. by Helen Waddell" (P23 B7 F3), 1–10
"Dialectic, Ideology, and Myth" (draft) (Q4 B9 F27–29)
"Dialectic, Ideology, and Myth" (index) (Q4 B9 F9)
Drucker, Peter F. "Drucker" (in pencil) (P23 B7 F4)
"Harvard Summer School Conference on the Defense of Poetry, Aug. 14–17, 1950," conference transcript (P33 B8 F22–23)
"Index for Order" (Q4 B9 F9)
"Index for Traditional Principles of Rhetoric" (Q4 B9 F9)

"Introduction to Devices—Situational" (The Rhetoric of Bureaucracy) (P20 B6 F22)
"Landmarks—" (index) (Q4 B9 F9)
"myth—" (P17 B5 F3)
"myth (from Cave Man to Excavation Man)" (P17 B5 F4)
"Notes on Joseph Campbell's lecture Myth and Ritual, as taken by a member of the Bennington Faculty" (P17 B5 F2).
"on myth" (P17 B5 F4)
"Order," also titled "Dialectic, Ideology, and Myth" (Q4 B9 F27-29)
"Outline (Sept. 1946)" (P23 B7 F2)
"Outline (April 27, 1947)" (Q22 B12 F33-34)
"The Poet of the Resistance" (P23 B7 F3), 1-9
"principles (categories)—of the analysis of good plays, as considered from the standpoint of Rhetoric" (Q17 B11 F22)
"problems of rhetoric (from letter to DM)" (P23 B7 F4)
"Prospectus" (P23 B7 F5)
"Range of Rhetoric—" (P23 B7 F1)
"The Rhetorical Situation" (P18 B5 F16-17)
"A Rhetoric of Motives" (fair copy) (Q4 B10 F2-10)
Salvadori, Max. "The Myth of the State: Lecture given at Bennington College on March 25, 1947" (P17 B5 F3)
"Scientific Rhetoric" (Q19 B11 F48)
"September 1946" (P23 B7 F2)
"to McKeon" (P23 B7 F3)
"Traditional Principles," also titled "Landmarks of Rhetoric" (B9 F23-26)
"Untitled" (P23 B7 F3)
"when on myth as vocabulary of essence" (P17 B5 F2)

Burke-3: Review
Arthur E. Jensen, "Kenneth Burke Not Easy to Read," *Boston Herald*, undated clipping (Q17 B11 F28)

Richard Blackmur Papers, Princeton University Special Collections, Princeton, NJ (RBP)

Correspondence
Kenneth Burke

Malcolm Cowley Papers, The Newberry Library, Chicago (MCP)

Ralph Ellison Papers, Manuscript Division, Library of Congress, Washington, DC (REP)

Stanley Edgar Hyman Papers, Manuscript Division, Library of Congress, Washington, DC (SHP)

Matthew Josephson Papers, Beinecke Rare Book and Manuscript Library, Yale University, New Haven, Connecticut (MJP)

Richard Peter McKeon Papers, Hanna Holborn Gray Special Collections Research Center, University of Chicago Library, Chicago, Illinois (RMP)

James Sibley Watson / The Dial Papers, The Henry W. and Albert A. Berg Collection of English and American Literature, The New York Public Library, Astor, Lenox and Tilden Foundations, New York (JWP)

Manuscript
Kenneth Burke, "Kinds of Criticism"

Shelby White and Leon Levy Archives Center, Institute for Advanced Study, Princeton, New Jersey (SWLL)

Manuscript
Beatrice Stern, "Notes on the Director's Fund," 16 December 1947

Published Sources

Abrams, M. H. *The Mirror and the Lamp: Romantic Theory and the Critical Tradition*. New York: Oxford UP, 1953.
Adams, Sarah Elizabeth. "Agitation with—and of—Burke's Comic Theory." *Philosophy and Rhetoric* 50.7 (2017): 315-35.
Anderson, Dana. *Identity's Strategy: Rhetorical Selves in Conversion*. Columbia: U of South Carolina P, 2007.
Anderson, Dana, and Jessica Enoch, eds. *Burke in the Archives: Using the Past to Transform the Future of Burkean Studies*. Columbia: U of South Carolina P, 2013.
Bal, Mieke. *Travelling Concepts in the Humanities: A Rough Guide*. Toronto: U of Toronto P, 2002.
Beasley, James P. "'Extraordinary Understandings' of Composition at the University of Chicago." *CCC* 59.1 (2007): 36-52.
Beasley, James P., and Jack Selzer. "Present at the Creation: Kenneth Burke at the First CCCC." *Rhetoric Review* 38.1 (2019): 39-49.

Beatty, Paul. *The Sellout*. New York: Farrar, Straus & Giroux, 2016.

Beauvoir, Simone de. *The Second Sex*. Translated by Constance Borde and Sheila Molvany-Chevalier. New York: Vintage, 2009.

Belk, John. "Snapshots of Identification: Kenneth Burke's Engagements with T. S. Eliot." *Rhetoric Society Quarterly* 44.4 (2014): 363–82.

Bell, Catherine. *Ritual Theory, Ritual Practice*. New York: Oxford UP, 1992.

Berger, Peter L. *The Sacred Canopy: Elements of a Sociological Theory of Religion*. New York: Anchor, 1967.

Bernal, Martin. *Black Athena: The Afroasiatic Roots of Classical Civilization*. New Brunswick: Rutgers UP, 2020.

Biesecker, Barbara. *Addressing Postmodernity: Kenneth Burke, Rhetoric, and a Theory of Social Change*. Tuscaloosa: U of Alabama P, 1997.

Bird, Kai. *American Prometheus: The Triumph and Tragedy of J. Robert Oppenheimer*. New York: Vintage, 2005.

Booth, Wayne. "Kenneth Burke's Way of Knowing." *Critical Inquiry* 1.1 (1974): 1–22.

Borch-Jacobsen, Mikkel. *The Freudian Subject*. Translated by Catherine Porter. Stanford: Stanford UP, 1982.

Borrowman, Shane, and Marcia Kmetz. "Divided We Stand: Beyond Burkean Identification." *Rhetoric Review* 30.3 (2011): 275–92.

Brock, Bernard L. "Epistemology and Ontology in Kenneth Burke's Dramatism." *Communication Quarterly* 33.2 (1985): 94–104.

———. "The Evolution of Kenneth Burke's Philosophy of Rhetoric: Dialectic Between Epistemology and Ontology." In *Extensions of the Burkean System*, ed. James W. Chesebro, 309–28. Tuscaloosa: U of Alabama P, 1993.

Brock, Bernard L., Kenneth Burke, Parke G. Burgess, and Herbert W. Simons. "Dramatism as Ontology or Epistemology: A Symposium." *Communication Quarterly* 33.1 (1985): 17–33.

Brunner, Edward J. *Cold War Poetry: The Social Text in the Fifties Poem*. Urbana: U of Illinois P, 2001.

Bruns, Gerald. *Inventions: Writing, Textuality, and Understanding in Literary History*. New Haven: Yale UP, 1982.

Bryant, John L. *The Fluid Text: A Theory of Revision and Editing for Book and Screen*. Ann Arbor: U of Michigan P, 2002.

Burke, Kenneth. "The American Way." *Touchstone* 1 (December 1947): 3–9.

———. *Attitudes Toward History*. 3rd ed. Berkeley: U of California P, 1984.

———. "Counter-Gridlock: An Interview." In *On Human Nature: A Gathering While Everything Flows, 1967–1984*, ed. Kenneth Burke, Angelo Bonadonna, and William H. Ruekert, 336–90. Berkeley: U of California P, 2003.

———. "Doing and Saying: Thoughts on Myth, Cult, and Archetypes." *Salmagundi* 15 (Winter 1971): 100–119.

———. *Essays Toward a Symbolic of Motives, 1950–1955*. Clemson, SC: Parlor Press, 2006.

———. *A Grammar of Motives*. New York: Prentice Hall, 1945.

———. "Homo Faber, Homo Magus." *Nation* 163 (December 1946): 666–68.

———. "Ideology and Myth." *Accent* 7 (Summer 1947): 195–205.

———. *Language as Symbolic Action: Essays on Life, Literature, and Method*. Berkeley: U of California P, 1966.

———. "Nous autres matérialistes." *Esprit* 127 (November 1946): 628–42.

———. *Permanence and Change: An Anatomy of Purpose*. 3rd ed. Berkeley: U of California P, 1984.

———. *The Philosophy of Literary Form*. Berkeley: U of California P, 1973.

———. "Revolutionary Symbolism in America." In *The Legacy of Kenneth Burke*, ed. Herbert W. Simons and Trevor Melia, 267–73. Madison: U of Wisconsin P, 1989.

———. "The Rhetorical Situation." In *Communication: Ethical and Moral Issues*, ed. Lee Thayer, 263–75. New York: Gordon and Breach Science, 1973.

———. *A Rhetoric of Motives*. New York: Prentice Hall, 1950.

———. *A Rhetoric of Motives*. 2nd ed. Berkeley: U of California P, 1969. Citations are to this edition.

———. "Rhetoric—Old and New." *Journal of General Education* 5 (April 1951): 202–9.

———. "Thanatopsis for Critics: A Brief Thesaurus for Deaths and Dyings." *Essays in Criticism* 2 (October 1952): 369–75.

———. *Towards a Better Life: Being a Series of Epistles, or Declamations*. 2nd ed. Berkeley: U of California P, 1966.

———. *The War of Words*. Ed. Anthony Burke, Kyle Jensen, and Jack Selzer. Berkeley: U of California P, 2018.

Bushell, Sally. *Text as Process: Creative Composition in Wordsworth, Tennyson, and Dickinson*. Charlottesville: U of Virginia P, 2009.

Campbell, Joseph A. *The Hero with a Thousand Faces*. New York: Pantheon, 1949.

———. *The Mythic Image*. Princeton: Princeton UP, 1974.

Camus, Albert. *The Myth of Sisyphus*. New York: Vintage, 2018.

Carter, C. A. "Kenneth Burke and the Bicameral Power of Myth." *Poetics Today* 18 (Autumn 1997): 343–73.

Cassirer, Ernst. *An Essay on Man: An Introduction to a Philosophy of Human Culture*. New Haven: Yale UP, 1944.

———. *Language and Myth*. New Haven: Yale UP, 1946.

———. *The Myth of the State*. New Haven: Yale UP, 1946.

Chase, Richard. *Quest for Myth*. Baton Rouge: Louisiana State UP, 1949.

Clark, Gregory. *Civic Jazz: American Music and Kenneth Burke on the Art of Getting Along*. Chicago: U of Chicago P, 2015.

———. *Rhetorical Landscapes in America: Variations on a Theme from Kenneth Burke*. Columbia: U of South Carolina P, 2004.

Cmiel, Kenneth, and John Durham Peters. *Promiscuous Knowledge: Information, Image, and Other Truth Games in History*. Chicago: U of Chicago P, 2020.

Cohen, Philip G. *Devils and Angels: Textual Editing and Literary Theory*. Charlottesville: UP of Virginia, 1991.

Condit, Celeste. "Framing Kenneth Burke: Sad Tragedy or Comic Dance?" *Quarterly Journal of Speech* 80.1 (1994): 77–82.

Coupe, Laurence. *Kenneth Burke: From Myth to Ecology*. Clemson, SC: Parlor Press, 2013.

———. *Kenneth Burke on Myth: An Introduction*. New York: Routledge, 2006.

Cousins, Norman. *Modern Man Is Obsolete*. New York: Viking, 1945.

Cowley, Malcolm. *The Flower and the Leaf: A Contemporary Record of American Writers Since 1941*. New York: Viking, 1985.

Crable, Bryan. "Burkean Perspectives on Transcendence: A Prospective Retrospective." In *Transcendence by Perspective: Meditations on and with Kenneth Burke*, ed. Bryan Crable, 3–32. Anderson, SC: Parlor Press, 2014.

———. "Burke's Perspective on Perspectives: Grounding Dramatism in the Representative Anecdote." *Quarterly Journal of Speech* 86.3 (2000): 318–33.

———. "Defending Dramatism as Ontological and Literal." *Communication Quarterly* 48.3 (2000): 323–42.

———. "Distance as Ultimate Motive: A Dialectical Interpretation of *A Rhetoric of Motives*." *Rhetoric Society Quarterly* 39 (July 2009): 213–39.

———. *Ralph Ellison and Kenneth Burke: At the Roots of the Racial Divide*. Charlottesville: U of Virginia P, 2011.

Crusius, Timothy W. *Kenneth Burke and the Conversation After Philosophy*. Carbondale: Southern Illinois UP, 1999.

———. "The Question of Kenneth Burke's Ethics." *K.B. Journal* 3.1 (2006): n.p.

Davis, Diane. "Identification: Burke and Freud on Who You Are." *Rhetoric Society Quarterly* 38.2 (2008): 123–47.

———. *Inessential Solidarity: Rhetoric and Foreigner Relations*. Pittsburgh: Pittsburgh UP, 2010.

Day, Dennis G. "Persuasion and the Concept of Identification." *Quarterly Journal of Speech* 46 (1960): 270–73.

Deppman, Jed, Daniel Ferrer, and Michael Groden. "Introduction: A Genesis of French Genetic Criticism." In *Genetic Criticism: Texts and Avant-Textes*, ed. Jed Deppman, Daniel Ferrer, and Michael Groden, 1–16. Philadelphia: U of Pennsylvania P, 2004.

Derrida, Jacques. *Archive Fever: A Freudian Impression*. Trans. Eric Prenowitz. Chicago: U of Chicago P, 2017.

Dosse, François. *History of Structuralism*. Vol. 1, *The Rising Sign, 1945–1966*. Trans. Deborah Glassman. Minneapolis: U of Minnesota P, 1997.

Doty, William G. *Mythography: The Study of Myths and Rituals*. 2nd ed. Tuscaloosa: U of Alabama P, 2000.

Doyle, Richard M. *The Genesis of Now: Self Experiments with the Bible and the End of Religion*. State College, PA: Metanoia P, 2019.

Dyson, George. *Turing's Cathedral: The Origins of the Digital Universe*. New York: Vintage, 2012.

East, James H., ed. *The Humane Particulars: The Collected Letters of William Carlos Williams and Kenneth Burke*. Columbia: U of South Carolina P, 2003.

Eliade, Mircea. *The Myth of the Eternal Return: Cosmos and History*. Princeton: Princeton UP, 2005.

Enoch, Jessica. "Becoming Symbol-Wise: Kenneth Burke's Pedagogy of Critical Reflection." *College Composition and Communication* 56.2 (2004): 279–96.

———. "Claiming Access to Elite Curriculum: Identification and Division at the Harvard Annex." *Journal of Curriculum Studies* 44.6 (2012): 787–808.

Feder, Lillian. *Ancient Myth in Modern Poetry*. Princeton: Princeton UP, 1971.

Fitzgerald, Robert. *Enlarging the Change: The Princeton Seminars in Literary Criticism, 1949–1951*. Boston: Northeastern UP, 1985.

Ford, Colby. "The Western Roundtable on Modern Art (1949)." http://ubu-mirror.ch/historical/wrtma/transcript.htm. Accessed 8 June 2021.

Foss, Sonja K., and Cindy L. Griffin. "A Feminist Perspective on Rhetorical Theory: Toward a Clarification of Boundaries." *Western Journal of Communication* 56.4 (1992): 330–49.

Foucault, Michel. "What Is an Author?" In *Language, Counter-Memory, Practice: Selected Essays and Interviews*, ed. Donald F. Bouchard, 113–38. Ithaca: Cornell UP, 1977.

Freud, Sigmund. "Dreams and Telepathy." 1922. In *The Standard Edition of the Complete Psychological Works of Sigmund Freud*, trans. James Strachey, 18:195–220. London: Hogarth, 1955.

Fromm, Erich. *The Forgotten Language: An Introduction to Dreams, Fairy Tales, and Myths*. New York: Rinehart, 1951.

Gaiman, Neil. *Norse Mythology*. New York: W. W. Norton, 2018.

Geiger, T. J. "Forgiveness Is More Than Platitudes: Evangelical Women, Sexual Violence, and Casuistic Tightening." *Rhetoric Society Quarterly* 49.2 (2019): 163–84.

Genette, Gerard. *Paratexts: Thresholds of Interpretation*. Trans. Jane E. Lewin. New York: Cambridge UP, 1997.

George, Ann. *Kenneth Burke's "Permanence and Change": A Critical Companion*. Columbia: U of South Carolina P, 2018.

George, Ann, and Jack Selzer. *Kenneth Burke in the 1930s*. Columbia: U of South Carolina P, 2007.

Girard, René. *The Scapegoat*. Trans. Yvonne Freccero. Baltimore: Johns Hopkins UP, 1989.

———. *Things Hidden Since the Foundation of the World*. Trans. Stephen Bann and Michael Metteer. Stanford: Stanford UP, 1987.

Gittens, Rhana A. "'What If I Am a Woman?': Black Feminist Rhetorical Strategies of Intersectional Identification and Resistance in Maria Stewart's Texts." *Southern Communication Journal* 83.5 (2018): 310–21.

Glenn, Cheryl. "Rhetoric and Feminism: The Possibilities of Women and Beyond." *African Yearbook of Rhetoric* 1 (2010): 42–51.

Glenn, Cheryl, and Jessica Enoch. "Drama in the Archives: Rereading Methods, Rewriting History." *College Composition and Communication* 61.2 (2009): 321–42.

Gorer, Geoffrey. *The American People: A Study in National Character*. New York: W. W. Norton, 1948.

Greetham, D. C. *Theories of the Text*. Oxford: Clarendon Press, 1999.

Greif, Mark. *The Age of the Crisis of Man: Thought and Fiction in America, 1933–1973*. Princeton: Princeton UP, 2016.

Griffin, Roger. *Modernism and Fascism: The Sense of a Beginning Under Mussolini and Hitler*. New York: Palgrave Macmillan, 2007.

Gross, Daniel M. *Being-Moved: Rhetoric as the Art of Listening*. Chicago: U of Chicago P, 2020.

Guerard, Albert. "Kenneth Burke and an End to Rhetoric." *New York Herald Tribune*, July 23, 1950, 8.

Harries-Jones, Peter. *Upside-Down Gods: Gregory Bateson's World of Difference*. New York: Fordham UP, 2016.

Hawhee, Debra. "Language as Sensuous Action: Kenneth Burke, Sir Richard Paget, and Gesture-Speech Theory." *Quarterly Journal of Speech* 92.4 (2006): 331–54.

———. "Looking into Aristotle's Eyes: Toward a Theory of Rhetorical Vision." *Advances in the History of Rhetoric* 14.2 (2011): 139–65.

———. *Moving Bodies: Kenneth Burke at the Edges of Language*. Columbia: U of South Carolina P, 2009.

———. *Rhetoric in Tooth and Claw: Animals, Language, Sensation*. Chicago: U of Chicago P, 2017.

Hawhee, Debra, and Christa J. Olson. "Pan-Historiography: The Challenges of Writing History Across Time and Space." In *Theorizing Historiography in Rhetoric*, ed. Michelle Ballif, 90–105. Carbondale: Southern Illinois UP, 2013.

Hayles, N. Katherine, *Unthought: The Power of the Cognitive Nonconscious*. Chicago: U of Chicago P, 2017.

Heath, Robert L. *Realism and Relativism: A Perspective on Kenneth Burke*. Macon: Mercer UP, 1986.

Hill, Ian. "'The Human Barnyard' and Kenneth Burke's Philosophy of Technology." *K.B. Journal* 5.2 (2009). http://www.kbjournal.org/ian_hill. Accessed 1 September 2020.

Horkheimer, Max, and Theodor W. Adorno. *Dialectic of Enlightenment*. New York: Continuum, 1993.

Huxley, Aldous. *The Perennial Philosophy*. New York: Harper, 1944.

Huxley, Julian. "Is War Instinctive—and Inevitable?" *New York Times Magazine*, February 10, 1946.

James, William. "The Moral Equivalent of War." *McClure's*, August 1910, 463–68.

Jameson, Frederic. "The Symbolic Inference; or, Kenneth Burke and Ideological Analysis." *Critical Inquiry* 4.3 (1978): 507–23.

Japp, Phyllis. "Can This Marriage Be Saved: Reclaiming Burke for Feminist Scholarship." In *Kenneth Burke and the 21st Century*, ed. Bernard L. Brock, 113–32. Albany: SUNY P, 1998.

Jay, Paul, ed. *The Selected Correspondence of Kenneth Burke and Malcolm Cowley*. New York: Viking, 1988.

Jensen, Kyle. "Genetic Rhetorical Criticism: An Alternative Methodology for Studying Multi-Versioned Rhetorical Works." *Quarterly Journal of Speech* 102.3 (2016): 264–85.

———. "Rhetorical Counteraction in Kenneth Burke's *A Rhetoric of Motives* and *The War of Words*." *Quarterly Journal of Speech* 104.4 (2018): 384–99.

———. "Rhetorical Listening in Principle: A Burkean Apology." *JAC: A Journal of Rhetoric, Culture, and Politics* 32.1–2 (2012): 185–219.

Jensen, Kyle, and Krista Ratcliffe. "Mythic Historiography: Refiguring Kenneth Burke's Deceitful Woman Trope." *Rhetoric Society Quarterly* 48.1 (2018): 88–107.

Jensen, Kyle, and Jack Selzer. "How the Media Encourages—and Sustains—Political Warfare." *The Conversation*, 28 September 2018. https://theconversation.com/how-the-media-encourages-and-sustains-political-warfare-100941.

Judt, Tony. *Postwar: A History of Europe Since 1945*. New York: Penguin, 2006.

Jung, Carl G. *Symbols of Transformation*. Trans. Gerhard Adler. 2nd ed. Princeton: Princeton UP, 1977.

Jung, Julie. "Systems Rhetoric: A Dynamic Coupling of Explanation and Description." *Enculturation: A Journal of Rhetoric, Writing, and Culture*. 7 April 2014. http://enculturation.net/systems-rhetoric. Accessed 16 June 2020.

Kelemen, Erick. *Textual Editing and Criticism: An Introduction*. New York: W. W. Norton, 2008.

Kennedy, George. *Comparative Rhetoric: An Historical and Cross-Cultural Introduction*. Oxford: Oxford UP, 1997.

———. "A Hoot in the Dark: The Evolution of General Rhetoric." *Philosophy and Rhetoric* 25.1 (1992): 1–21.

Kermode, Frank. *The Sense of an Ending: Studies in the Theory of Fiction*. New York: Oxford UP, 1966.

King, Jeff, and Maud Oakes. *Where the Two Came to Their Father*. Ed. Joseph Campbell. Princeton: Princeton UP, 1991.

Kraemer, Don J. "Between Motion and Action: The Dialectical Role of

Affective Identification in Kenneth Burke." *Advances in the History of Rhetoric* 16.3 (2003): 141–64.

Langer, Susan K. *Philosophy in a New Key: A Study in the Symbolism of Reason, Rite, and Art.* Cambridge: Harvard UP, 1941.

Leja, Michael. *Reframing Abstract Expressionism: Subjectivity and Painting in the 1940s.* New Haven: Yale UP, 1993.

Lentricchia, Frank. *Criticism and Social Change.* Chicago: U of Chicago P, 1985.

Lepore, Jill. *These Truths: A History of the United States.* New York: W. W. Norton, 2019.

Levine, Caroline. *Forms: Whole, Rhythm, Hierarchy, Network.* Princeton: Princeton UP, 2017.

Lévi-Strauss, Claude. *The Naked Man.* Trans. John and Doreen Weightman. Chicago: U of Chicago P, 1981.

Lewis, Robin Coste. *Voyage of the Sable Venus: And Other Poems.* New York: Knopf, 2017.

Lincoln, Bruce. *Theorizing Myth: Narrative, Ideology, and Scholarship.* Chicago: U of Chicago P, 2000.

Lloyd, Keith, ed. *The Routledge Handbook of Comparative World Rhetorics: Studies in the History, Application, and Teaching of Rhetoric Beyond Traditional Greco-Roman Contexts.* New York: Routledge, 2021.

Luhmann, Niklas. *Social Systems.* Trans. John Bednarz Jr. Stanford: Stanford UP, 1996.

Mao, LuMing, ed. *Comparative Rhetoric: The Art of Traversing Rhetorical Times, Places, and Spaces.* New York: Routledge, 2014.

McCullough, David. *Truman.* New York: Simon and Schuster, 1992.

McGann, Jerome. *The Textual Condition.* Princeton: Princeton UP, 1991.

McGee, Michael Calvin. "The 'Ideograph': A Link Between Rhetoric and Ideology." *Quarterly Journal of Speech* 66.1 (1980): 1–16.

McMahon, Robert. "Kenneth Burke's Divine Comedy: The Literary Form of the Rhetoric of Religion." *PMLA* 104.1 (1989): 53–63.

Merkur, Daniel. *Psychoanalytic Approaches to the Study of Myth: Freud and the Freudians.* New York: Routledge, 2005.

Meyers, Peter Alexander. *Civic War and the Corruption of the Citizen.* Chicago: U of Chicago P, 2008.

Miller, James E., and Bernice Slote. *The Dimensions of Poetry: A Critical Anthology.* New York: Dodd, Mead, 1962.

Monk, Ray. *Robert Oppenheimer: A Life Inside the Center.* New York: Doubleday, 2012.

Mumford, Lewis. *The Condition of Man.* New York: Harcourt, 1944.

Murray, Jeffrey W. "Kenneth Burke: A Dialogue of Motives." *Philosophy and Rhetoric* 35.1 (2002): 22–49.

Nichols, Marie Hochmuth. *Rhetoric and Criticism.* Baton Rouge: Louisiana State UP, 1963.

Nicotra, Jodie. "Notes from the Abyss: Variations on a (Mystical) Theme in Burke's Work." *Burke in the Archives: Using the Past to Transform the Future of Burkean Studies*, ed. Dana Anderson and Jessica Enoch, 160–77. Columbia: U of South Carolina P, 2013.

Niebuhr, Reinhold. "Social Myths in the 'Cold War.'" *Journal of International Affairs* 21.1 (1967): 40–56.

O'Gorman, Ned. "Longinus's Sublime Rhetoric, or How Rhetoric Came into Its Own." *Rhetoric Society Quarterly* 34.2 (2004): 71–89.

———. *Spirits of the Cold War: Contesting Worldviews in the Classical Age of American Security Strategy.* East Lansing: Michigan State UP, 2012.

Olson, Christa. *Constitutive Visions: Indigeneity and Commonplaces of National Identity in Republican Ecuador.* University Park: Penn State UP, 2013.

Ovid. *Metamorphoses.* Trans. A. D. Melville. Oxford: Oxford UP, 2008.

Pan, David. *Sacrifice in the Modern World: On the Particularity and Generality of Nazi Myth.* Evanston: Northwestern UP, 2012.

Parker, Hershel. *Flawed Texts and Verbal Icons: Literary Authority and American Fiction.* Evanston: Northwestern UP, 1984.

Powers, Richard. *The Overstory.* New York: W. W. Norton, 2018.

Ratcliffe, Krista. *Rhetorical Listening: Identification, Gender, Whiteness.* Carbondale: Southern Illinois UP, 2005.

Rickert, Thomas J. *Ambient Rhetoric: The Attunements of Rhetorical Being*. Pittsburgh: Pittsburgh UP, 2013.

Riesman, David. *The Lonely Crowd: A Study of the Changing American Character*. New Haven: Yale UP, 1962.

Ringer, Jeffrey. "The Consequences of Integrating Faith into Academic Writing: Casuistic Stretching and Biblical Citation." *College English* 75.3 (2013): 272–99.

Rountree, Clarke. *Judging the Supreme Court: Constructions of Motives in Bush v. Gore*. East Lansing: Michigan State UP, 2007.

Rowland, Allison L. *Zoetropes and the Politics of Humanhood*. Columbus: Ohio State UP, 2020.

Rueckert, William H. "A Field Guide to Kenneth Burke—1990." In *Encounters with Kenneth Burke*, 55–98. Urbana: U of Illinois P, 1994.

———. *Kenneth Burke and the Drama of Human Relations*. 2nd ed. Berkeley: U of California P, 1982.

Schneider, Eric D., and Dorion Sagan. *Into the Cool: Energy Flow, Thermodynamics, and Life*. Chicago: U of Chicago P, 2006.

Schrödinger, Erwin. *What Is Life?* Cambridge: Cambridge UP, 2012.

Seigel, Marika A. "'One Little Fellow Named Ecology': Ecological Rhetoric in Kenneth Burke's *Attitudes Toward History*." *Rhetoric Review* 23.4 (2004): 388–404.

Selzer, Jack. *Kenneth Burke in Greenwich Village: Conversing with the Moderns, 1915–1931*. Madison: U of Wisconsin P, 1996.

Shillingsburg, Peter L. *From Gutenberg to Google: Electronic Representations of Literary Texts*. Cambridge: Cambridge UP, 2006.

———. *Resisting Texts: Authority and Submission in Constructions of Meaning*. Ann Arbor: U of Michigan P, 1998.

Skodnick, Roy. "Counter-Gridlock: An Interview with Kenneth Burke." *All-Area #2* (Spring 1983): 4–32.

Slochower, Harry. *Mythopoesis: Mythic Patterns in the Literary Classics*. Detroit: Wayne State UP, 1970.

Smith, Michelle. "The Dramatism Debate, Archived: The Pentad as 'Terministic' Ontology." In *Burke in the Archives: Using the Past to Transform the Future of Burkean Studies*, ed. Dana Anderson and Jessica Enoch, 143–58. Columbia: U of South Carolina P, 2013.

Stauffer, Donald. "The Key Is 'Substance.'" *New York Times Book Review*, 11 June 1950, 30.

Steinberg, Peter L. *The Great "Red Menace": United States Prosecution of American Communists, 1947-1952*. Westport, CT: Greenwood P, 1984.

Stewart, J. A. *The Myths of Plato*. London: Macmillan, 1905.

Strenski, Ivan. *Four Theories of Myth in Twentieth-Century History: Cassirer, Eliade, Lévi-Strauss, and Malinowski*. Iowa City: U of Iowa P, 1987.

Sutherland, Kathryn. *Jane Austen's Textual Lives: From Aeschylus to Bollywood*. Oxford: Oxford UP, 2005.

Virgil. *The Aeneid*. Trans. Sarah Ruden. New Haven: Yale UP, 2008.

von Hallberg, Robert. *American Poetry and Culture, 1945–1980*. Cambridge: Harvard UP, 1985.

Walker, Jeffrey. *Rhetoric and Poetics in Antiquity*. New York: Oxford UP, 2000.

Walsh, Lynda. "A Zero-Sum Politics of Identification: A Topological Analysis of Wildlife Advocacy Rhetoric in the Mexican Gray Wolf Reintroduction Project." *Written Communication* 36.3 (2019): 437–65.

Weaver, Richard M. *Ideas Have Consequences*. Chicago: U of Chicago P, 1948.

Weiser, M. Elizabeth. *Burke, War, Words*. Columbia: U of South Carolina P, 2008.

———. "National Identity Within the National Museum: Subjectification Within Socialization." *Studies in Philosophy and Education* 34.4 (2015): 385–402.

Wells, Susan. "Richards, Burke, and the Relation Between Rhetoric and Poetics." *Pre/Text: A Journal of Rhetorical Theory* 7.1–2 (1986): 59–75.

Wess, Robert. *Kenneth Burke: Rhetoric, Subjectivity, Postmodernism*. Cambridge: Cambridge UP, 1996.

———. "Kenneth Burke's 'Dialectic of Constitutions.'" *Pre/Text: A Journal of Rhetorical Theory* 12.1–2 (1991): 9–32.

———. "Pentadic Terms and Master Tropes: Ontology of the Act and Epistemology of the Trope in *A Grammar of Motives*." In *Unending Conversations: New Writings by and About Kenneth Burke*, ed.

Greig E. Henderson and David Cratis Williams, 154–75. Carbondale: Southern Illinois UP, 2001.

Williams, William Carlos. "Spring and All [By the Road to the Contagious Hospital]." https://poets.org/poem/spring-and-all-road-contagious-hospital. Accessed 1 June 2020.

Wolin, Ross. *The Rhetorical Imagination of Kenneth Burke*. Columbia: U of South Carolina P, 2001.

Worsham, Lynn. "Kenneth Burke's Appendicitis: A Feminist's Case for Complaint." *Pre/Text: A Journal of Rhetorical Theory* 12.1–2 (1991): 67–95.

———. "Toward an Understanding of Human Violence: Cultural Studies, Animal Studies, and the Promise of Posthumanism." *Review of Education, Pedagogy, and Cultural Studies* 35 (2013): 51–76.

Wright, Mark H. "Burkean and Freudian Theories of Identification." *Communication Quarterly* 42.3 (1994): 301–10.

Zappen, James P. "Kenneth Burke on Dialectical-Rhetorical Transcendence." *Philosophy and Rhetoric* 42.3 (2009): 279–301.

———. "On Persuasion, Identification, and Dialectical Symmetry by Kenneth Burke." *Philosophy and Rhetoric* 39.4 (2007): 333–39.

Zappen, James P., S. Michael Halloran, and Scott A. Wible. "Some Notes on 'Ad bellum purificandum.'" *KB Journal*. https://kbjournal.org/node/201. Accessed 1 September 2020.

Index

anagogic interpretation
   psychoanalytic, 81
   socio-, 82–83, 86, 88, 119–20, 170, 176
Aristotle, 6, 58, 63–64, 151, 185
   definition of rhetoric, 37
   entelechy, 48
   formal devices, 6, 140, 148–50, 152
   definition of scientific rhetoric, 51
   topics and commonplaces, 137, 198, 206
atomic warfare, 18, 21, 36–37, 46, 78, 112, 196

bureaucracy, 48, 50–51, 63, 66, 75, 187, 191, 194

Campbell, Joseph, 44, 145, 165, 197, 199–201, 204–5
Cassirer, Ernst, 42, 44–45, 122–23, 199–201
collaborative expectancy, 70, 150, 186
courtship, 82, 84, 105, 120–22, 172
   concept of, 65, 69–70, 80, 84, 122
   principle of, 105, 118–19, 122, 135
   rhetoric of, 65, 135, 175–77
   rituals, 135–36
Cowley, Malcolm, 19, 27, 83, 93
   correspondence with, 2, 5, 17–18, 24, 28–33, 40–41, 62–63, 72, 78–79, 87
   on myth, 44, 100

dialectic principle, the
   Burke's preoccupation with, 181, 186
   capacities of, 54, 62, 101, 103–5, 107–8, 112–13, 116, 120–21, 128, 133–34, 143, 147, 149, 151, 169, 176, 178, 180
   concept of, 120–21, 135, 157
   definition of, 103, 105, 133
   functions of, 24, 70, 81–82, 108, 120, 124, 128, 133–34, 143, 151, 168–69, 174, 176–77, 208
   Marx's insights into, 172, 174
   mythic figurations of, 45, 102–5, 114–15, 130, 176, 179
   pre-linguistic unity and, 204
   rhetoric study of, 106, 112–14, 134, 138, 150, 170, 173
   universal features of, 28, 133, 186
dissociation, 50, 55, 114–16, 149
division
   bridging, 38, 115, 131
   conscious, 23
   cultural, 5
   human, 64
   identification and, 53–54, 103, 107, 113
   linguistic, 64–65, 115, 128
   as logical priority, 101, 103, 130
   mediating, 122
   myth of, 111
   original, 103–4, 108, 118, 124
   problem of, 38, 112
   redress, 131
   social estrangement, 118
   state of, 23, 113
   ultimate, 114
   unrecognized, 23, 112

Eliade, Mircea, 115, 134, 180, 199–201
Ellison, Ralph, 19, 63, 192, 208

Freud, Sigmund, 44, 69, 81, 100, 127–28, 186–87, 193, 202–3

Grammar of Motives, A, 18–20, 22, 28, 57, 71, 90, 186, 189, 196
    dialectic, 200, 205
    diseases and cures, 184
    logical priorities, 100
    media devices, 190
    paradox of substance, 133
    referenced in RM, 132
    reviews of, 32–33
    revision of, 20, 41
    scope and reduction, 138–39
    substance, 43
    war, 202

hierarchic principle, 105, 122, 124, 133–35
    goadings of, 5
    manifestation of, 170
    mysteries created by, 118
    mythic representation of, 99, 100–111, 173
    tracking, 169–70, 173, 174–76
hierarchy
    Burke's personal, 5
    concept of, 65, 69, 80, 82, 84, 88, 108, 125, 128, 172
    continuation of, 134
    culminating stage of, 175
    Machiavelli on, 123
    metaphorical view of, 112–14
    morbidities of, 79
    motives of, 160
    principle of, 122
    reversal, 120, 134
    social, 120
    social estrangement, 135
Hyman, Stanley Edgar
    background on, 93, 190
    concerns about "The War of Words," 2–3, 72, 74–75, 152
    correspondence with, 5, 18, 54, 61, 63, 70, 78, 83, 207
    invitation to lecture, 33
    response to Rosenfeld, 32

identification
    appeal of, 64
    in *ATH*, 197, 201
    audience, 34
    autonomous activity, 157
    as bridging device, 118, 122, 172
    bureaucratic, 62, 134
    classical rhetoric, 108, 150
    concept of, 4, 6, 26, 35, 37, 53–55, 64, 97, 102, 109, 127–28, 193, 202–3
    conscious, 109, 160
    consubstantiality, 107, 202
    corporate, 142
    definition of, 6, 58, 106, 202–3
    dialectical resource, 66, 70, 101
    dimensions of, 128, 204
    dramatization, 151, 206
    factional, 26, 59
    form of, 179
    Freudian, 69, 127–28, 202
    group, 34, 69
    human consciousness, 186
    identification:persuasion, 140–43, 146
    implicit, 120
    myth, 56, 71, 109, 147, 199
    naive, 115
    nonconscious, 6–7
    organizing term, 43–44, 54, 56
    part-whole, 34
    persuasion:identification, 139–40, 146, 150
    poetic, 128, 133, 136–37
    principle of, 128, 131–33, 137, 149, 150, 175, 203, 205
    principle of rhetorical identification, 138–39
    of property, 104
    realistic vs. idealistic, 69
    rhetorical, 59, 115, 128, 133, 137, 142
    scope of, 157
    social, 176
    symbolic, 165, 202–3
    topic of, 17
    tracking, 7
    ultimate, 105, 205
    ultimate order, 123
    universal grounds of, 59, 103, 107, 113, 170
    variants of, 69
    the war of words, 120
identity
    concept of, 43, 69, 132, 202
    corporate, 142
    definition of, 45, 197
    mythic, 47, 56
    national, 122, 142
    poetic forms of, 133
    politics, 181
    transform, 45
    ultimate, 136

Josephson, Matthew, 5, 19, 27, 189–90, 196

"Kinds of Criticism," 27–28

"Logomachy, The," 5, 25, 37–38, 50, 190

Mannheim, Karl, 44–45, 65–66, 102, 116–18, 170
McKeon, Richard, 18–19, 42–43, 61, 190, 195–99, 206
Milton, John, 116, 120, 131, 136
    identification with Samson, 53–56, 107–8, 170
    symbolic transformation, 59–60, 101–2, 155–56
minimum grounding in unity, 40, 197
mystification
    concept of, 108, 113, 172
    Marx on, 173, 196
    special vs. general, 114–16, 122
mythic images
    cataloging devices associated with, 178–80
    definition of, 4–5, 64, 101, 103–4, 114, 130, 143
    dialectic method, 118
    failure of representation, 103–4, 204
    garden of Eden, 64, 100
    identifying, 113, 117, 168–69, 171
    imagining new, 185
    inventing, 172–73
    investigating limits of, 176–78
    Marx's proletariat as, 171–72
    reconfiguring, 110
    tower of Babylon, 64, 100, 124, 130
    tracking, 174–75
    universal principles, 170
    the war of words, 97, 102–7, 121–22, 130, 136, 147, 156, 182
    whore of Babylon, 121

nationalism, 18, 46, 124, 193

Oppenheimer, Robert, 16, 73, 77, 79, 83, 197–98, 207–8
"Order," 68, 79, 82–83, 86, 176, 193, 195

positive, dialectic, ultimate terms, 65–66, 109, 116
pre–linguistic unity, 103, 111, 128, 130–31, 156, 203–4
principle of courtship, 118–19, 122, 135
    pure persuasion
    concept of, 70, 79, 105, 193, 122, 205
    definition of, 121, 131, 177–78
    examples of, 130, 208
    section on, 67–68, 84, 121, 190

rhetorical devices
    bland strategy, 70–72, 153, 158–60, 162

    definition of, 147–48
    deflection, 70–71, 153, 191
    general theory of, 146
    making the connection, 153, 179
    reversal, 71, 154
    say anything, 71, 76, 99, 124, 152, 154, 179, 207
    say the opposite, 71, 154
    shrewd simplicity, 70–71, 153, 191
    spiritualization, 2, 71, 73, 137, 154, 190–91
    spokesman, 70–71, 154, 172
    undo by overdoing, 153, 162
    yielding aggressively, 71, 153, 162
rhetorical education, 39, 101, 143, 146, 148, 157, 206
rhetorical situation
    local, 34, 56–57, 180, 201
    modern, 6
    postwar, 22, 35, 39, 50, 55, 78, 176
    theory of, 55
    universal, 55, 57, 66, 114, 201
    war of words, 25, 34, 55, 57, 105, 119, 124, 166
    "Rhetorical Situation, The," 25–26, 37, 48–49, 51–52, 57, 63, 66, 194–95

scapegoat, 114, 134, 142, 160, 166, 175, 192
second-order reality, 108–10, 201
"Scientific Rhetoric," 48, 51, 66, 75–76, 194
Symbolic of Motives, A, 20, 22, 39, 62–63, 69, 76, 78, 88, 93, 132–33, 186, 197

"Traditional Principles of Rhetoric," 61–63, 65, 79, 108, 114, 140, 149
transcendence, 5, 101
    dialectical–rhetorical, 193
    as formal operation, 45
    linguistic, 116
    Platonist, 80
    ultimate identification, 205
transformation
    definitional, 41
    definition of, 101
    as formal operation, 45
    historic, 200
    linguistic, 165
    as logical priority, 101, 107, 111, 121, 166, 197
    methods of, 37, 111, 132, 149
    poetic, 60, 108, 118, 120, 131, 163, 200, 204
    rhetorical, 167, 193, 204
    total, 205

ultimate order, 65, 118, 120–21, 123–24, 138, 171–72, 174–76, 178

Virgil, 44–46, 50, 56, 59, 65, 100, 119, 191

Watson, James Sibley
    correspondence with, 2, 17–23, 26, 28–29, 32–35, 38–40, 42–44, 49–51, 53, 56–63, 70–92, 161–62, 191, 195–97, 206
    feedback on new opening for RM, 56
    feedback on "Order," 65, 80, 128
    feedback on pure persuasion, 68–69
    feedback on RM, 91
    feedback on socioanagogic interpretation, 86, 120
    feedback on "The War of Words," 72, 88
    illness of, 86
    response to nuclear attacks, 21–22
"World of Publicity, The," 62–63, 179, 198

www.ingramcontent.com/pod-product-compliance
Lightning Source LLC
Chambersburg PA
CBHW032336300426
44109CB00041B/1067